A Practicum in TESOL

CAMBRIDGE LANGUAGE EDUCATION
Series Editor: Jack C. Richards

This series draws on the best available research, theory, and educational practice to help clarify issues and resolve problems in language teaching, language teacher education, and related areas. Books in the series focus on a wide range of issues and are written in a style that is accessible to classroom teachers, teachers-in-training, and teacher educators.

In this series:

A Practicum in TESOL

Professional Development through Teaching Practice

Graham Crookes

University of Hawai'i at Manoa

CAMBRIDGE
UNIVERSITY PRESS

PUBLISHED BY THE PRESS SYNDICATE OF THE UNIVERSITY OF CAMBRIDGE
The Pitt Building, Trumpington Street, Cambridge, United Kingdom

CAMBRIDGE UNIVERSITY PRESS
The Edinburgh Building, Cambridge CB2 2RU, UK
40 West 20th Street, New York, NY 10011-4211, USA
477 Williamstown Road, Port Melbourne, VIC 3207, Australia
Ruiz de Alarcón 13, 28014 Madrid, Spain
Dock House, The Waterfront, Cape Town 8001, South Africa

http://www.cambridge.org

First published 2003

Printed in the United States of America

Typefaces Times Roman 10.5/12.5 pt. and Helvetica   *System* LaTeX 2_ε [TB]

A catalog record for this book is available from the British Library.

Library of Congress Cataloging in Publication Data

Crookes, Graham.
A practicum in TESOL : professional development through teaching practice /
Graham Crookes.
    p.   cm. – (Cambridge language education)
Includes bibliographical references and index.
ISBN 0-521-82305-6 – ISBN 0-521-52998-0 (pbk.)
1. English language – Study and teaching – Foreign speakers.   2. English teachers –
In-service training.   I. Title.   II. Series.
PE1128.A2 C73   2003
428'.0071–dc21   2002035085

ISBN 0 521 82305 6 hardback
ISBN 0 521 52998 0 paperback

To my parents, Brian and Vicki;
my wife Hildre;
and to Alison, Paul, and Ellen.

Contents

Series Editor's Preface

While the practicum is considered a core course in most TESOL teacher education programs, compared to many other areas of professional theory and activity it has received relatively little serious study, in terms of conceptual orientation, content, or practice. Hence, as the author of this book states, it remains undertheorized and under-researched. What little research it has received has primarily been descriptive in nature.

This book seeks to do several things. First, it describes how a course in teaching practice can be organized. Based on extensive experience in teaching the practicum course in a MATESOL program, Dr. Crookes explores the issues involved and describes how many of the practical questions that arise can be addressed. Simplistic answers are avoided, however, in favor of a further probing of the questions and an introduction to a rich knowledge base in educational theory and philosophy as a source for insight and clarification. A parallel agenda of the book is to open up the whole nature of teacher development in language teaching and evaluate the assumptions, values, and practices on which it is constituted. The perspective presented as this process of reflective analysis takes place can be described as one grounded in critical pedagogy. Thus, throughout the book the author offers a critical questioning of commonly held assumptions and practices and leads us to further examine our ideas about many aspects of teaching, including its social, moral, and political dimensions. And lastly, Dr. Crookes seeks to present an approach to the practicum that is collaborative and that facilitates long-term teacher development and does not merely provide substance for a one-semester practicum experience.

This is not, then, simply another "how to" book of techniques. Although valuable insights are presented throughout concerning the basic issues involved in the organization of teaching practice, including relations with mentor teachers, lesson planning, observation, motivation, classroom management, and the role of teacher development groups, the development of teaching skill is viewed as a complex phenomenon involving many layers of learning. Beyond the level of practical learning are issues that involve the development of personal theories and teaching philosophies. The development of social and interactional skills and the recognition that teaching has a moral and political dimension are also involved. Dr. Crookes is hence concerned with exploring both the outer and inner worlds of teaching and teacher development, and in the process he invites us to revisit many of the working assumptions from which we operate in teacher education. His ability to draw on his extensive knowledge of the fields of educational psychology and the philosophy of education adds both breadth and depth to his narrative.

This book is therefore an important addition to the literature on teacher learning in language teaching and to our understanding of how the practicum course in TESOL can be conceptualized and taught. It will be a valuable source book for both teacher educators and classroom teachers. It offers a fresh and challenging perspective on the nature of the practicum, written from the unique perspective of a leading scholar and theoretician in the field of applied linguistics who is actively involved in both classroom teaching and teacher education. It is hence a welcome addition to the Cambridge Language Education Series.

Jack C. Richards

A Practicum in TESOL

Introduction

In this Introduction, let me first say what this work is for and how it arose. I'll then give a quick orientation to the structure of the text, introduce myself, and finally present a few key background areas.

This book is designed to accompany a period of teaching practice, or practicum, for teachers of English to speakers of other languages. It should also be of use and interest to any group of ESL or EFL teachers working together to improve their practice or develop their understandings of teaching. It reflects my experiences as a teacher and teacher educator in many locations and over twenty years, and it addresses issues which I believe transcend local contexts. At the same time, I should mention that it also naturally reflects my experiences at my home institution, where I work particularly with student teachers completing the MA in English as a Second Language (ESL) at the University of Hawai'i. These students are an international group of individuals who are still within the first part of their career, with classroom experience in ESL or EFL, in a variety of different countries, typically ranging from one to five years. The teachers I have worked with in short courses in other locations have generally been teachers in midcareer. In conducting regular teaching practica, I usually work with a course lasting about 15 weeks, in which developing teachers either work directly with a cooperating teacher, or in their own class, and I (as supervisor), the cooperating teacher, and their peers observe them regularly and provide feedback on their classroom practice.[1] At the same time, they attend weekly meetings providing supporting material for this intensive period of reflection and professional development. Our concerns range from organizing a course and planning lessons to one's moral and social responsibilities as a teacher; they also include how the latter relate to the former.

When I first began to conduct classes of this sort, more than a decade ago now, there was surprisingly little material in the area of TESOL, ES/FL, or ELT[2] for developing teachers that went much beyond the "tips for teachers" model, and first efforts at research in the area were merely descriptive (e.g., Richards & Crookes, 1988; cf. Johnson, 1996). As TESOL has continued to grow, and as applied linguistics professionals have drawn more on the

1

field of education, more resources have become available; though scholars continue to comment that how S/FL teachers develop is still a topic little understood (Cumming, 1989; Freeman, 1996), and the practicum remains an undertheorized and underresearched area. I think this area is so crucial to the needs of generations of ES/FL professionals that a wide range of perspectives and orientations in support material should be on offer to developing ES/FL teachers and teacher educators, including, of course, the present one.

The structure and content of this book

As I hope you can see from the Contents page, the chapters reflect a deliberate sequence of ideas. Starting off, I will urge readers, in the first chapter, to think about what it is they are trying to achieve in a period of professional development. Some setting of goals might be facilitated through flipping through the book and dipping into it at some points, rather than trying simply to begin at the beginning and move steadily forward. I next introduce what is for me an underlying concept: the idea that teachers can improve by working together, and accordingly I review the techniques that can be used to gather the material for such development: observations of classes and one's own reflections on teaching; I also address the important process of sharing them with other teachers, preferably in a group setting. Elements for structuring those reflections come in succeeding chapters. I draw on material originating in the philosophy of education – an area which provides personal or values-based structures for organizing what one knows, thinks, or believes about teaching and learning generally. I also suggest a review of what formal content readers may have accumulated or may be accumulating from academic coursework in TESOL, SLA, SL Studies, and so on, or (of course) from independent study in those areas. These are interleaved with three chapters on various more down-to-earth matters to do with general (nonskill–area-specific) aspects of classroom practice, which while basic do in fact intersect with, and should reflect, our views about our educational practices. Continuing my emphasis on teachers helping teachers, a review of social skills serves to connect the classroom, and issues of student-teacher rapport, with professional life, where we work with or sometimes against our colleagues, and for which similarly social skills are needed. All this reflection won't happen, of course, without appropriate institutional structures, so unless teachers working with this book are prepared at some point in their career to attend to those, there won't be much point in our joint engagement with these issues. Hence the final chapters address what is needed, at the institutional level, if long-term professional development is going to occur as an integral part of our careers. The reader may wish to pick and choose, of course – but that's the long and the short of it.

Sections of the text

Besides the main expository sections of this book, there are two other types of text here. Most important, there are substantial extracts from the reflections and comments of student teachers I have worked with. Some of these are quite experienced teachers, some less so. I personally have found their reflections and comments extremely valuable in advancing my own thinking; I hope you will, too.

The other kind of text is headed *Warm-up*, *For Discussion*, and *You try it*. ... These short sections are particularly appropriate when the book is being used by groups of teachers, whether with or without a group or discussion leader (or supervisor). The first of these is simply to get the reader thinking at the beginning of a chapter. The sections headed *For Discussion* simply contain discussion questions pertinent to the section or subsection they terminate. Much benefit can be obtained through sharing views of material one is reading or studying with another person, and comparing different perspectives and experiences. Talking through the ideas of a section can also assist by moving the reader to a more active use of them. Sections headed *You try it* ... are written more directly to the individual reader (whether part of a group or not) and relate principally to encouraging you to apply some idea just discussed in the text. Occasionally in both of these text sections I write specifically about how the main material in a chapter could be worked with, prior to suggesting some discussion topics or activity. In all these cases, aiding reflection is the goal, and there are no right answers.

For groups working with this book: in some cases, where an activity is suggested the actions proposed may take time, and their feasibility will definitely vary according to the circumstances of the group. In some instances, however, it may be possible to choose one such activity after concluding reading a chapter, and then have group members report back on their attempts to carry it out at the beginning of a subsequent meeting.

Positionality

In the sciences at the beginning of the new century there is an increased consciousness of the importance of context in determining or limiting knowledge claims. Closely related to this is a rise in acceptance of the local, personal, and interested (i.e., not *dis*interested) nature of knowledge. For me, this means that it is essential that the author of a work such as this disclose himself to readers, rather than assume common interests and understandings, or take refuge in impersonal, anonymous, yet authoritative prose. In addition, in the context of material which will stress personal and professional development, it may be desirable to see individuals as not fixed, but "positioned," in a shifting web of relationships that temporarily define a person.[3] Consequently, and with that caveat, I'm white, male, middle-class, raised in London, and have lived most of my adult life outside my country of birth. I've taught in high schools in London and Sarawak, in the business training sector and English conversation schools in Japan, and in the English for Academic Purposes sector in the United States. While my Masters is in ESL, my Ph.D. is in Educational Psychology.[4] I've been primarily based in EFL/ESL teacher education as an academic and teacher at the University of Hawai'i since 1988. In that role and status, I've had experiences working with teachers at other U.S. institutions, and further afield, in Singapore, Australia, Colombia, Japan (again), Denmark, and Kyrgyzstan. These days I'm particularly concerned, professionally, about the poor working conditions of many ES/FL teachers, and the lack of support for professional development in the administrative structures in which they are involved. Broadly, in my work I'm trying to find ways of fostering S/FL education that will lead to a better world.

Some scene-setting comments . . .

General aspects of S/FL teaching practice

Many parts of a language teacher's professional expertise are not exclusively associated with the teaching of a specific domain, "skill," or aspect of the language. Accordingly, the program of professional development contained in or implied by this book does not specifically relate to, for example, the teaching of reading, or literacy, or oral communication skills, or content ESL, or any other equivalent area. There are many handbooks, not to mention journal articles, which provide advice or empirical evidence concerning how best to handle such matters. I believe there are also *general* aspects of practice which deserve attention (cf. Shulman, 1987), and that is what this book addresses.

Professional development and a practicum

There is not enough time in a practicum, or for that matter in an MA or Certificate course, to do all the teacher development that might be desirable.[5]

Consistent with this, the basic qualification in most areas of teaching is really little more than a license to begin: it implies that the relevant authorities would be willing to accept a person as a teacher, at a basic level of competence, and does not imply that this person knows all there is to know about teaching (cf. Reynolds, 1992). While an MA, particularly when it is taken after other certificate-level qualifications in ES/FL, is an indication of a fair measure of proficiency as an educator, those who hold it and have gone on in their career may sometimes reflect (as I do) on how little they really knew after completing the course, compared to what they know now.

A way to address the problem of the brevity of supervised teaching within formal coursework (whether BA, Certificate, or MA) is to see the formal period of practice and learning as just *one* brief period within what should be a more extensive period, indeed career, of less formal learning. But few of us will have those careers or learn as much from them as we could if there is not an initial emphasis, in our first periods of teacher education, on structuring our teaching so as to learn from it – engaging, that is to say, in reflective practice – and on structuring our career and our working conditions, so as to be lifelong learners. And that is a major underlying concern of this book.

Teaching as performing a social role

Becoming a teacher means, among other things, learning to perform a particular social role. In performing the social role of "teacher," an actor necessarily engages with a script partly constructed by the expectations of our audience of students, fellow-teachers, administrators, and (possibly) parents and community members. As Cazden (1988, p. 44) says, "School is always a performance that must be constituted through a group of actors." I think it is this conception of teaching which is recognized by the beginning teacher as fundamental (and why such teachers-under-construction can be impatient with what they call "theory"). Knowing a large amount about, say, the psychological processes involved in acquiring reading strategies in a second language is of little importance if one cannot enact the teacher role in front of students.[6] Enacting that role includes knowing what can (initially) be said and done, and doing so in a way that will elicit the complicity of the students, who often know their role better than does the beginning teacher.

However, even as one is gaining a command of the basic or historically well-established aspects of the role, one can begin to refine technique and rewrite the script (cf. Grossman, 1992). For me, technique includes not only standard aspects of ES/FL pedagogy, but also those aspects of human interpersonal communication skills that can facilitate complex communication, which in turn range from those needed to transmit information clearly, to those through which one sustains the relationships that support communication.   .

The possible need to rewrite the script is suggested by a number of factors. For most of us, the basic understanding of "school" comes to us from our own experiences as children and young adults. Much has changed in the world since that time. And if the state of the world as a new century begins is not one to be complacent about, perhaps the old script of "school" is implicated in that. The right to rewrite the script is something that the more highly paid professional actors ensure is entered into their contracts. In a parallel manner, we can also hope that the more professional teachers reflect on the roles they have stepped into and explore the full range of possibilities available within them, and consider to what extent they may want to or be capable of altering them (given the constraints they are under: Ritchie & Wilson, 2000). Teachers' explorations are partly dependent on understanding how their roles relate to the rest of the script – that is, to the other characters in the play and the thrust of the storyline. In the real world as it encompasses teaching, this means the nature of schooling and of education, and what it means to be a teacher in terms of both one's effect upon students and also of one's effect upon society. The university-based S/FL teacher education curriculum has a role to play in developing this understanding (Hudelson & Faltis, 1993). To drop the metaphor, life is not a play, and people can get hurt, or helped, by what we do. Teaching is not a technical exercise, but a moral[7] enterprise enacted through social means.

Teacher learning/reflective teaching

The present book is intended to support teacher learning. A variety of understandings of how teachers, including ES/FL teachers, learn has coexisted in the professional literature and the minds of teachers for as long as this topic has been discussed. Probably those which have been most treated by academics at any one time have been those most consistent with the dominant understandings of learning at that time. One feature of modern scientific disciplines is their much greater size, complexity, and diversity than ever before. This allows a much greater range of theories to coexist; or, for a single phenomenon to be explored from multiple perspectives. Teacher learning can be conceptualized as having both individual and social dimensions. Hitherto, much of the small literature in our field on teacher development has crowded under the heading of "reflective teaching," in which a somewhat individual perspective is taken.[8] Presently, there are increasing efforts to look at the social aspects of teacher learning, on various grounds, including that teachers do learn from each other, and may possibly learn better when they have more opportunities to interact in a mutually supportive fashion. In this book, I assume that both social and individual perspectives on ES/FL teachers learning can be useful, though I don't probe the details very much. This book does not set forth any one psychological or social theory of teacher learning, nor does it depend on just one – as a survey, it is not that kind of work. On the other hand, I do strongly advocate social structures that support teacher learning, both at a micro or "group" level (in Chapter 2), and a macro or "institutional" level (in Chapter 11).[9]

Personal development and boundary crossing

Professionals working in the areas of ESL and EFL are far more conscious than we used to be of the context- and culture-specific nature of many aspects of teaching and learning, even of English, which, as an international language, is now often seen as no longer the property of any one culture. Accordingly, this book reflects my own specific experience of S/FL teacher education, and that of my students, at an international university. The catchment area of my university includes the Pacific rim, but overall my program is one whose student teachers come from all parts of the world. Most of them, most of their teachers, and indeed most members of the S/FL teaching fellowship are in an interesting position as the twenty-first century opens, with respect to the increasingly rapid process of globalization characteristic of this time. They are people already comfortable (to some extent) with a social position that interrupts the line separating one culture from another. Some of them may be comfortable with straddling a similar conceptual line that separates one culture-determined aspect of an individual's identity from another.[10] If current trends in world sociocultural change continue, we may expect far more people to have to work with such challenges to a unitary concept of self.

Many second or foreign language teachers will have created, or re-created themselves as cultural boundary crossers.[11] They have undergone a process of second language socialization, which, as Roberts (1998, p. 37) says, "is not a straightforward case of becoming communicatively competent within a fixed sociocultural group. It is rather a hybrid process of both learning to belong and yet remaining apart – of having several social identities and affiliations to several languages." They will thus recognize the importance of engaging in a steady process of personal change as they continue through their career and through the stations of their life's development. In becoming teachers, we take on the responsibility for facilitating the change and growth of others, whether we like it or not, and in the early stages of our career we ourselves are changed, accordingly. In continuing to discharge our professional responsibilities, particularly in positions of increasing professional demand and power, I believe we also are responsible for continuing our personal development and self-actualization[12] as individuals in a rapidly changing, increasingly multicultural world society.[13]

At the cultural and social level, humans regularly have to grapple with a calling into question of behaviors and views that previously seemed fixed. Even supposedly elementary aspects of classroom practice can come in for renewed scrutiny by the teacher in midcareer, reexamining the previously unquestioned assumptions of earlier professional training. At a broader level, questioning of previously taken-for-granted matters continues, as ever, in the world of the arts, sciences, and philosophy; including in the research areas that contribute to the supposed "knowledge base for ES/FL teaching."

In concluding this subsection, I would like to mention the valuable role of skepticism in the development of a professional. It was skepticism that moved the European middle ages into the modern world,[14] with the resulting enormous advances in technology and the physical conditions of life. Skepticism is also highly desirable in S/FL teachers as a means of defense against the many popular fads that have coursed through the business in recent decades. Skepticism, along with a questioning and critical attitude about one's own accepted practices, as well as about the institutions we find ourselves in, can be a valuable basis for reflective development and for professional reconstruction, at the individual, group, and institutional level, which I hope this book will support.

YOU TRY IT...

As the author, I've briefly introduced myself to you the reader. If you are using this book, or a part of it, with other teachers, might I suggest that you make sure you all have been adequately introduced? As you will find (if you haven't already flipped forward in the book), I hope to encourage quite a bit of teacher-to-teacher collaboration and discussion through discussion sections in the text. This sort of thing is less effective if you don't really know or feel comfortable with the teachers you are talking to. So if you are using this book with others, make sure you and they know each other.

And at this point, I should introduce some less academic voices – a group of individuals without whom this book would not exist – my past students. You will hear their voices from time to time throughout this book, as they comment on various topics in it, or, in some chapters, extend the coverage of material and ideas that I initially present.

Acknowledgments

I am most grateful to Anne Burns and Sandy McKay, who provided valuable comments on successive versions of this work, and to Jack Richards, without whose confidence in my efforts from an early stage this book would probably not have gotten very far. And naturally, I am very happy to acknowledge the support and insight of successive groups of teachers-in-development who have worked with me. Their words appear throughout the book, and a special thank you to all of them who allowed fragments of the dialogues we've had to appear for the benefit of other teachers. I regret that anonymity means no personal acknowledgments, but I at least remember who you are.

1 *Organization and Goals*

- What should the content of a practicum-related course be?
- Are goals important in professional development?

Warm-up
Write down one goal you have for your development as a teacher, then share it with another developing teacher.

We don't always consciously seek out the things that most affect our development as teachers. Some of the things that have made me grow as a teacher have been my failures. Accidents can help, too – I have often not sought a particular book on a topic I needed help with, but encountered it by chance. But I think there is a lot to be said for having goals. In this chapter I have one major aim in mind: to encourage or help you to set at least tentative goals for a period of professional development focusing on teaching practice and what underpins it. Since this book is intended to support your attainment of such goals, let me first comment on the content, organization, and tone of the chapters that follow, so that they can be helpful in terms of your goals.

Elements and organization of a course to accompany practice teaching

The program of study and reflection implied by this book can be conceptualized as relating to "those skills and values useful in developing as an ES/FL teacher which cannot be assigned to specific conventional parts of ES/FL teaching." This eliminates from separate consideration the so-called four skills of listening, speaking, reading, and writing, and also those areas of content or disciplinary knowledge that form the core of applied linguistics or second language studies and their source disciplines of psychology, linguistics, anthropology, and sociology. Which leaves: what you do to be an ES/FL teacher, in the classroom and outside it; how you work with your colleagues, your school, and your society; and how you base this, as a reflective human being, in your values and beliefs. Values and personal growth, then, form part of the curriculum for ES/FL teacher development, in my opinion, and they appear as part of the content and intent of this book. (Though not always emphasized in TESOL teacher education, they have a long history elsewhere.[1]) And finally, this book also includes attention to the processes and prerequisites for continuing professional development, both institutional and personal, beyond the formal practicum itself.

The material of this course is presented in a linear sequence, and has the authoritative form of the written word. Rather than necessarily following its sequence, and rather than accepting its authority, however, I suggest you be "strategic" in engaging with it. Depending on your level of experience, some of it may be more and some of it less useful to you; and your working contexts may make some of the ideas discussed here more easily applicable than others. What use you make of it will not only depend on your present development as a teacher, but also how you see yourself developing, which is likely to be guided to some extent by your goals. Though some cultures may place more emphasis than others on the learners' own goals being a driving force for his/her learning, the possibility that you have broad goals for a period of professional development seems likely. I think it is important to articulate them, but first, let us briefly review the topic of goals itself. We could look at goals from a variety of perspectives (philosophical or cultural, for example), but I will simply take a few points from the understanding of goals provided by psychological research (recognizing that it may include cultural perspectives itself). I then go on to specific exemplars of how goals have been referred to in teacher development.

Goals

Older psychological research identified goals as having a variety of positive effects on learning. It investigated the topic of goals from three main viewpoints: the characteristics of goals (such as their specificity), their content (personal, social, etc.), and the individual's orientation to goals of different types (challenge on the one hand versus grades on the other; see Schutz, 1994, for review). A wide range of social science research on goal-setting is reviewed in Baumeister, et al. (1994, p. 62; see also Locke & Latham, 1990; Walker & Quinn, 1996), from which I extract the following:

Both long-range and short-term goals are valuable for effective self-management. Having long-term goals is important for orienting oneself and providing continuity across one's efforts . . . [cf. e.g.] De Volder and Lens (1982). Long-range goals may help one transcend the immediate situation and its unpleasant demands or distracting temptations. Long-range goals alone can be daunting, however . . . Bandura & Schunk (1981) showed the benefits of having proximal . . . as well as distal goals. People who pursued a set of proximal goals gained a sense of self-efficacy by the fact that they were frequently approaching and reaching these goals. In that way, they avoided the discouragement that comes from seeing how remote one's ultimate, long-range goals are . . . Thus, it is most helpful to have both proximal and distal goals. Manderlink and Harackiewicz (1984) found that distal goal setting increased people's intrinsic motivation, whereas proximal goal setting led to more positive expectations for success. People who have both types of goals will tend to enjoy the benefits of having a long-term plan that structures their activities and provides a continuous source of motivation, as well as receiving the encouraging feedback of making progress toward these goals.

We probably should see this work as providing useful evidence that goal-setting does help adults succeed in doing tasks, including learning, and that it also helps them develop personally and professionally. At the same time, I would suggest that this line of research included a general, largely un-examined assumption, that "self-directed behavior" is universally needed to achieve academic success, as well as success elsewhere in life. That is, this work takes as axiomatic the idea that individuals independently choose goals for themselves and direct their energies toward them, in a largely independent manner. While this may be true for adults in the dominant cultures of Europe and North America, it may not do justice to cultures where people are more interdependent. Nevertheless, it can provide a jumping-off point for this discussion.

Let us get closer to home now, and consider goals in the context of teacher development. In the area of teacher development, what procedures are used or have been advocated for goal-setting? Good and Brophy (1987, p. 531) emphasize a focus on explicit behaviors. "Make explicit plans," they say, continuing,

Teachers who attempt to improve their teaching must be able to decide what they want to do and how to determine if their plans are working. Too often, our halfhearted New Year's resolutions are never acted upon because they are vague. Resolutions such as . . . "I want to be a more enthusiastic teacher" are seldom accomplished simply because they are not concrete suggestions that guide behavior.

They would recommend a more explicit goal – in this case, " 'I want to tell students why a lesson is important before it begins and model my sincere interest in the content' " (p. 531). Presumably it is possible to be explicit without being behavioral.

However, Duke (1990), on the basis of a one-year project on teacher goal-setting in the context of professional development, reports that the teachers he worked with (in U.S. mainstream education) had considerable difficulty setting goals. They were not accustomed to setting goals for their professional growth, and it was necessary to devote considerable time and energy to designing exercises and providing a supportive, collaborative environment in order to make this possible.

Courses for teacher development probably should, then, encourage participants to reflect on their goals. Here is an example of how a text in this area does so: Posner (1996, p. 17) encourages preservice teachers about to have their first experience with the field to articulate their concerns as well as identify goals:

EXERCISE 2.2 Expressing personal goals and priorities
People's goals affect their actions, expectations, and perceptions, even (and maybe especially) when they are unaware of these goals. Expressing goals makes their examination possible, thereby providing an opportunity for reassessment.
  Write a few sentences describing how you expect to benefit from your field experience . . .
  Now look at what you have written. You might want to compare your goals with the following generic goals:

1. To find out what teaching is really like (i.e., career exploration)
2. To see if I like teaching (i.e., exploring personal preferences)
3. To see if I can really do it (i.e., self-testing)
4. To learn some skills and modify certain habits and characteristics (i.e., training)
5. To develop my own approach or style (i.e., personal style)
6. To apply what I've learned in college to real students and to real classrooms (i.e., theory into practice).

Despite my caveat concerning the older psychological research in this area, we may note that the possibility of this sort of practice in teacher education is not confined to "Western" countries. For example, Kwo (1996, p. 314) reports on one Hong Kong EFL preservice teacher education course that began by way of a questionnaire given to students including the following:

1. *Orientation*
• Why have you chosen to do [this] . . . program? (In considering your career, what are your options?)

- What do you see as essential qualities of a teacher which you are striving to develop? (List them and describe role models, if any)
- What do you expect from the . . . course? (What would you like to be the objectives of the course?)

A sort of compromise between the idea that goals for a period of learning may be set by the learner, and the idea that they should be set by the teacher, can occur if teachers-in-development are encouraged to specify their goals while being aware of an instructor's. Here, to exemplify this, is a quote from a recent syllabus (of mine) designed for use with the present book:

Participants will develop their own goals for the course. Past goals (developed by me, with input from successive groups of students) included the aim that participants develop

1. a conceptual map for SL teaching techniques which are not skill-area specific
2. their conscious understanding of the processes of SL teaching
3. their ability to reflect on their use of classroom teaching procedures and lesson planning
4. a critical stance towards the components of teacher education contained in the practicum.

I'd like to see you articulate your own goals and share them with the class.

In using this remark in a syllabus, I assume that my students (like you, the reader) are motivated professional adults, and thus might prefer to choose goals for themselves, or at least jointly negotiate them, rather than merely accepting those imposed on them by administrative structures and the instructor. At the same time, given the work of Duke just mentioned, it is probably advisable for us to devote time and thought to the matter of goal-setting, rather than take it for granted. And of course, experiences themselves, even if not driven by goals, are important and valuable, too.

YOU TRY IT ...

If you are using this book in connection with a period of teaching practice or some other form of professional development, try to determine some goals for yourself that you will aim at during this time. You may wish to use Posner's example as a basis, though remember he is addressing the preservice student teacher.

In developing a goal or goals, here are some things to bear in mind:

1. Obviously, you must make sure your goal makes sense. You must believe in the rationality or appropriateness of your goal.

2. For some goals, such as long-term life goals, you may find it helpful to visualize what it would look like to attain that goal.
3. Writing a goal down (in a literate culture) is said to enhance one's sense of commitment to it; and sharing it or divulging it to others may increase this further (cf. Shell, 1999).

If possible, share these goals with other teachers and your instructor. How do your goals compare with those in Posner's, Kwo's, or my extracts? Are your goals more specific, or more abstract; are they more long-term, or more immediate? If you are one of a group of teachers using this book, what differences are to be found among the goals of the group – can any of those differences be related to the amount of teaching experience already accumulated or the circumstances of that teaching experience?

Student teachers comment . . .

Here is (my reduction of) what a group of participants in an ES/FL practicum class I ran had to say when first pressed to report their goals.

Several students specified the fairly obvious goal of developing as a teacher (to "improve," to be "competent," "to further my education," and "to become a more reflective teacher"), and then went on to specify in more detail what they meant, or some of the things this implied for them. For example, one student teacher wanted to develop an experiential approach during the course of the practicum.

[My] main goal is to improve as a teacher, and thereby improve my teaching. To me, this means making learning more enjoyable and interesting for my students (and, by extension, more effective), and that's why a more experiential approach is something I'd like to attempt. This is the way I think I would like to learn another language (or anything, for that matter). . . . So, yes, what I need is to get a few books on the subject, find out in more detail what it involves, and try to work it into my lessons. Yes, I can see this as one of my goals for the course.

Several teachers mentioned getting clearer about their own views. This could be with regard to methodological principles:

I feel my teaching approach (style) tends to be a potpourri of techniques and philosophies that I read or hear about, there is no continuity or structure. I'm not consistent at all and this disturbs me greatly.

Or a philosophical principle: one student wanted to explore the implications of

one of the greatest Japanese scholars, Takeji Hayashi [who] said that teaching is equal to learning.

And one typical target for clarity is:

I'd like to be able to articulate my teaching philosophy.

An important point made by one *experienced* teacher concerned choice of perhaps *new* goals:

I believe a lot of what I am going through here is the result of lack of experience with these particular skill areas and perhaps these particular learners (here I mean ESL vs. EFL). At my former school . . . I could teach any aspect of the curriculum to any level of student . . . and I had enough experience in this domain and enough knowledge of the student population to effectively create a learning experience that I knew would be successful. The change of skill area and of student population has brought me back to stage one – that of discovering what and how to teach and also how to make it work. In order to grow as a teacher, I requested these skill areas, so I have no one to blame but myself.

For several less experienced teachers, a goal was simply to see how it was to be a teacher. One wrote,

I've been a student for such a long time and this is going to be the first time that I participate in a language classroom as a teacher. The simple fact that I am no longer one of the students in class makes me excited about discovering a new aspect of myself as a person.

In some cases, a crossover or interplay appeared between goals my student teachers had for their own students and goals they had for themselves:

the more immediate classroom goals which allow you to guide the education of your students and the long range goals associated with "self actualization" are both integral part of being an educator.

And again

My goals for this course are to learn how to develop clear, concise, and reachable goals for myself and my students.

Finally, a valuable questioning of the goal orientation is offered by one student:

Whenever I am asked to state what my personal goals are, I don't really know how to respond . . . I don't want to give the impression that I'm indecisive . . . but personally I think my discomfort with stating goals stems from my personal philosophy. . . . I don't really believe that it is always necessary to develop a set of goals. I have found that sometimes not knowing where you're going to go, or not striving for a certain destination, can be quite fruitful. It's sort of like trusting that the process will lead to its own destination.

Understanding your curricular context

When teachers are also learners (as in any instance of teacher development), they have the possibility of turning their experience of learning to use in reflecting on their teaching. Not all adult learning can inform, say, the teaching of a second language to high school students, of course. But in some cases there is the possibility of heightened awareness, if not transfer. Sometimes this sort of thing is referred to as "double-loop learning" (Woodward, 1991). A classic example in the ES/FL context might be when teachers learn about implementing group work via an experience of learning using groups (as opposed to receiving a lecture on the topic).

If now I make some effort to heighten your awareness concerning the pedagogical context of a focus on learner goals, your own teacher development process may be more efficient, and the utilizability of the experience in your own teaching may also be enhanced. Therefore, it may be of use to consider some of the historical and conceptual strands of thought in curriculum and pedagogy involved in a shift from a position in which the teacher sets goals unilaterally, to one in which goals might be the subject of discussion between teacher and student.

In the dominant model of educational course planning used in post-secondary institutions in the 2000s (in my part of the world), course goals are generally made explicit. For elementary and secondary schools they may be set by curriculum experts or a ministry of education; in the post-secondary sector they are often set by the instructor or the institution.[2] Having explicit goals is considered good practice, as it makes the success of the course to some extent open to evaluation: were the goals met? Very detailed procedures for having experts (teacher or curriculum specialists) deriving and specifying curricular and course goals have become a central feature of mainstream curriculum theory over the past 50 years (at least in the English-speaking world), though widely established in practice perhaps only in the last twenty.[3]

Positions contrary to this, curricular orientations which allow student autonomy or choice, have coexisted in western education systems with these just-mentioned more hierarchical and authoritarian arrangements at least since the Romantic movement of the eighteenth century (Shotton, 1993). They appear with more prominence at different times and places. In the United States, they were associated with the progressive movement in the 1930s; more recently, in many countries and across all age ranges they were temporarily prominent in the 1960s (Della-Dora & Blanchard, 1979). While this position has often been associated with more radical philosophies of education, such as libertarian (Smith, 1983) or alternative education (Kozol, 1982) or critical pedagogy (Crookes & Lehner, 1998), the basic idea seems firmly established, and far less radical, in professional and in-service forms of education. Here one may find, for example, the "learning contract" widely used (in which students contract for a specific grade in exchange for specific amounts of study: Boak, 1998).

Some of these ideas have been incorporated under the heading of social constructivism (Berger & Luckmann, 1966) at the curricular level:

In this social constructivist view, curriculum is constructed within the social context of the classroom or school. It has been, and is being, enacted or experienced through teachers' and students' joint negotiation of context and meaning . . . In viewing curriculum in this way, the enactment of individual lessons can be seen to be an important unit of curriculum, and the curriculum as socially constructed events in which teachers and students engage to negotiate different aspects of the curriculum, including topics to be included, ways of approaching them, goals, and means of assessment (Feldman, 1996, n.p.).[4]

In addition, in the wider TES/FL world, there has been a tradition of pedagogy and curriculum (e.g., Benson & Voller, 1997; Dickinson, 1987; Holec, 1980; Littlejohn, 1983; Tudor, 1996) coming under the heading of learner autonomy, which has over at least twenty years (and was? awkward possibly influenced by the many social changes in Western Europe in the 1960s) argued for the importance of the learner as an individual in charge of his/her learning.

Finally, a third strand should be acknowledged: adult education, with its theoretical tradition of "andragogy" (Knowles, 1982). This recognizes, to a much greater degree than does mainstream (child) pedagogy, the often self-directed and autonomous nature of the way adults learn in the real world. The expectations and capacities they consequently bring to the classroom can lead to greater use of interactive and nonlinear forms of program design (Kowalski, 1988; cf. Brookfield, 1985, 1986; Mezirow, 1991; Rajal, 1983). These ideas also relate to the overlapping domain of professional education, of which teacher education is a prominent subcategory (Eraut, 1994).

Of course, on the other hand, it is clear that these ideas, which are by no means dominant in Western educational systems, are also even less common in non-Western systems (cf. Polio & Wilson-Duffy, 1998).

FOR DISCUSSION

1. If you are presently teaching an EFL or ESL course, has a needs analysis been used as the basis for establishing course goals? If not, on what basis are they set, and why?

2. Under what circumstances do you set goals for yourself? How do you achieve them, and what support do you use or make use of to do this?
3. Under what conditions, if any, do you think it could be desirable for your students to contribute to determining the goals for a course you might be teaching?
4. I believe that the teacher should at least consider to what extent s/he wishes to share the institutionally-assigned authority to set goals with students; and also, to what extent, if any, institutional pressures and cultural expectations might allow this. In a minority of cases, the teacher will be in a setting where there is a tradition of allowing students input in this area, but my guess is that in the majority of cases, the student teacher will find the administrative system unaccustomed to such initiatives, and the students likewise. What is your situation? What options are available to you? How does your situation compare with other teachers'?

2 *Writing, Observing, Interacting, and Acting Together*

> • What might some benefits be in working collaboratively with other teachers during a practicum?
> • What personal and interpersonal practices are needed to work with other teachers on one's teaching?
> • What problems might occur, and how can these be resolved or prevented?

Warm-up

In your experience as a teacher, have you worked with other teachers on curriculum, instruction, or related matters? If so, how did it go?

In the Introduction I implied that a teaching practicum should draw upon the developing teacher's previous experience as both teacher and learner, and potentially concern their self-concept and personal development. I also suggested that it should not be something completely distinct from what happens in a teacher's subsequent professional life. The practicum is a short-term, intensive opportunity for professional growth, occurring (we hope) under relatively favorable institutional conditions. In it, with institutional support on the one hand, and an extensive commitment of personal time and attention, on the other, teachers attempt to move forward in various aspects of their professional lives. In this chapter, I would like to follow up on the work readers have done in specifying their goals, and review processes that could enable a practicum to have a long-term outlook, as well as work well for a teacher in the short-term. These processes relate to how teachers reflect and think individually, as well as how they do this with others.

Let me first explain why I am concerned about the duration of (most) practica, and why I want to support teachers' processes of learning in connection with a practicum that would facilitate long-term teacher development. Around the world, teaching practice courses for ES/FL teachers tend to be comparatively brief compared with the idea of a lifetime career.[1] For example, in professional development courses for ES/FL teachers at university graduate level in North America, teaching practice courses are often taken along with several other courses during a single semester and they are usually a standard 45 contact hours in length. Courses for teaching practice located in a department or college of education may require one full-time semester in a school, supplemented with formal meetings. These courses will typically contribute to an MA-level degree. In many other English-speaking countries, those who are taking ES/FL teaching practice courses at university are probably doing so in something like a one-year Certificate course, in which their teaching practice will be a full-time term on-site (as in the UK).

It could be said, then, that the amount of supervised teaching experience to be found in the coursework of most ES/FL teachers is relatively little upon which to build a career or to develop as a teacher. As a teacher educator, I find this worrying. As someone with responsibility for such practice teaching courses, or practicums, I have asked myself how I can structure them to compensate for their brevity, and wondered what content can be most useful, long-term. A central part of my response to this problem is to advocate that a practicum should manifest aspects of a "teacher development group," so that students can begin to think about (and experience) a structure they can utilize after their formal training is over – a structure which facilitates long-term continuing teacher development.

Teacher development groups are small-scale, informal gatherings of teachers to work together on their professional concerns. They may be meetings organized to share experiences or they might involve discussing readings, books, articles, and so on. Under favorable circumstances they might include discussion and feedback based on mutual observation. These groups work against the individualist conception of teaching dominant in Western educational systems that prevents teachers from gaining assistance from those most immediately able to offer it – their fellow teachers (cf. Shimahara, 1998a). I believe that teachers, for the sake of their own continued professional development, and possibly for the sake of their own mental and emotional health in a demanding business, should become aware of and capable of participating in and running teacher development groups.

Upon graduating or finishing a course of teacher education, a teacher does not stop learning; s/he simply moves from intensive, concentrated, and formal learning, to far less intensive, informal learning. Under the worst conditions, some teachers (on the outside at least) appear to cease to learn – giving rise to the familiar distinction between a teacher who has twenty years' experience and the teacher who has one year of experience 20 times.

But I will take the perhaps overly optimistic view that given the option that teachers have of creating their own teacher development groups in their workplace, they can move from an intensive, short-term practicum, to an extensive, long-term engagement with a group of like-minded individuals and continue to work on their practice (cf. Clair, 1998; Edge, 1992, 1993; Underhill, 1992; see also Appendix A).

Within this general context, basic and increasingly standard techniques of professional growth apply. Reflection is central to these approaches – personal reflection through writing, by way of journals; interpersonal means of reflection, such as observing another's class and giving them feedback or merely using the experience to think about one's own class; or group means: the teacher development group discussion and investigation.

In this chapter, I will review these processes for reflection and their supporting structures. While more is now available in our field than before about writing and observing as means for professional development, and acting together to investigate practice is becoming a growth area, less advice is available concerning small group process, so I will give most space to this important area.

Writing

The idea of using forms of personal writing as an aid to learning and personal growth is probably age-old, though it was not part of my upbringing as a school student nor my education as a student teacher. It is certainly very popular, not to say ubiquitous these days. I urge readers who are using this book as part of a program of professional development to use personal writing to reflect on their practice while reading these chapters. One of the earlier discussions of reflective teacher writing for our area is Porter et al. (1990). They emphasize the role of personal writing which aids learning through various means, including seeing writing as a discovery process, for exploring new ideas, and making connections.

Definitions

The following set of definitions, from Holly and McLoughlin (1989, p. 263), may be helpful:

Log   A log is a regularly kept record of performance. Facts, unencumbered by interpretation, are recorded systematically. Social scientists and educators use this "objective" and empirically based process to record facts important to their work. A teacher writes in the manner of a log when recording what happened in a class. A lesson plan is a plan for what is intended to take place, while the recording of what did take place is a factual recounting of the events (that is, a description of teaching).

Diaries   A diary is defined as a record of personal experiences and observations over time. In contrast to the log, it is by definition a personal document – one in which the writer includes interpretations, opinions, feelings, and thoughts. A diary typically contains a spontaneous type of writing. Although diaries have been published, the intent is usually to talk to oneself through writing. Facts can be recorded but they are usually tied to the writer's thoughts and feelings about daily events.

Journals   A journal includes facts similar to a log, and it can include spontaneous and personal thoughts and feelings as does the diary, but it is more than these. A journal is a comprehensive and systematic attempt at writing to clarify ideas and experiences; it is a document written with the intent to return to it, and to learn through interpretation of the writing. The journal, like the log and the diary, is kept over time. It is not necessarily a record of events as they happen. Patterns or topics that recur in the writer's experience can be written about. A teacher who is writing a journal about teaching might notice a pattern, and reflect on similar examples and write about these. The teacher then might use the journal to explore and work on problems in a systematic way.

In personal writing we may distinguish, then, to some extent, between journals, logs, and diaries. Porter et al. (1990) favor journals as the best type of writing for professional growth and particularly suggest they be used as a means of communication between student teacher and supervisor. This communication, at its simplest, has the supervisor writing back to the journaling student teacher, on hard copy journal entries, and increasingly, e-mail journals are possible and potentially more convenient. Porter et al. note that a journal should not be an accounting of personal matters, nor merely a place to take notes. While this is reasonable, I am reluctant to discourage teachers writing a journal for the purpose of aiding professional development from addressing any topic, in any way, for fear of stopping the writing/thinking process. A writer's personal ruminations may be important in themselves. Particularly when the journal is being used as a form of communication between a student, or a teacher-in-development, and a supervisor, personal content may allow for greater mutual understanding and rapport. In my experience, journal entries often encompass elements of several other similar genres.

I recognize that if you are someone who has never kept a journal or a diary before, developing the self-discipline necessary for this may be difficult. I myself come up with many reasons for not doing it, or for breaking off having once started. Changes of routine can throw me off, and my tendency to do most of my professional writing at a computer inhibits me from journaling in the traditional way; yet I think it is important to make the effort. A key point for me is the possibility of reflection. One may be growing, as a teacher, but if there is no record of one's naiveté to return to, one may not have a sense of progress! More positively, I would affirm the conception of writing as discovery as central to the journal as a means of professional development. Some experts in linguistic self-exploration have said, "how do I know what I think until I see what I say?"[2] When in our crowded professional lives, sometimes combining the role of student and teacher, do we have a chance for "exploratory talk" (Barnes, 1971), in which we try out ideas to see how they sit with us?

The broader contexts of journaling: narrative theory and teacher research

The keeping of personal reflective writing has a wider and increasingly influential theoretical context that should be considered as well. Personal reflective writing that goes on over time is a form of narrative; and narrative has been identified as both an archetypal form of knowledge (e.g. Bruner, J., 1986) and as a way we represent ourselves to ourselves, that is, a way we figure out who we are or who we are becoming. Given my emphasis on the congruity between self-development and teacher development, personal narrative seems particularly important in this light. During a practicum, participants may be making a particular effort to review their values, their reasons for being a teacher, and so on, for which, again, journaling can be very useful. (See Chapter 3.)

    The importance of narrative, both in the world of ideas and in general, for personal growth has been emphasized by many (e.g., Witherell & Noddings, 1991). Narayan (1991, pp. 113–4) swiftly stakes out some of the academic ground relevant to this topic, as follows:

Narrative has colonized territory in a number of fields. Though clearly sweeping in behind the vanguard of the "text" analogy, the use of narrative instead of text emphasizes the subjectivity of active agents and the negotiated unfolding of events. That narrative is a means of making sense of one's own and others' experience has been recurrently argued by theologians (Crites, 1971; Goldberg, 1982; Hoffman, 1986); psychologists (J. Bruner, 1986, 1987; Coles, 1989; Polkinghorne, 1988; Schafer, 1983); philosophers (MacIntyre, 1981; Ricoeur, 1984); historians (Clifford, 1986; Mink, 1978 . . .); and anthropologists (E. M. Bruner, 1986; Rosaldo, 1989) – to cite only a prominent selection of authors and publications. Most generally, these theorists agree that the progression of events in narrative captures the dimension of time in lived experience. By arranging the flux and welter of experience around a narrative line, we make sense of our pasts, plan for our futures and comprehend the lives of others.

Making sense of one's life, from a writing perspective, is akin to finding one's voice, a benefit of journaling identified by teacher educator Cooper (1991, p. 105):

> I was privileged to watch this process in my students when I taught a class called Shaping Meaning: The Reading and Writing of Diaries and Journals. One student in my class wrote about the importance of finding one's own voice through writing, telling, and listening to each others' stories: "Hearing all of your voices in your journals and speaking in class gives me confidence. The fact that you sound so good to me helps me assume that you are hearing me that way too."

Another of the many beneficial effects of journal writing, according to Cooper, is that of caring for the self (an additional philosophic context provided by Noddings' ethic of care – see Chapter 5). Cooper remarks that

> writing our own stories works to combat [a] depletion [of care] by reminding us of who we are, while it focuses on and attends to our needs. Diarists report that when they sit down and put pen to paper, their most immediate and pressing concerns emerge before them on the pages. There is a feeling of surprise, "Oh, so that's what's bothering me" that emerges from [this] process of engrossment (p. 105).[3]

Making sense of professional practice can result in contributing to professional knowledge, too. Now, journaling can be both individual and interpersonal. I mentioned the "dialogue journal," in which entries in a journal are written not only for oneself but for another, who responds in writing, in terms of student teacher and supervisor; but it is obviously a possibility in a teacher development group context, or even if there is only a single colleague with whom one is working on teacher development. One can also think of writing in a full group format, in which a teacher development group as a whole decides to write on a particular topic. But for what audience, and what kind of writing, one might ask? The results of this kind of writing can also benefit other teachers, and be a form of "teacher research." Journal writing, even including the making of journal entries that have more of a diary character, is actually part of a long tradition of scientific work. Even the stereotypical "white-coated scientist" keeps a lab journal, recording the progress and implementation of lab work; and in the hands of anthropologists, the journal and associated "field notes" are both the raw material and the partly-cooked basis for theorizing and further exploration. Teachers working on their practice are similarly engaged in a process both of exploration and experimentation. (I will return to this matter in the final section of this chapter.)

1. If you have not kept a journal before, starting one may require some assistance. Let me assist by providing a partial list of things that you could write about:

   successes in use of classroom techniques

   practical problems that may have come up in the class, particularly ones you have not yet solved

   the administrative context of your class, particularly as it affects you or your students

   matters arising from working with a cooperating teacher

   your day-to-day life, particularly as it affects your work as a teacher or your development as a student teacher

   how you are or are not manifesting your principles as a teacher in your class

   your image of yourself as a teacher

   material you are reading or studying (could be the present book!) and how it plays into your development as a teacher

   Now choose one topic and write a brief journal entry about it. Use the first person, draw on your own experience, and don't feel that your comments have to be polished or final in any sense.

2. If you are using dialogue journals, you may wish to check with the person you are writing to concerning their expectations for the entries. Even if you are writing to a teacher educator, it may be quite unnecessary to write formally, or with great attention to accuracy. The personal, first-person, spontaneous aspects of the writing are likely to be more important, and a focus on surface accuracy will probably interfere with the "thinking" nature of the writing. At any rate, discuss this with whomever you are writing to or for.

Here is a brief extract from an e-mail dialogue journal between a relatively inexperienced teacher and her supervisor just as an illustration. The writing (like much email) is personal and relatively informal. Sentences are not necessarily well-constructed or even as clear as they might be, since they reflect the flow of thought and are unlikely to be revised much or at all prior to being sent.

[Student Teacher]: ... things are fresh in my mind in terms of what I have learned, and then I have flashes of "Oh...now I

	understand" as well as further queries into what it is all about. The students themselves make it really worthwhile to me – they make me laugh and teach me a lot too.
[Supervisor]:	Is the concept of a "multistrand" syllabus helpful? Most published textbooks try to utilize a variety of different syllabus "building blocks" all at once; most theoretical discussions of the topic refuse to consider this option. However, so long as you are primarily dependent on your textbook, you will have to consider the first of these, I think.
[ST]:	I am not familiar with the term "multistrand." Could you please provide a brief description for me? (old topic. . . .)
[S]:	[provided elsewhere] Notice that you have already espoused a values position if you are assuming that it is your sole responsibility to know what the students need to know. (You may actually have different values; since we aren't communicating synchronically interactively excuse me on this one! Teaching what students actually need has an efficiency argument behind it; but from a values point of view, how should you interact with your students regarding their needs [interests, wishes] and why?)
[ST]:	Oh, the students' needs are extremely important as well. I believe that there is a trade off. What they want is not always what they need, and what I think they need is not always correct either. There should be some negotiating and interaction in the classroom. Though I have been instructed through a more authoritarian system and may have those tendencies as a result, the other (more liberal) part of myself is very attracted to creating a classroom that allows everyone equal voice. The classroom for me seems like a good place to explore ideas and stretch the mind in a challenging way that is fun. I like to walk out and feel like I have really learned a lot, or seen another way to look at something. I hope that I can provide that "high" feeling, too. I do not have to be the one who is the sole source – it should be more synergistic.
[S]:	Yes; fair enough and don't worry too much at this stage of the game. This is definitely the sort of thing that can't

be learned all at once. Even now, however, you could experiment with in-class activities (not to mention the journals you have been using) in which you find out what it is that students need, or think they need, and the activity types they like.

[ST]:   I would still really like to talk with you about syllabus design. [continues . . .]

Observation and feedback

Karen, an experienced female American teacher:

This week I had a number of people in, observing my classes. Tuesday, Lisa came to my ESL 100 class; Wednesday, you sat in on my ELI 82 class; Thursday, Brian and Ellen both came to the ESL 100 class; and Friday, Yumiko sat in on my ELI 82 class. It is not nearly as nerve-wracking as one might think; it's actually nice to go over your lessons with someone and get some input, questions, or suggestions beforehand and then to discuss the class afterwards. I feel the most pressure from wondering how students will react, but most of the time they're not too affected by having visitors or at least that's how they appear.

Patrick, an inexperienced male American teacher:

Well, I say that I had thought I wouldn't be nervous, but . . . Monday morning before class I began thinking about my lesson and about Lenny watching me, and I began getting extremely self-conscious. I thought about my lesson plan, about my assignments, and about my own teaching all morning before coming to school and to class. I criticized everything to myself, thinking about what Lenny may see and "discover" about me. I had thought I was doing a good job so far, but this was the true test.

When I saw Lenny sitting in the class it really hit me for a moment. I had planned with him beforehand to do the free-write first (which is what we always do) before introducing him to the class. While the students were doing their free-write, I sat at my desk shuffling papers and thinking about Lenny observing the class. Each time he wrote something on his pad, I could see him in my peripheral vision, and I tensed up wondering if he was writing about me. Finally after the free-write I introduced Lenny to the class and he made some comments to the students. As he explained his mission, I could feel myself relaxing bit by bit. When he finished giving his spiel, I began my class lesson and quickly forgot all about him. After class I thought about this and realized that I was concentrating so much on delivering my message to the students that I forgot all about my anxiety about Lenny watching me. This is how the next observation sessions went. Usually I was anxious before class and upon entering, but once class started I got so wrapped up in the lesson that I didn't have time for anything else. However, each day just after class I again thought, "What did Lenny see and write about me?"

Well, I had thought that I was nervous before, but I hadn't really felt anything until it came time to go meet with Lenny about his observations. I knew that it was a good thing and that I would learn some valuable things about my teaching, but I was still so nervous. When I got to his office and just before we began talking I thought about how easy it was to have him observe me . . . this was actually the difficult part. Now I would have to hear about everything I did wrong. But, that was just me being silly because Lenny is a nice guy who puts things well and gives very good criticism.

Classroom observation is an archetypal feature of teaching practice, and probably the most common feature across practica. It is also one which induces anxiety, particularly when, as is most common, the observer is a master teacher or administrator. Nevertheless, teachers report a high degree of benefit from being observed or observing expert teachers (Richards & Crookes, 1988) At the same time, long-term programs of teacher observation, the sort of thing that can go on beyond the confines of a practicum, might also be conceptualized in terms of peer observation. One's fellow teachers are always available, and work on peer observation also suggests that teachers find this beneficial (e.g., Lockhart, 1990). Regular classroom observation conducted in a nonjudgmental fashion is an important part of school-based programs intended to facilitate long-term professional development (cf. Peters & March, 1999). It is thus extremely important for observation to be effective and comfortable, not only for the practicum experience but for the long-term development of teachers. In learning or developing the skills of observing and giving feedback, and handling the personal and institutional issues that arise, teachers can acquire orientations and practices which will be needed as they continue to develop, and help other teachers develop, beyond the confines of a practicum.

There have been and still are many discussions of observation as a component of developing skills in the classroom. In the past, considerable emphasis was placed on the development of checklists or observation schemes, some of which were used as the basis for detailed feedback and extensive accounts of what might be good practice (e.g., Fanselow, 1987). While the psycholinguistic tradition in ELT research tries for good reasons to identify aspects of classroom practice which might best facilitate S/FL learning regardless of context, many aspects of S/FL classroom teaching have never been subjected to much systematic investigation of this kind. At the same time, different cultures, classrooms, and teachers disagree as to what is important, and alternative academic traditions in ELT research question the applicability or validity of the broad generalizations aimed for in the former tradition. Suggesting or reviewing preexisting observation schemes or tools is therefore not my intention here.[4]

I am more concerned with helping set up observation so that it has the potential for a long-term, egalitarian, developmental collaboration. In this I am in line with Peters and March (1999, p. 9) who remark

> Because every teacher is part of a larger community, he or she is far more likely to take the continuous growth process seriously if it is shared with a partner or two. . . . When asked to identify the most important and reliable source for growth, [teachers have] consistently identified fellow teachers.
>
> Throughout the literature, the professional growth model of choice is consistently the peer partnership of the collaborative network model. Its acceptance has become such an icon of both the school reform and the professional growth cultures that *not* to endorse it would be unthinkable.

In conceptualizing teacher development as growing out of something like a teacher development group, it follows that such a group of teachers (whether experienced or less experienced) should review *their own* opinions about what is good practice, as an initial phase in deciding what to look for when observing each others' classrooms. Subsequently, egalitarian, descriptive, and relatively non-judgmental observation would be the target. The objective of such observations can be to share perspectives, provide general feedback, or, subsequently, to provide data on specific aspects of practice which may be nominated by the individual teacher, or of concern to the group as a whole.

Toward ground rules and procedures for observation

There are many published sources we can turn to for suggestions on observation protocol. In an exchange quite some years ago in the *TESOL Quarterly*, Master (1983) and Zuck (1984) briefly set out some useful opinions on how to handle observation (admittedly, for administrative purposes). Their points serve here as the beginnings for readers' own deliberations concerning what procedures you would like to follow as you observe and are observed by fellow teachers (as well as supervisors, perhaps).

Some of Master's main points were:

- There should be enough time for the teacher to develop rapport with a class before an observation is conducted.
- It's good not to sit at the back of the room. At the side, where one can observe the whole class [teacher as well as students], is recommended.
- The observer should check with the teacher concerning whether [s/he] should be prepared to take an active role in the class if requested.

- Note-taking should be minimized to avoid distraction.
- Immediate feedback after the close of the lesson should be aimed for. A good format would begin with a description of the point of the lesson (as far as the observer can tell), then cover procedures used, and then comment on "the teacher's handling of the class."

In her response, Zuck (1984) made several comments. She was concerned that there be dialogue about the observer's understanding of "good teaching." She emphasized the importance of multiple visits. She advised that the teacher should explain the purpose of the observation to the students. Key information about the class should be provided by the teacher to the observer *before* the observation. These might include: (1) goals of the lesson, (2) relation to previous learning, (3) relation to subsequent classes, and (4) any problems anticipated. A copy of the materials should be made available to the observer. In giving feedback, the observer should begin by soliciting the teacher's views as to how the lesson went. Both Zuck and Master advocate that the observer should provide the teacher with a written report.[5]

More recently, Nunan and Lamb (1996) provide a brief exemplification of the process of peer observation in a group of concerned, professionally developing EFL teachers in Japan (cf. also Schecter & Ramirez, 1992). This is noteworthy and useful particularly because of its sensitivity to interpersonal aspects of observation. Master and Zuck were working with observation between senior and junior teachers or staff. Nunan and Lamb's teachers were all peers. The procedures they mention are mostly consistent with those of Master and of Zuck, but an interesting point emerges from the status identity. Feedback from superior to junior is legitimated by that difference, but the egalitarian and individualist culture of teaching makes teachers not only uncomfortable being observed by each other initially, because of its rarity, but also uncomfortable giving feedback. The teachers cited by Nunan and Lamb solved this problem by agreeing ahead of time, in their "peer observation interest group," to identify and comment on three things they would have done the same as the teacher they observed, and three things they would have done differently.

Finally, from among the many approaches to teacher observation that exist, I also want to draw attention to the extended approach to peer observation of Peters and March (1999). It deserves attention because it integrates peer observation with school reform programs (a concern I take up in Chapter 11). Space does not allow more than a brief summary, but these specialists advocate (as do many others) a detailed preobservation conference, in which the observer should gain a thorough understanding of the teacher's general views about teaching as well as of the objectives of the class to be observed and the section of the course that the class is in. Taking notes on the class (the in-class data collection) should be done in as nonevaluative a manner as possible, and these notes should be recopied into "a legible script, omitting any editorial remarks or value words" (ibid., p. 17). On the basis of this script, a postobservation conference should be held, in which the observer would identify "strengths, questions and concerns" (from his/her perspective), and then a jointly developed "action plan" could follow. In this final outcome it also connects to concepts of action research (see below, this chapter).

The Peters and March model is commendable for its thoroughness, use of broad range of preexisting research, and its setting within the wider context of school reform and even action research. In particular, its emphasis on the observer gaining an understanding of the views of the teacher s/he is about to observe is noteworthy. What a teacher-observer sees happening in a class to a considerable extent depends on her/his beliefs concerning good, desirable, or effective teaching. If these are not congruent with those of the teacher observed, a productive outcome is less certain; and if they are not conscious, again, the observer may have less to offer the observed. Hence, as discussed in the next couple of chapters, the importance to developing teachers of becoming clear, or at least clearer, about these views and values. Overall, Peters and March suggest, a consistent program of teacher peer observation could contribute to long-term professional development throughout an institution and over teachers' careers (rather than being confined to one or two teachers at the very beginning of their professional career).

YOU TRY IT...

1. If you are working with a group of fellow teachers, a good place to start with this topic is by sharing any experiences you have had being observed, or observing another teacher. It would be particularly important to articulate any negative experiences. It seems to be the case, unfortunately, that teachers are not accustomed to being observed and that when they are observed it is most often an evaluative experience accompanied by feelings of anxiety and discomfort. After this, consider what the characteristics of regular mutual peer observation should be in your particular context(s).

2. As a preparation for observing or being observed, consider what are some of the things you would like to see, and some of the things you would *not* like to see, in an ES/FL classroom. Also, consider what your expectations are of ES/FL classrooms that you might be likely to observe in the near

future. How are your expectations likely to affect the way you make sense of what you might see in an ES/FL classroom?

3. Since this observation is in support of a practicum, review the table of contents of this book for topics you might choose to use to guide an observation. You could try to focus on aspects of the class that are indicative of the teacher's philosophy of teaching; their views about SL learning; how they framed or paced the lesson; any use of a lesson plan or obvious improvisation; efforts to motivate the class; how they handled relationships or manifested rapport; and so on. In addition, of course, you should attend to whatever your observee tells you is important for him/her.

4. If you are presently teaching, arrange to be observed by one of your peers. Follow some approximation to the procedures summarized above, including scheduling a postobservation conference. If possible, audiotape the conference for later review. Listen to the audiotape to identify successful and less successful ways of giving and seeking feedback on your teaching. Does drawing up an "action plan" for subsequent teacher development seem appropriate or feasible in your situation? Why/why not?

Talking

Practicum participants, and teachers-in-development generally, should be familiar with the skills for successful participation in a teacher development group, whether as an ordinary participant, or as a facilitator or organizer. Let's consider some aspects of facilitation[6] first.

Within the context of a teaching practicum, the skills of facilitating a group discussion have two justifications. First, they are a necessary part of any teacher's toolbox for running their own classrooms, and second, they are also beneficial to the running of practicum-related meetings. When a practicum supervisor can step back from the traditional discussion-leading part of this role, meetings of practicum participants may take on a more participatory character, as if they were indeed egalitarian teacher development group sessions.

In running a discussion group, having a leader (whose role may rotate) is often considered desirable. This individual performs a number of functions which facilitate the discussion, including, but not limited to

initiating discussion
stating or selecting topics
nominating speakers

making sure the group is on topic
time keeping
summarizing
keeping notes
concluding.

Participants in a practicum have probably developed abilities in this area by virtue of their classroom experience, but may not have reflected on the need to use such skills in peer discussion. They may not necessarily feel competent to run a discussion unless mandated to do so by the course instructor. Some advice or consciousness-raising may be necessary.[7]

It is not essential that all the functions of facilitation be confined to one person. In a meeting of practicum participants, for example, one possibility is for the group leader to distribute functions (e.g., time-keeper, note-taker) among participants, and roles can be rotated. If this procedure is adopted, its use does not imply that the participants are incompetent to perform all the functions simultaneously. However, exercising just one or two may allow participants to give attention to their performance of these duties while still being actively involved in discussion. An additional reason for distributing functions among participants who have had little experience in chairing a discussion is that it aids the chair – for this person, it frees up cognitive resources, something desirable when learning or carrying out a new or unfamiliar task.[8]

FOR DISCUSSION

If you have facilitated a group discussion, share with others what are some of the more important things to be done as a facilitator. What do you find, or have you found difficult? If you haven't facilitated but have been a part of small group discussions, what things make them less effective, in your experience? If a group is made up of members from different cultures, genders, or differing first language backgrounds, what might be some key aspects of facilitative practice?

Alternatives to "regular" facilitation; participation patterns

People's participation in discussion in a group is often affected by their differing expectations about participation, or by status or power differentials, which can lead to some speaking a lot while others are unwillingly silent. Power and expectation imbalances may be related to gender, in particular. Also, however, in our field it is not unusual to find groups of teachers with mixed cultural backgrounds and also widely differing command of the language(s) used for discussion. It may be necessary, accordingly, to give explicit attention to such expectations and practices.

One way to do this is by considering the variety of possibilities which exist concerning group facilitation. One source for alternatives to mainstream group participation patterns is feminist group process practices. These were developed by feminists because of the importance that egalitarian discussion or "consciousness-raising" groups have had in the women's movement (cf. e.g., Schniedewind, 1993).

One alternative structure, for example, is "rotating chair" (Wheeler & Chinn, 1988, pp. 25–26):

Rotating Chair is a mutually shared responsibility for facilitating group interactions. Whoever is speaking is the chair. . . . The woman who is speaking is responsible for passing the chair to the next individual who raises her hand. The chair is passed by calling the name of the woman you are recognizing to speak next. If more than one woman indicates a desire to speak, preference is given to the woman who has not spoken or who has not spoken recently.

Passing the chair by calling of names is an important tool for a large group to help everyone learn everyone's name. More important, in a group of any size it is a symbolic gesture that signifies honoring each individual's identity, and respecting the presence of each woman for who she is. For the group, calling the next speaker's name is a clear signal that you have finished speaking, and that you are indeed passing the chair along.

A woman is under no obligation to relinquish the chair to someone else until she has completed the ideas and thoughts she wishes to share. At the same time, each speaker has the responsibility to facilitate an opportunity for all women who wish to speak to each issue. Each speaker avoids making long, repetitive or unrelated comments that prevent access to the chair for other women. . . .

Each woman desiring to speak is assured that she will have the opportunity to do so. A woman with a soft voice knows that she doesn't have to shout to get attention. A woman who is unaccustomed to speaking in a group is assured of having a space and the time to practice those skills. A woman who speaks slowly, or who pauses to gather her thoughts, is assured that nobody is going to jump in and grab the attention of the group before she completes what she wants to say.

One of the most serious difficulties I face as an instructor (whether doing teacher education or teaching ES/FL) is dealing with widely differing expectations of classroom interaction and participation. Presently, as a teacher educator, my regular student body includes both native and nonnative speakers of English.[9] Some of the former are young, shy, and lacking experience. Some of the latter are highly experienced and confident. Some in both groups come from cultures or subcultures where the student is expected to be quiet in class, while the teacher talks. Some come from cultures where there are marked differences in participation patterns by gender or age, others from cultures where this is not so obvious in academic settings. It is probably advisable under these conditions for all participants to have the chance to say what their expectations and preferences are concerning classroom participation.

One manual of group process provides a set of example problems that may arise in group discussion, by way of the following list of pitfalls:

Hogging the show. Talking too much, too long, and too loud.
Problem solver. Continually giving the answer or solution before others have had much chance to contribute.
Speaking in capital letters. Giving one's own solutions or opinions as the final word on the subject, often aggravated by tone of voice and body posture.
Defensiveness. Responding to every contrary opinion as though it were a personal attack.
Nitpicking. Pointing out minor flaws in statements of others and stating the exception to every generality.
Restating. Especially what a woman has just said perfectly clearly.
Attention seeking. Using all sorts of dramatics to get the spotlight.
Put-downs and one-upmanship. "I used to believe that, but now ..." or "How can you possibly say that?"
Negativism. Finding something wrong or problematic in everything.
Focus transfer. Transferring the focus of the discussion to one's own pet issues in order to give one's own pet raps.
Self-listening. Formulating a response after the first few sentences, not listening to anything from that point on, and leaping in at the first pause.
George Custerism. Intransigence and dogmatism; taking a last stand for one's position on even minor items.
Avoiding feelings. Intellectualizing, withdrawing into passivity, or making jokes when it's time to share personal feelings.
Speaking for others. "A lot of us think that we should ..." or "What so-and-so really meant was ..."

The full wealth of knowledge and skills is severely limited by such behavior. Women and men who are less assertive than others or who don't feel comfortable participating in a competitive atmosphere are, in effect, cut off from the interchange of experience and ideas. Those of us who always do a good deal of the talking will find we can learn a lot by contributing our share of the silence and listening to those around us (Moyer & Tuttle, 1983, pp. 25–29).

I'm glad to say I haven't seen all of these behaviors in groups of student or in-service teachers; but I've seen enough of them to want to raise the matter. Moyer and Tuttle introduce the problems in the context of gender-related differences in participation, but then go on to observe that these behaviors are actually not confined to one gender. Also, their observations derive from their experience of one Western culture, and we should be hesitant to generalize them. However, they may serve to draw attention to the dangers of such behaviors, wherever they emanate from.

At the same time, the emphasis on the assumed importance of equal oral participation in a diverse group may be problematic. It might be that if a student teacher, or teacher doing an in-service program, is accustomed to learning through listening, they may find sharing as yet not well formed views unpleasant. Such individuals may prefer to be silent as group talk proceeds, in which case, there will indeed be imbalances in participation, though not for the reasons Moyer and Tuttle are initially concerned with.[10] On the other hand, descriptions of teachers in ES/FL working together to develop include accounts which mention these issues (e.g., Bashiruddin et al., 1990; Bailey, 1996; cf. Chiseri-Strater, 1991). Bashiruddin et al. found that in a mixed group of MA Applied Linguistics students attending seminars at a British university, "women contributed [orally to the discussion] approximately half as often as men despite roughly equal numerical representation" (p. 82) even after the contribution of high status individuals such as faculty (all men, in any case) had been removed from the data. Bailey's report concerns an ES/FL teacher education class composed of both native and nonnative student teachers. She reports that

A recurrent problem in this course over the years has been that international students are often silenced in both the whole class discussions and the small groups ... During [the] first few weeks, group members reported that the students from the United States tended to dominate the group discussions (p. 267).

A student teacher comments ...

One thing that concerns me is that, in some respects, the nondominant speaking group (in our case non-native speakers) is dependent on the dominant speaking group to police itself. Either there is a reliance on the teacher to be sensitive and aware or on the students. In my experience, most instructors tend to put the onus for participating on the non-participatory student. Men (in mixed group discussions) are usually very reluctant to view their discussion pragmatics as oppressive or deficient in any way and blame women for being too timid. Native speakers also share this tendency, blaming non-native speakers for not talking. Many of my students have related incidents to me where professors and other students have told them, in no uncertain terms, you better jump in and make your point or you're not going to do well in this class. My ESL students have also told me that both their classmates and teachers are often intolerant of any difficulties in expression and will gloss over their comments or questions. . . . It may have more of an effect . . . if all [the] classmates (especially the non-native speakers) had some sort of strategy to deal with . . . any . . . speaker who does not yield the floor or who frequently strays off topic. . . .

In the ESL class, the situation is a little different because the teacher is (or should be) more sensitive to these types of communicative differences. And, while the teacher may have students with varying levels of proficiency in English, everyone, except perhaps the teacher, is a non-native speaker. Here it seems more a matter of drawing out the less confident, less outgoing students. There seems to be less of an issue of control and domination by certain group members and more of an issue of getting comfortable speaking up in class.

For discussion

1. Have you observed any of these behaviors in groups you've been in? If so, what do you think should be done if they occur in the future?
2. Have you ever been part of a group containing highly fluent speakers of a language discussing something where the language is one you are not entirely fluent in? How was your participation different from that in groups made up of speakers of your first language (or any other languages you are fully native-like in)?
3. One option that is available in some classes or groups is to allow for group email-based communication as a supplement to oral discussion. If you have experienced this, share your experiences. What are the strengths and weaknesses of this form of communication as a way of coping with oral participation diversity?
4. If you are using this book in association with a group of student or in-service teachers of mixed language backgrounds, first split into those of the locally dominant language and those of others and compare views about participation patterns. Then reform groups and share findings and opinions.
5. In Bailey's (1996) study cited earlier, the problems of participation are addressed through the concepts of "voice" and "scaffolding." "It appears that a discourse sequence for voice must include at a minimum . . . three interactionally coordinated moves" (p. 263). The problems were addressed because "the concept of creating a voice for all class members has become an important part of the course, with both the instructor and the facilitators actively scaffolding international students' participation." What do you think is meant by scaffolding and voice in this instance? (Hint: Is there more to having a voice than just speaking?)

1. I don't really want *my* students to have to go back to raising their hands when I'm running a class, because it reinforces a hierarchical difference I'm trying to get away from. But there's no reason why a group of teachers working without a supervisor-type in their discussion group shouldn't try it. Try discussion with hand-raising, and without. Try it with each speaker nominating the next person to speak by name, and without. Try it with a specified pause length after each contribution, and try it where each speaker *must* interrupt to gain the floor.
2. Here are some of Moyer and Tuttle's suggestions for altering participation pattern imbalances. What do you think of them? Can they be reformulated to address native-speaker/nonnative-speaker participation imbalances?

   Here are some specific ways we can be responsible to ourselves and others in groups:

   Limiting our talking time to our fair share. With ten people in the group, we are entitled to roughly one-tenth of the total talking time.

   Not interrupting people who are speaking. We can even leave space after each speaker, counting to five before speaking.

   Becoming a good listener. Good listening is as important as good speaking. It's important not to withdraw when not speaking: good listening is active participation.

   Not giving answers and solutions. We can give our opinion, believe our ideas to be valuable, but not more important than other's ideas.

   Not speaking on every subject. We need not share every idea we have, at least not with the whole group.

   Nurturing democratic group process. Learning democratic methods and adopting democratic structures and procedures will improve our group process.

   Interrupting others' oppressive behavior. We should take responsibility for interrupting a ... [person] who is exhibiting behavior which is oppressive to others and prohibits ... growth.... We need to learn caring and forthright ways of doing this.
3. With adequate ground rules for participation, a group of teachers might just jump in to discussing an issue in their teaching. But another form of oral interaction that comes up often among groups of teachers is sharing short accounts of practice – narratives, or, if you will, telling stories (White, 1991). Try to select an incident or aspect of your practice that made you think or about which you are concerned, and, in reporting it, structure the account so that it ends with something useful to other teachers. This could be a moral, and it could also be a form of theory,

that is, a theoretical statement grounded in practice but slightly abstracted from it. Other possible endings could include an appeal for assistance, for joint reflection, or for relevant sources of information.

Simply select an incident that occurred in your recent teaching practice, and formulate it as described above. To do this, however, note that you will have to reflect on it and make sure you are clear on what you learned. Try experimenting with conventional discourse markers for "moral tales." (End by saying, "And so, the moral of the story is. . . .") See if your peers can come up with a different moral for your story!

Writing and acting together

As discussed, journaling is a good means of reflecting on one's practice. Reflection alone may be sufficient, particularly if we are trying simply to get clear on what it is we are doing, or what our beliefs are as teachers. But in addition, exchanging recent experiences (or "talking story," as we say in Hawai'i) with other teachers, and sharing anecdotes about crises we've experienced as teachers (what White, 1991, calls "war stories") can be valuable, too.

For less experienced teachers, a period of practice teaching can be uncomfortable because *many* aspects of their teaching are problematic, and often not all of those problems can be solved. Alternatively, a student teacher may feel that his or her problems are unimportant because they don't seem to be faced by a cooperating teacher or more experienced colleagues. Within a group of less experienced teachers, however, some may well be experiencing the same problems, and could benefit from finding out how one teacher solved them. If a less experienced teacher raises a problem in a teacher development group, they may get a range of valuable suggestions, but not all of these may work. In any case, it is useful to other group members to hear back concerning the outcome of trying out such suggestions. If our reflection is stimulated by or in connection with a problem, then at its conclusion we may need at least one more step – action.

I, like many others involved with S/FL teacher education, believe that this business of trying things out and reporting the outcome to others is central to developing as a professional; so important that it deserves a label and support. The two labels one often finds attached to it are "action research" and "teacher research" (Crookes, 1993). I am pleased to say that it is experiencing an even greater upswing in interest within ELT in the last few years (Burns, 2000; cf. Burns & Hood, 1995; Ellis, 1999; Freeman, 1998; Nunan, e.g., 1993) and is finding a place within both general practice and in the preparation of student teachers (Richards & Lockhart, 1994; cf. Gore & Zeichner, 1991). One of the short definitions commonly used in introducing the topic is that of Kemmis and McTaggart (1988, p. 5):

Action research is a form of collective self-reflective inquiry undertaken by participants in a social situation in order to improve the rationality and justice of their own social practices, as well as their understanding of these practices and the situations in which these practices are carried out.

What this terse definition is referring to is a series of steps and practices jointly engaged in by teachers and other professionals. First, there may be a period of reflection, stimulated by a specific problem, a general concern, or a need to find out more about a situation or aspect of practice. Then there will be some gathering of relevant information, or "data," whether in a small-scale or in a more sustained fashion. Typically, in educational settings, this involves observing classrooms or students, or it may involve talking to students, teachers, or other participants in the school or community setting; and it may often include collecting written texts, whether syllabus documents or student work, and so on. There must then be some attempt to analyze this data. And then some course of action intended to improve the situation, ameliorate the problem or address the concern will be taken. But this is not the end of course; it is only the beginning of a cyclical process. For the action must have its effects considered and analyzed, which again requires some data gathering and analysis. Often one attempt on the problem is not sufficient, and a revised action will be taken on the basis of the conclusion of the first of several cycles of reflection, action, and data gathering and analysis. At some point in the process, teachers involved in this sort of professional action will communicate what they have found "so far" to others who would be interested – very often fellow teachers, and again, sometimes other members of the educational community. The whole process is sometimes seen as a very thorough and concrete form of professional reflection. Ideally, as the Kemmis and McTaggart quote makes clear, it sees teaching as socially located and doesn't ignore the importance of the social context, which can often make or break our work as teachers.

In recent work with student teachers, I've come to feel that one of the aspects of action research that is most important to emphasize is its collaborative dimension (particularly as in some discussions of this topic in our field, this is minimized: e.g., Wallace, 1998). Collaboration in action research can take place in several directions. In particular, one can involve one or more of one's fellow teachers, or student teachers, and/or one can involve one's students, directly. When you have one of your fellow student teachers in to observe you, take notes on your teaching or your class, and discuss your practice with you, this can provide a valuable second perspective. If schedules and resources permit, sustained visits and meetings of this kind can really contribute to rapid progress. But this is rarely possible. However, one category of observer is *always* available – the students! It is possible to invite the students into the process, as observers, as notetakers, as active providers of data. Some student teachers (and many experienced teachers too) will feel reluctant about sharing with students that they have a problem, or problems, in their teaching practice, which they are trying to improve. Student teachers sometimes feel that their control both of the role and the content is sufficiently shaky that to share their uncertainties with the students could be damaging. In some cases this may be true; but on the other hand, many students will know that their teacher is inexperienced or has an explicit status as "student teacher" in any case. In a sense, inviting students in to problem-solve an aspect of practice is more challenging for *experienced* teachers, who may well feel that they, as veterans, are supposed to know what to do and have all the answers. In either case, part of the problem arises if the classroom is conceptualized as solely the teachers' responsibility. But as I have mentioned earlier, classrooms are co-constructed, and so are their difficulties.

Another rationale for an action research perspective within a practicum follows from the view of Kagan (1993, p. 138) that "acquiring knowledge of pupils and ... using that knowledge to mitigate one's image of self-as-teacher" are two of the three "most fundamental" tasks in learning to teach.[11] An action research perspective doesn't exclude the possibility of beginning by trying to understand a situation. It may begin with a concern, rather than a problem; and for beginning teachers, as well as for more experienced teachers working with groups of students they are unfamiliar with, a fundamental concern may simply be "what's going on here?" Becoming familiar with students, their backgrounds, their perspectives on learning, and their culturally-based expectations, can enable a teacher to act far more skillfully than s/he can if s/he knows little or nothing of this area, and is arguably a major aspect of teacher development (Yee, 1990).

Another metaphor may be helpful: a cybernetic one.[12] Some aspects of teaching, particularly ES/FL teaching, are difficult because we can't be sure if our teaching is having the desired effect. The causal links aren't strong and the results, if and when they appear, may not reflect what we did. We are trying to draw conclusions about our practice solely from the data provided by student learning or lack of it. However, part of the problem is that often we are not taking up all available data, and what is most easily available is not easily interpreted. The feedback loop between us and students' learning can be improved if we involve them in it. The most common way that teachers keep channels of communication open between them and their students is to monitor them closely during class, but while often effective, this still may provide insufficient explanation or allow for diverse perspectives. One of my students remarked

the experienced teacher advises that a way to read a student's mind is to read his/her facial expression. In the case of determining the nature of or reasons for students' silence in the classroom, I was often unable to discern the cause by facial expression. I wanted to acquire "intellectual empathy" (see Grimmett & Erickson, 1988, p. 124) but often students would show neither comprehension nor lack of it on their faces, and I had no clue what their silence meant. If I were to ask them, I would only receive the same expressionless faces on many occasions.

One of the practices increasingly found in ES/FL classrooms is student journals. Teachers regularly ask their students to write, either in first or target language, about aspects of students' learning, their attitude to the class, what is motivating them (or not) and so on. And if the teacher writes back on these entries, we then have "dialogue journals" (as mentioned earlier). From an action research point of view, under favorable conditions, one can share with the class that some aspect of it is problematic from the teacher's point of view, and seek the students' perspective on this. Analyzing this data, along with one's own reflections, possibly student teacher or other colleagues' observations, one may come up with solutions to the problem. Going one step further, again under favorable conditions, students themselves may suggest actions that will ameliorate problematic aspects of a class, materials, and so on. Finally, it is obvious that when solutions are arrived at, other student teachers (at least) might want to know. The teacher development group is an appropriate venue, and simple oral reports to one's colleagues are the most common way that action research is disseminated. I do think that when we as teachers don't pass on the results of our struggles, a lot of the effort we go to is wasted – no one else benefits from it. So for me the final "dissemination" phase is very important. Informal written reports, too, of teacher research, are often produced for small-scale distribution either in hard copy or increasingly by e-mail.

Reading

Because of the authoritative nature of academic prose, it may not be obvious that I take a teacher research perspective on topics presented in the remainder of the book (in line also with my advocacy of a skeptical viewpoint earlier). That perspective includes a "valorization" of the teacher's perspective and problem-solving capacity. Which is to say, when I present the results of my scavenging in the archives of educational research, I don't expect the reader to take them as indisputable. Indeed, in some cases the discussion questions encourage readers to try out such ideas themselves, recognizing that they or their implications may not necessarily work in the specific circumstances readers find themselves in. The cultural distance, too, between much research (both that done on ES/FL learning and teaching, as well as general educational research) and the specific ELT contexts of readers, further warrants skepticism and test. This position was presented very articulately in an introductory book on research in S/FLA/T, by Johnson (1992, pp. 6–7)[13]:

Notions of what it means to "apply" research vary widely . . . It is often assumed that research is conducted, teachers read research, and then teachers attempt to apply the findings of research . . . Holders of this traditional consumer view of applying research tend to see teachers as passive recipients of information, not as readers who construct their own meaning from the events and texts with which they transact or interact. The consumer model is inadequate for several reasons. First, the direct application of research findings to practice is usually ill advised, even if it were possible. Studies are usually not conducted in situations that are similar in important ways to the environment in which the teacher practices. It is usually wrong to assume that phenomena that occur in one situation with one group of students . . . will occur in the same way in another situation with another group of students . . . Research findings cannot necessarily be generalized across settings . . . While there are certain universal aspects of second language acquisition, other aspects of the process vary according to the individual and according to social and cultural circumstances . . .

   Second, the consumer model of applying research is inadequate because readers of research may gain different insights from the same study. For example, from a study about L2 writing, one reader may be intrigued by what students can learn through talking about writing, while another reader's attention is captured by an approach to assessing writing development that is new to her. Each reader, then, constructs a unique meaning, gaining different insights from the same study, and will use those insights to revise personal views and practices in unique ways. . . . It is more productive to take the attitude that research provides an impetus that encourages us to reflect continually on language use and learning processes, to rethink practice, and to take action to improve practice.

3 Developing a Philosophy of Teaching

> • What is a philosophy of teaching?
> • Why do we need one?

Warm-up

To get you started, here's a basic question: Why are you (or why do you want to be) a teacher and why, specifically, a teacher of languages?

This chapter takes for granted the idea of personal goal-setting for professional growth, and the conscious use of individual and group strategies for fostering it, reviewed in the first chapters. We turn now to a central, and possibly difficult matter, that of developing an overall understanding of one's work as a S/FL teacher. In my view, even the least experienced teacher needs to begin to tackle this directly, and not put it off until after "basic pedagogical techniques" have somehow been acquired. Rather, the two processes can go hand-in-hand. The more experienced of us can usually benefit from a review of our thinking in this area, too. This chapter and Chapter 5 are intended to work closely together to aid this.

Introductory

It is important for ES/FL teachers, as for any other teachers or professionals, to be able to articulate their basic views and values concerning their practice, that is, their philosophy of teaching.[1] As with all aspects of professional activity, unless one can state what one is trying to do, it is hard to critique or develop one's practice. In our ES/FL contexts this is all the more necessary, because as specialists in cultural boundary crossing, we spend much of our professional lives in situations or working with materials in which values, beliefs, cultures, or philosophies may disagree or conflict. This chapter presents a first pass over the topic of philosophy of education within an

ES/FL teaching context, a domain of relevance for the development or clarification of a teacher's professional value system, and their personal philosophy of teaching.

In this matter it is necessary to recognize and address separately the different constituencies of readers who may make use of this book. I believe that there can be considerable differences in the background and initial training that certain groups of native and nonnative[2] EFL teachers bring with them, which will play into their philosophy of teaching; the domestic orientation of ESL teachers to a marginalized population represents another important and distinct orientation as well. I will comment on these three groups in order (and run the risk of gross oversimplification of their backgrounds, for which I hope they will forgive me).

Because English is the dominant language of international communication, the training of teachers of EFL for the international sector[3] is not necessarily closely associated with national educational policies. In some EFL countries, much of the English teaching of adults takes place outside of state education institutions. Even in ESL countries, much instruction takes place in private language schools. Our students' explicit instrumental needs for English, to complete their education or to get a better job, or possibly to engage in international travel or communication, have been the primary driving force for the dominant conceptions of curriculum, at least as expressed in the academic literature of our area, and of the content of most commercial materials. Teacher education for this sector of the field has therefore often assumed its role to be to prepare ES/FL teachers simply to deliver language instruction with no other major concerns. Native English-speaking teachers of ES/FL with an international orientation have often entered the profession themselves with a relatively limited amount of prior preparation, and largely unaware of the philosophical or values content of the courses of preparation taken by their nonnative colleagues with whom they work alongside.

The nonnative speaker of English who trains to be an English teacher at first in their home country will quite likely include in their first degree work, if it has a specific concern with education, coursework in philosophy of education and, in more traditional countries, moral (and possibly religious) philosophy. The reason is obvious – state education systems, when training language teachers, are preparing them to have a powerful influence on the youth of a country, and they wish to prepare or inculcate their teachers accordingly. Elementary and secondary teachers do not just transmit content, they provide models of behavior and exert discipline, and – though the term is no longer much used in the West – in many countries they still stand *in loco parentis*; they may even have respect.

Somewhat similarly, the ESL teacher in the United States, for example, is more likely to have taken coursework that addresses the role of the bilingual child in society. S/he might well be a member of an immigrant group or sympathetic to the large number of minority groups for whom developing English skills, along with preserving and developing their first language competence, is an important means to cope with the culturally-alien environment that surrounds them. This individual is closer to the nonnative EFL teacher in terms of what their experience and professional education may provide concerning moral or political resources from which to construct a philosophy of teaching.

The different institutions in which these three different groups of ES/FL teachers work also offer different takes on professional values. State and national educational policy documents usually contain sets of statements about what education should be, or what values the educational system should embody. These often reflect fundamental beliefs about morals and citizenship held by the educational policy-making bodies of particular countries. From a slightly more critical perspective, it can be said that state education systems reflect the views of the most prominent social or political groups in a particular society, so the educational values appearing or desired in education systems may be seen as having a political as well as a moral character. Private educational institutions sometimes have overt value systems, as when a school has been set up by a religious order. Or there may be an unacknowledged set of values, as when a language school operates in the private sector, responds primarily to "market forces," and sees its role as an uncontroversial one of serving the client-student in delivering the foreign or second language to be learned. In addition, schools, whether private or public, are usually contested sites, in which a range of values may contend for official or unofficial expression.

Individual teachers may have conscious or only partly conscious value systems. Some may believe that their professional responsibility is to keep their personal beliefs out of the classroom; others may feel that this is impossible, to some extent; others may feel that if they are not acting in accordance with their values then they are not living correctly.

This is a complex and, in many respects, sensitive area. However, conceptual analyses of professional practice suggest that it is impossible to act, as a teacher, without having theories (including values) which inform teaching actions, at least to some degree (see e.g. Carr & Kemmis, 1986; Ross, Cornett, & McCutcheon, 1992). The question then to be considered, beginning with this chapter is: Which theories, or sets of values, or perspectives, at which levels of analysis or discussion, might ES/FL teachers draw upon? We must also ask how ES/FL teachers can effectively explore and develop such matters. The aim of the exercise is to begin to develop, or further refine, one's "philosophy of teaching."

What might be in a philosophy of teaching?

When I originally drafted this section, and reflected at first on what questions might be answered by, or in, a philosophy of teaching, a few questions came to my mind immediately:

How should one teach?
How should one treat students?
What does it mean to be a human being; or, relatedly, What is human nature?
What should be the role of the teacher (given answers to the above
    questions)?
What is my world view, as a teacher?

As Wiseman, Cooner, and Knight (1999, p. 24) remark, "Developing a personal philosophy involves clarifying educational issues, justifying educational decisions, interpreting educational data, and integrating that understanding into the educational process." Answers to questions such as those above (by no means an exhaustive list!) would indeed assist in those activities of clarification, justification, and so on.

The material from which one might find information to address such topics could come from a number of sources. Naturally, one's personal life experiences are influential, and we could consider here experiences as a student (for many adults this is counted in decades of years), as well as any previous experience as a teacher, with other teachers, and under the influence of various educational institutions. Additional formal sources, exist, of course; for example, systems of religion or politics, as well as scientific theories. Philosophy of education has particular potential for one attempting to develop a philosophy of teaching because, as a domain of study, it has already in many cases attempted to mediate between the larger systems of meaning that humanity has developed and the specific concerns of teachers trying to make sense of their positions and practices.

Many of the statements a teacher might make when asked about their philosophy of teaching are likely to contain the equivalent of the word "should." They presuppose that there are right and wrong ways of proceeding, as a teacher, which is to say, there are moral and immoral pedagogical practices, or more generally, that teaching is a moral activity. The professional and academic literature of TESOL touches upon morality comparatively rarely, perhaps because in a time of cultural change and conflicting values, morality has in some areas come to be thought of as a matter of personal preference, and in any case more concerned with one's private life. And indeed, there is no reason not to look at teaching from a perspective (or in terms of a value) such as that of "efficiency." Given the preponderance of a concern for efficiency in our professional literature, however, I would not wish to ignore the potential of moral perspectives in developing a teacher's philosophy of ES/FL teaching, a viewpoint that is of course presupposed by the existence of codes of ethics for all the professions. This part of the discussion will be taken up in Chapter 5.[4]

Many of my students comment that they find developing and/or articulating their philosophy of teaching to be difficult, even though they may be somewhat experienced as teachers, and even though they may be presently teaching. If you are an experienced teacher, you may have so thoroughly internalized some principles related to your practice that it may be difficult to express them. Whether or not you have extensive teaching experience, if you are currently teaching, you may be so involved in teaching every day that getting the distance that may be needed to articulate your principles may be difficult too. Finally, while it may be possible to state certain views or values about teaching in general and about specific practices, the idea that they have to tie up, be fully coherent, or somehow be part of a "system," may be inhibitory.

On the other hand, another reason why this may be difficult is that teachers have not actually been asked to do it before at any stage in their career. They may not have been provided with any models, and they may not have been provided with adequate or indeed *any* resources from which to construct an integrated statement of their professional beliefs.

It appears to be the case (see e.g. Goodman, 1988) that the development of a philosophy of teaching, like any other complex cognitive structure guiding professional practice, is a comparatively slow process, in which reflective thought, reading, searching for relevant information, and dialogue with peers and with more experienced individuals would be necessary. Besides thought and talk, treating it as something to be written is productive. However, students and teachers I have worked with say (and my own experience confirms) that it is not something that can be swiftly written up over a few days at the end of an intensive period of study. Even a period of supervised teaching, which should provide some of the wherewithal for deep reflection, may not be sufficient for more than a first draft. Teacher educators Wiseman et al. (1999, p. 24) comment, "The development of a personal philosophy requires self-examination and honest comparison and consideration of what we are about as teachers. It is a continual process that involves seeking answers to hard questions over a long period of time." And in a study of preservice teachers' development, Loughran and Russell (1997, p. 176) comment,

> developing and articulating a teaching philosophy is [a] valuable outcome ... that cannot be transferred in any simple way from teacher educators' minds to their student teachers' minds. A teaching philosophy is something that must be individually cast and recast as it is constructed from and translated into the experiences of practice.

On the basis of a study of the development of preservice teachers' practical philosophies of teaching, Goodman (1988, p. 134) recommends that

> preparation programs develop strategies for helping students reflect upon their own and their fellow students' perspectives. This reflection must include more than just what individuals "believe".... It is important for teacher education to help students consider the meaning they give to their words, how these meanings may differ among a given group of individuals, and what experiences influence their ideas and actions.

YOU TRY IT ...

Any task that seems large and complex can be rendered more manageable through being considered as a series of smaller tasks, or steps. Not having time pressure can help. The material that is presented here, and in Chapters 5 and 7, should be seen as *one* source supporting the construction, reconstruction, or development of a philosophy of teaching. Your own reflection, particularly in writing, along with discussions you may have with peers or seniors, are an important additional source. Your own teaching (if you are teaching) is a potentially very valuable source. Reflective dialogue with your peers, journaling, and other techniques for reflection discussed in Chapter 2 should all be deployed in the pursuit of this goal.

Three points for beginning development of a philosophy of teaching:

1. If you are teaching, audiotape a class and listen to the tape. Use it to stimulate note-taking concerning the principles or beliefs you appear to be operating under. Some of those most easy to capture may concern classroom technique: "Wait a few seconds to give students time to answer"; but others may be more abstract, like "I am trying to respect my students," or "I treat students firmly but fairly." Try to focus on the second category, without excluding the first when they come up.

   Review your notes with a peer teacher or with a senior, possibly a teacher educator, and try to find areas where statements appear to go together.

2. If you are not teaching, think about classes you have taken recently, or if possible, observe a class. What assumptions did your teacher seem to be working under, concerning effective pedagogy, his/her relationship to the students, his/her expectations of how they learned? Also make a note of any statements implied or visible in the institution you took the classes in concerning the responsibility of the institution to its students and to the country you are in. If possible, review curriculum documents or mission statements.

   Review your conclusions with a peer teacher or with a senior, possibly a teacher educator; try to deduce what the underlying assumptions, or even the philosophical positions are, that are implied by these experiences.

3. If you have a cooperating teacher, simply ask them about their philosophy of teaching. If you think they would have time, you could ask them to make a few written notes about it first, and then interview them or have a discussion based on their notes.

4. "Consider the impact of your own biography on your choice to become a teacher [and begin] . . . the development of an autobiography of your career choice. [If appropriate, include] . . . your childhood experiences, the teacher and family influences . . . the teaching experiences [or other life experiences] that contributed to your decision to become a teacher" (Wiseman et al., 1999, p. 25). How have your views as a teacher changed since your first days as a teacher?

Now read on; use the next subsections as resources to develop or refine your initial statements.

Toward "a philosophy of teaching"

As we begin to move into this area, there are two (mis)understandings of the term "philosophy of teaching" that I should like to head off. First, we can find plenty of published reflections on ES/FL teaching closely associated with "Methods" which present themselves using the term philosophy of teaching. A statement of preferred methodology does not do justice to the potential of this term or topic.

The second understanding that I think is too limited for our purposes is that derived from one influential school of philosophy – "analytic philosophy." When this approach to doing philosophy is applied to education, we have "analytic philosophy of education"; and scholars in this area regard the primary task and content of philosophy of education to be solely the analysis and clarification of educational concepts, such as "teaching" (Hamm, 1989).

This leads to a position such as that of Passmore (1980, p. 16):

The philosophy of teaching is that part of the philosophy of education which concerns itself, not with the formal structure of educational theory, not with those problems in social, political and moral philosophy which arise out of the character of the school as an institution and its relation to society, but primarily, at least, with teaching and learning – with problems which arise in *any* attempt to teach systematically in *any* social system which places *any* value whatsoever on the transmission, by way of formal teaching, of knowledge, capacities, attitudes.

However, analytic philosophy is only one of many schools of philosophy, and no longer has the preeminence it once had in the English-speaking world, and this narrow conception of "philosophy of teaching" will not alone serve the purposes of S/FL teachers in the circumstances of the early twenty-first century, though we may sometimes draw on its analyses.

What I want to encourage, instead, is an understanding that begins with the sense of the term philosophy of teaching that often shows up at important points in a teacher's career, such as a job interview. There, a teacher may be asked what his/her philosophy of teaching is. In such circumstances, one may outline a general collection of statements ranging from why one wants to be a teacher, various values that one has concerning education, through to preferred forms of classroom practice (cf. Goodman, 1988). In my view it is crucial to be aware of one's views in these areas (cf. Freeman, 1991). At a minimal level, employers will often appreciate a job applicant who can be articulate about them, providing of course that in the more sensitive of these areas the job seeker and the employer agree about what is important. More substantially, I would assert that some conscious understanding of this area is vital to one's development as a teacher. Ideally, a personal philosophy of ES/FL teaching worthy of the name should go deeper, and be extensive. Particularly at a time when one is trying to engage in a systematic process of personal development as a teacher, a more complete, coherent, and extensive construction would be desirable.

This personal or micro sense of the term ("a" or "your" philosophy of teaching) can be linked to a macro sense of the term ("the" philosophy of teaching), similar to that of Passmore's, but not merely confined to problems and definitional clarification, and indeed bringing in the matters he rules out.[5] In the latter sense, philosophy of teaching is indeed a subsection of the academic discipline I have already referred to known as philosophy of education. My hope is that through engaging with resources to be found in that area, considered broadly, teachers can use the resources of philosophy of education to aid in the development of their own philosophy of teaching. We should, that is to say, specifically bring in conceptual issues that arise when we consider the institution in which we work, school itself, and its relationship to the wider social order. We can develop our philosophy of teaching by drawing on these resources. Then we can integrate with it (to the extent we feel appropriate, or agree with them) empirical findings that research in SLA/T[6] has accumulated which may additionally guide our practice as teachers (a source to be drawn upon in Chapter 7).

Note, incidentally, that empirical, research-based theory, an important basis for ES/FL teacher education curricula, does itself have philosophical underpinnings. Much of the curriculum content of ES/FL teacher preparation derives from scientific investigations of ES/FL learning and teaching. The new ES/FL teacher typically lives in a society (an increasingly global one) in which the technological manifestations of scientific method structure our existences. While it is common knowledge that science as a set of social practices developed recently in the history of recorded civilization, it needs to be mentioned that science as it is generally understood grew out of Western philosophy.[7] And it did so partly in the pursuit of questions that both philosophers as well as scientists were concerned with (indeed the two groups of individuals were not originally separate); and finally note that many of the findings in what are now called the social sciences are still inextricably involved with philosophical positions and cultural beliefs (cf. e.g., Manicas, 1982, 1987). As ES/FL teachers are consumers (when they have time) of the results of social scientific investigations and theories, it is important that they be able to recognize the philosophical underpinnings of these theories in developing their own practical philosophies.

To continue our review of the resources philosophy of education offers teachers developing their practical philosophies of teaching, let me point out that though philosophy of education written in English has tended to mean *Western* philosophy of education, globalization, not to mention the international nature of TESOL, makes it important that we consider both Western and non-Western philosophies of education. As a whole, this area can be approached in a number of ways, including at least (1) with respect to movements or trends in the field of education ("philosophies of schooling": Power, 1982); (2) in terms of systems or schools of philosophy as applied to education; (3) and by way of perennial issues that must be addressed by teachers and concepts of which they should have a deep understanding.[8,9] Let us begin with option (1).[10]

Philosophies of schooling

One theme running through this book is that teachers should know what they are doing, and accordingly that there is much to be gained, as a professional, from articulating one's beliefs, or finding out about them. In the present instance, we all have come to teaching with the results of our apprentice-ship of observation – we all, that is to say, have gone through many years of being educated while observing our teachers and schools. The education systems we experienced, though they did not represent unitary sets of values or philosophical positions, nevertheless probably reflected some identifiable aspects of educational philosophy. In addition, the educational systems within which we work, or to which we will return or enter, certainly do contain such sets of values. One way to begin is to identify the values and beliefs which were likely operational in the education we received. We could then move on to discussing the values as they may be involved in our current situation. We may discover, in some cases, that we as teachers have been created by preexisting ideas about teaching, rather than coming to them and committing to them freely. To this end, I will briefly review the philosophies of schooling prominent in modern times, so that readers may be helped to locate their own educational experiences and practices as part of identifiable historical trends with philosophical dimensions.

Historical perspectives

Some experts, ignoring the role of context, have argued that three basic distinctions can be made in approaches to education (e.g., Bowyer, 1970). First, the simplest conception of education is "transmission": a means of transmitting information or skill. It has a simple, utilitarian objective of passing on the means whereby we may live and know our surroundings. Second, there is education for the nonutilitarian purpose of "salvation." This exists within all societies, but particularly in those with a strong religious character, the purpose of education is in some sense otherworldly. Third, one may consider education for "self-development." In societies not focused heavily on the spiritual, this stands in place of the second conception. These aspects of education can be seen as coexisting in most societies at most times.

However, context, in the sense of the culture and society in which the education is taking place, is essential. In a sense, there *is* no simple "transmitting of information." Education presented simply as transmission is likely to reflect overarching needs of dominant interests – of the state, or of business, or of the people; and we may thus see self-development as standing in opposition to, or in tension with, for example, state development. Education to serve the needs of society has itself inner tensions – mainly between those who wish it to serve the present needs of a society, and those who, possessing a critique of it or a hope for its future development, see progress as involving improvement in people's social and political systems. Aspects of these lines of thinking can be traced, in the West, back to Plato at least.

Two main poles between which educational traditions oscillate have been identified: (a) traditional, conservative, or custodial; as opposed to (b) progressive, liberal, or humanistic.

The development of modern (Western) concepts of schooling can be traced to the period in European history known as the Enlightenment. During this time philosophers such as Locke and Rousseau developed concepts of the individual and of the child new to modern European civilization. Education and citizenship were tied together in the minds of some figures such as Jefferson, who in the 1820s advocated forms of education, including higher education, accessible to the ordinary man: "I know of no safe depository of the ultimate powers of the society but the people themselves. [We must] inform their discretion by education." This was to be through "a system of general instruction which shall reach every description of our citizens, from the richest to the poorest."[11] In addition, school as a modern Western institution developed concurrently with the development of the nation-state. As powerful central governments developed and as mass schooling became a possibility, the state took control of schooling; besides the state, other powerful groups like business and labor took a close interest in it.[12]

During this period, too, European nations colonized almost all of Africa, Asia, and the Americas, with subsequent powerful effects on the education systems of most present-day ex-colonial nations, including their philosophical systems and values.[13] In the later phases of this process, Anglo-American colonialism was a strong force for the spread of English and the development of English as a second or foreign language in many countries. A late manifestation of the relationship between the teaching of English and the power of the English-speaking nations in the twentieth century is the visibility and influence of Anglo-American academics in the field of TESOL. Consequently, we should not be surprised if European or Anglo-American trends in schooling should also manifest themselves in TESOL, even though it is an international enterprise. They may also appear in English instruction in EFL countries.

I should note here that "education" includes both formal and informal education. Formal education tends to be associated with school, and school in turn tends to be seen as an originally Western entity. It is thus dangerously easy to overlook the philosophies of nonformal, non-Western education (Reagan, 1996). While recognizing the importance of the latter, I will not attempt to review it here. As for *formal* non-Western education: during the discussion that follows the question needs to be asked: To what extent do non-Western school systems manifest "indigenous" ideas, and on the other hand, to what extent have they taken on board not only the Western institution of school, but also philosophical ideas or values that go along with it?[14]

THE EIGHTEENTH CENTURY IN EUROPE

The education systems of modern nations[15] in the last 30 or 40 years reflect changes that can easily be traced to ideas expressed in Europe during the eighteenth century. This was a time which spawned great reform movements, not to mention political revolutions, which not only set up the states themselves, but also struggled over their form, direction, and content of their educational systems. One area of debate with philosophical roots concerned the extent to which the child would be molded by the school, and to what extent s/he would be allowed to grow or develop. Some educational theorists began to question the idea that the teacher's responsibility was simply to transfer knowledge into the individual mind. As a result, the idea that the child has an inherent potential that should be allowed to grow or flower in school became more accepted, in association with a broad set of ideas associated with the Romantic movement. This view was particularly associated with the writer Jean-Jacques Rousseau (1762).

Rousseau articulated a number of ideas which play into views of education today. Like many of his contemporaries, Rousseau was willing to imagine a "state of nature" in which individuals lived free from the effects of culture or society. In this state, humans were inherently good. Society, on the other hand, was inherently corrupt. Education, now as then, is often seen as fitting the child for society, but Rousseau tried to set down means whereby the inherent goodness of the individual would not be ruined by the need to prepare him or her for citizenship.[16] This included advocating a perspective in which the teacher teaches according to his/her perceptions of the child's readiness for learning, takes a generally child-centered approach, and has a concern for the student's motivation. A similarly radical belief in the child was also to be found in other educational writings at that time, including in the influential work of the English libertarian William Godwin, who saw the child as an inherently autonomous moral being, and thus one who should in no way be subject to coercion while being educated (Godwin, 1793 a, b).

THE NINETEENTH CENTURY (SPREADING FROM EUROPE)

Rousseau's ideas were the stimulus for other important work, including that of the German philosopher Kant, on education. Those who developed and responded to his work included major early educational reformers such as

Pestalozzi, Froebel (originator of the *Kindergarten*), and Herbart. The influence of Froebel and Herbart on educational systems and practices was substantial, not only as might be expected in Germany, but also in Latin America, Japan, and eventually in the United States. In the United States they influenced the work of the philosopher John Dewey; and they have been identified as having set the stage for the modern development of "philosophy of education" as an academic area. While the details of these influences need not concern us, I think it is important to know that the currents of modern educational thought (including in non-European countries[17]) have strong philosophical sources in distinguishable movements within the European Enlightenment. Insofar as present-day practices in TESOL have any connection with trends in educational thought, they are likely to manifest at least some underlying philosophical assumptions. In particular, for now I will simply note that two important positions appear in the work of these individuals. Herbart was among those who first introduced the ideas of the embryonic field of psychology into education; and Froebel was one of the first educational theorists in the West to work on personal development or self-realization, what we would these days call a humanistic understanding of learning (Kelly, 1969).

THE TWENTIETH CENTURY

The concept of personal development goes comfortably with another major movement of the early twentieth century in education, the progressive movement, associated with Dewey, and with the philosophical school of "pragmatism." Educators in this tradition believed that education should help the child to develop as a human being, and also that school should be a force for the improvement (in democratic and peaceful ways) of society as a whole. Though the progressive movement was strong in the educational communities of the United States and elsewhere (including China and Japan: Smith, 1991), there were other countervailing pressures. The early twentieth century was a time of increasing importance of science and technology, and a popular faith in them as a force for progress. This caused schools to come under pressure to train young people in such areas, as well as to apply the concepts of science (and technological innovations) to educational techniques themselves. Educational specialists who advocated making education into a science, and the application to it of techniques learned from management science (e.g., Taylorism), indirectly supported conservative currents against progressive or humanistic developments of school systems and pedagogy. Wherever and whenever governing elites have sought cultural and political homogeneity in the process of nation-building, schools have been agents for the transmission of particular forms of social theory (or religion). Throughout much of the twentieth century, national schooling attempted to instill respect for authority and acceptance of common ethical codes.

Because of the involvement of school with state-building, wherever there has been cultural or political resistance to forms of authority, or wherever there have been pluralistic societies, schools have been contested sites. This was true during the anticolonial struggles of the period after World War II, and it was also true internally in the more developed nations. In the 1960s and 70s, state education systems in the developed nations (even including Japan, e.g., Duke, 1973) came under the influence of those who wished to question established societal values. Programs and institutions offering alternatives to state schools grew, and the term "alternative education" came into use to describe the other pole, the educational trend which continues to counterpose the interests of the individual, or of humanistic conceptions of society, against those of the state, bureaucracy, or business.

NON-WESTERN SCHOOL SYSTEMS AND THEIR PHILOSOPHIES

The West still fails to take with sufficient seriousness the claims to primacy of Chinese civilization. Superficial acknowledgment of facts concerning where many modern technological developments appeared first (paper, movable type, gunpowder, and the compass) are not attached to an understanding of the breadth of social and political development implied by them (even though this was well-understood in Europe early, by Enlightenment scholars such as de Quesnay and Voltaire). Thus it needs to be emphasized that Chinese civilization constitutes the first manifestation of broad, state-supported education along with a meritocratic test-based use of education as a system for personal advancement in society.

That having been said, however, it also must be acknowledged that as a result of Western colonialism or economic influence, many non-Western countries either took up Western structures and concepts of school as an institution, or had them imposed. As a result, some traditions of schooling are shared to quite a large extent between such otherwise disparate countries as China, Korea, Japan, on the one hand, and the United States and the UK on the other; not to mention across countries who shared a particular experience of colonialism (e.g., Francophone Africa). Intense interest in Western schooling was apparent in East Asian countries by the late nineteenth century, and, for example, by 1916 "an estimated 10 million Chinese" had received at least an introduction and possibly "a substantial education of a Western variety" (Sheridan, 1975, p. 115; cf. Hayhoe, 1992). At the same time, some of the same tensions between state needs, the interests of the individual, and societal critiques manifested themselves in the philosophies and underlying goals of schooling. For example, in Japan, the Imperial Prescript on Education of 1890 identified development of national identity as the main educational goal, which became during its most militaristic period, education for industrial production and military preparedness. By 1947, this had switched to aims such as "the full development of personality" (Fundamental Education Law), and broadly, "education for individual development and idealistic personalism" (Kida, et al., 1983, p. 57; cf. Lincicome, 1995; Shimahara, 1995).[18]

However, I would not wish to suggest that there are *no* differences. One must look for the culturally different values underlying the apparent sameness of school building, groups of 30 or 40 children and one adult, rows of desks, and so on. Recent ethnographies of school systems (e.g. Lewis, 1995; Shimahara & Sakai, 1995) as well as studies of indigenous epistemologies (Gegeo, 1998; Schoenhoff, 1993; Wautischer, 1998) are important sources for finding out about one's own, or, in the case of many EFL teachers, one's host country's "ethnopedagogies"; that is, philosophies of schooling and school practices which draw on indigenous/non-Western concepts of development, learning, or the function of education. It may be that the philosophies of schooling of non-Western as well as Western countries are complex mixtures of old and new ideas, continually struggled over and rarely clearly manifested.

FOR DISCUSSION

1. Think back to your time as a student in elementary and secondary education. How (apparently) did school operate for you, in terms of guiding principles that you might have been experiencing the practical manifestations of? (Any parents discussing this question might consider the principles presently appearing in their children's schools.) Possible pointers: institutional factors; school rules; the structure of the institution; any "ought" statements your teachers made, and so on.

   This may be difficult. If so, you could proceed by recalling specific teachers who had a positive or negative impact, and then see if you can deduce some principles from these cases.
2. Let us see if we can trace the influence or lack of influence of any Romantic ideas of schooling in your personal history. As a student, have you ever been subject to "coercion"? As a teacher, do you ever find yourself exerting "pressure" on a student, whether moral or psychological?

Do you regard your students as "morally autonomous"? If you teach adults as opposed to children, how does this differ?
3. To what extent do you agree with Rousseau's basic idea of human nature? To what extent are your educative practices driven by the need to fit your students for society alone? As a teacher, are you now (or do you expect in the future) to be responsible to the state?
4. Can you think of examples where non-Western school systems manifest "indigenous" ideas? What do you think of the proposition that non-Western school systems have taken on board not only the Western institution of school, but also philosophical ideas or values that go along with it?
5. On "ethnopedagogies" – Are you aware of any classroom techniques or educational concepts that are done in school in one, let us say, non-Western culture, that do not appear in the West? If so, what cultural traditions or concepts do they manifest or are they based on?
6. Which aspects of your teaching, or what actual practices, manifest cultural, or culture-specific values?

YOU TRY IT ...

This would require some library work, web searching, or even correspondence: Look for a fairly high-level statement made by authorities responsible for education in your area. This might be a university mission statement, guidelines from the Ministry of Education, or even remarks by a politician or cultural leader. With a partner, analyze it for evidence that it accepts or adheres to any of the traditions in schooling considered so far. What other principles or assumptions does it make that would play into discussion of a philosophy of teaching?

Historical perspectives and TES/FL

But what of TES/FL in this history? Musumeci's (1997) work is the only book-length historical treatment of S/FL teaching that is both substantive and up-to-date.[19] As well as offering a detailed analysis of an important period in the European tradition of second/foreign language education, she also provides a useful view of the handful of other treatments of the topic, particularly Kelly (1969) and Titone (1968).[20] She concentrates on Jesuit educator Ignatius Loyola and on perhaps the most famous early S/FL pedagogue in Europe, Comenius. Though she doesn't delve deep into the philosophical background, what is important is, in brief, her reidentification of two poles between which advice to S/FL teachers has oscillated during the whole of the modern period in European history, which Titone calls the "formal" and the "functional" approaches. For much of the period between the fifteenth and seventeenth centuries, S/FL teachers emphasized natural language learning for and through communication; during the 1800s the emphasis gradually shifted, particularly under German or Prussian influence, to approaches emphasizing structure, drill, and translation. Against this in turn the late nineteenth-century "Reform Movement" language specialists revolted, and the effects of their efforts to change matters echoes down through to the present day in the various "communicative approaches." I find the excerpts from Comenius's writing that Musumeci presents useful because it shows him as foreshadowing the democratic tradition in schooling: he echoes Martin Luther in calling for mass education, and for general education particularly in literacy, and he has a vision for a new society in which every village will have a school. According to Titone, Comenius's ideas, together with those of Rousseau, were to be found in the S/FL specialists who represented the best of the functional tradition, especially in Germany, before the pendulum swung against them in the early 1800s.

As Musumeci notes, Kelly's (1969) thematic treatment primarily focuses on teaching methods, to demonstrate that many so-called new approaches are just old ideas coming round again. But he does also devote a unit to the question of "where did these ideas come from?" Kelly is informative concerning the conceptual antecedents of the Direct Method[21]:

Herbart's theories of education and learning were the basis of the teaching practice of the Direct Method. As language was a matter of organized perception, teaching it involved observation lessons . . . which gave the pupil direct experience of the language and its reality. The five steps of the Herbartian lesson can be seen in every treatment of the Direct Method: they were preparation (revision of old material), presentation (imparting new facts), association (of the new with the old), systematization (recapitulation of the new work in its context), and application (practice) (1969, p. 312).

Another great name in the philosophy of schooling comes in at the beginning of the oral-aural tradition: Kelly attributes to Pestalozzi the first formulation of the "principle of complete reliance on oral-aural training in the first stages of a new language" (p. 313).

My impression is that within the "Western world," language teaching, second language teaching, and TESOL, considered from the viewpoint of philosophies of schooling, have tended to reflect the various contending trends in the rest of Western education at any given time.[22] For example, the interest in our field in so-called innovative approaches in the 1960s and 70s is a fairly clear parallel to interest in the mainstream education world in alternative education and free schools.

However, when one looks at the contacts between different cultures occurring under the aegis of ESOL education, there have been some striking philosophical mismatches. Historically, this has become clear in connection with the role of schooling and especially TEFL in state development in the period following World War II, when the conception of economic underdevelopment was widely applied to the newly independent states, or ex-colonies. Education, and English education in particular, seemed important in fostering economic development and modernization, and EFL specialists became closely involved with many aid and development projects, and associated efforts in educational innovation. The theory of schooling espoused by the TESOL expert has by no means always been congruent with the dominant theory of schooling in the foreign culture (cf. Coleman, 1996). In particular, virulent debate has been concealed within academic language in discussions of the applicability of communicative approaches to TESOL within, for example, the state sectors (as opposed to elite tertiary institutions) of EFL countries.

I would reiterate that any ES/FL teacher who is trying to construct or reconstruct a personal philosophy of teaching needs to know the historical inheritances with which s/he is working. In addition, as many of us work at the new interfaces between traditions that globalization is throwing up in the twenty-first century, it is obviously important to understand the potential clash of philosophies that may occur. To exemplify this, I will here highlight one such clash. Tollefson (1991; see also Clarke & Silberstein, 1988) has discussed in highly critical terms the role of EFL in state-supported "modernization" programs in Iran and China during the 1970s. He argued that even though humanistic methods might have been espoused by some expatriate instructors, the ignoring of the political and economic realities of their actions made their work ideological, serving only the interests of the dominant groups in those countries during those times. Overall it would seem that philosophies of S/FL teaching, as both this modern case as well as the distant past case of Comenius suggest, are quite capable of drawing from the political traditions of a particular time, and having political implications and effects as well.

A temporarily concluding thought

[A teaching] philosophy [cannot] be exemplified to its fullest degree in every educational encounter . . . Such an insistence would be so intimidating to practitioners as to prevent *any* attempt to implement a philosophy. We should regard this rationale as a variable that can be realized to a greater or lesser extent at different times, in different settings, with different groups. Even within one class session the extent to which this philosophy is realized will vary with the nature of the individuals concerned, the exercises pursued, and the educator's conduct. Nonetheless, it is vital that a clear rationale be articulated so that practitioners may have a benchmark for judging the extent to which their activities exemplify fundamental purposes, principles, and practice. Without a clear rationale (even if full implementation is not always possible), practice will be condemned to an adaptive, reactive mode (Brookfield, 1986, p. 288).

None of us are able to base every teaching act on principles. Having worked through this section you should not (according to Brookfield) be paralyzed if circumstances prevent you from always sticking closely to your philosophy of teaching. But if you don't have one, perhaps you will never be sure if what you're actually doing, is what you want to be doing.

FOR DISCUSSION

1. Situation A. Imagine that you are a nonnative speaker of English and teach EFL within the state high school system of a country in which English is a foreign language. What are the likely sources of values in your teaching?

   Situation B. Imagine that you are a native speaker of English and teach EFL at a private university in an EFL country. What are the likely sources of values in your teaching?

   What are the key differences, if any, between these two situations? Does it matter whether a teacher is a citizen or a resident (who can vote) of the country where s/he is teaching?

2. Consider your ES/FL classroom practices. As a teacher, are you (or is your school) identifiable in terms of the formal or functional poles?

3. Try to describe your teaching (or the teaching of someone you are familiar with) in the same terms Kelly uses to describe the Direct Method of the nineteenth century. How much is the same, and how much is different? In what sense could you describe yourself as inheriting a particular historical tradition as an ES/FL teacher?

YOU TRY IT ...

1. As I noted earlier, writing one's philosophy of teaching can be challenging and time-consuming, particularly for the less-experienced teacher. Draw on the historically-oriented discussion of this section to begin to

write a section of your statement of your philosophy of teaching in terms of the concepts you have been exposed to in your schooling and inherited from the school systems you have been (or perhaps still are) part of. Identify and develop in this writing any educational concepts that seem particularly culturally important. Share drafts with your peers. If you wish, retain drafts for extension and revision following Chapters 5, 7, and 12.

2. This would require some additional reading: Try to find an account of teaching that presents a very strongly positive or negative view of teachers or schooling. This could be a newspaper article, or something more substantial (e.g., Said, 1999; Ashton-Warner, 1963). Use it to identify values, traits, traditions, or patterns of behavior you would want to emulate or avoid as a teacher.

4 Aspects of Classroom Technique

> • What are the aspects of ES/FL classroom teaching that apply across most curricular areas?
> • What characteristics does expert ES/FL classroom instruction have?

Warm-up
Think of a really good language teacher you have observed in action. Write down some of the things that the teacher did in running that class; do you do them, too, or are they aspects of your own practice you need to work on?

Chapter 3 began the process of developing (or reviewing) your philosophy of teaching; the material of the present chapter will continue it; and is intended to assist you in integrating your knowledge of SL learning and teaching with your classroom practice. It is common for formal S/FL teacher development programs to devote separate and explicit attention to such material, and a period of focus on "teaching practice" itself may draw on that information, though not expound on it systematically or explicitly. The problem for the teacher in development (and his/her supervisor, if one exists) is to make sure that such material seems or becomes relevant, and also becomes part of a teacher's practice.

However, at the same time, there are aspects of classroom practice which cut across or lie above, conceptually, these matters of how actually, "ESL reading" (and the like) should be taught. These aspects I call nonskill–area-specific, and while I think they are very important for successful practice, they appear to be under-researched and less frequently discussed in the literature of second and foreign language teaching. To some extent, perhaps, this is because some of these issues are common to all classroom teachers, and therefore discussion of them is to be found in the general education literature. But we ES/FL teachers nevertheless have our own special challenges in the area of technique. This is the area we now take up. The emphasis on these underresearched, yet vital aspects of classroom practice begins here and is interleaved through the next chapters up to Chapter 9: planning the lesson, managing its implementation, and keeping it alive (i.e., motivating).

Many of these areas, like teaching as a whole, have aspects which overlap with acting and public speaking. A successful teacher is quite likely to deploy a variety of techniques of good formal as well as informal communication; a less experienced teacher may benefit from a review of these. Significantly, perhaps, for EFL teachers, the extent to which they may be somewhat culture-specific has not been adequately looked into. It is not clear to me that all of them will necessarily be influenced by one's more general philosophical views about teaching. However, I do believe it is worth scrutinizing one's practice in these areas. We need to check our use of classroom techniques, to see if there is any possibility that what we are doing is incongruent with what we believe (particularly in the absence of research evidence as to the general or specific utility of practice in some of these areas). The main areas I will first consider concern how a lesson is structured and presented by the teacher, and the teacher's use of vocal and nonvocal means in this regard.

Framing

How a teacher starts and closes a lesson is often said to be important in aiding learning (Doenau, 1985). In this respect, a clear statement of the goal or objectives of the lesson is an orthodox opening, and a brief review of what the lesson has been about or intended to achieve is a common closing move. The justification for advising or suggesting this sort of behavior to teachers is by way of arguments concerning our human cognitive capacities and the difficulty of learning from activities whose purpose we do not understand, or the utility of summary statements given our limited cognitive resources.[1] The research most apparently relevant to this area is that on "teacher effectiveness," a body of work which attempts to relate specific teacher behaviors to learning outcomes. However, these studies were principally conducted in U.S. elementary schools during mathematics and reading classes (Reynolds, 1992). Richards and Lockhart (1994) concur that little work on this topic in ELT contexts has been done, and can draw upon only two studies of second language classrooms: Wong-Filmore, 1985, which is again of U.S. elementary classrooms, besides McGrath, Davies, and Mulphin, 1992 (adult ESL and other FL classrooms in the UK). (To these may be added Lopes (1995, a study of a Brazilian classroom), which I draw from below.) McGrath et al. comment on the "atheoretical nature" of the treatments of this topic in applied linguistics literature; their own data does not deal directly with effectiveness, but in their questionnaire sample of 160 learners, the learners themselves reported beginnings to be "important," with functions such as attention-gaining, reducing anxiety, motivating, and establishing lesson theme mentioned. Drawing on the additional interviews (with 17 students) in the study, the authors comment,

what comes out very unequivocally . . . is the importance of atmosphere and the contribution of a lesson beginning to this [as a result of] . . . affectionate greetings on the part of the teacher, set interaction routines such as asking what people have been doing . . . personally directed questions . . . games involving active participation or any other kind of activity in which stress levels are low (p. 104).

Students also recognized that an appropriate beginning, such as a review, can aid concentration.

Though this is indicative, lacking empirical data on effectiveness, I will also assert that lesson beginnings and endings are important because they contribute to the successful constituting of a lesson as a social event, one intended to support learning, in accordance with audience expectations. If a teacher does not fulfill to some extent his/her generally accepted role as master of ceremonies, will a lesson really be perceived as "a lesson"? Further, insofar as a lesson is an identifiable speech event in a given culture, it will have, or need, openings and closings as do other somewhat formal, or "ceremonial," speech events. At the same time, however, one must recognize that all social roles are interactionally constituted: one cannot be a master of ceremonies (MC) without power, but if the participants in the ceremony do not allow the MC to use that power, there will be no ceremony. The audience must to some extent conspire with the MC to allow the show to go on, and what the ceremony looks like will partly depend on the audience's wishes.

This metaphor (lesson as ceremony) in turn has its weaknesses. While recognizing the social and even ceremonial aspects of a lesson, I would prefer that its ritual aspects (cf. Rampton, 1999) be subordinate to its learning aspects. And then, students too can have instructional or structural responsibilities – framings and closings may be desirable for learning reasons, but they don't always need to be the sole responsibility of the teacher (as Shor, 1992, points out).

Lesson beginnings are a time to formulate the topic of the main discourse which constitutes the lesson. This can be seen as an interaction between teacher and students, having usually a fairly one-sided characteristic, arising from the common classroom power imbalance (Lopes, 1995, p. 351):

The teacher typically, as the more competent/powerful member of the interaction, orients the organization of discourse by indicating the topic, hoping that this process will engage the student and be conducive to learning. Therefore, topic formulation has the function of organizing the interaction in the light of the teacher's agenda.... Pupils' engagement with the teacher's topic constitutes a crucial point in the lesson since its development depends on teachers and students sharing a frame of references on the basis of which common knowledge can be built.

The teacher then needs to consider, first, what are some accepted ways of performing openings and closings, and second, whether they can be independently justified on pedagogical grounds. Lopes cites Heyman (1986) claiming that "classroom topics are formulated in the form of statements or of questions" (p. 352). I would add that sometimes they may not be stated at all, thereby leaving room (unfortunately) for students to have a different understanding of the lesson intent than does the teacher. Lopes documents a case in which through misunderstanding (rather than malice) students contribute, in response to the teacher's statement, an alternative topic, so that for some time at the beginning of the lesson the two sides are talking past one another in regard to what the lesson is really about. In this case, the teacher refuses to accept the students' contributions to an implicit negotiation of topic. Lopes (p. 361) leaves us, as S/FL teachers, with food for thought:

In view of the fact that the group of learners involved in the interaction ... are considered poor learners, this paper draws attention to the need to consider whether their reluctance to accept the teacher's topic, as more passive pupils would do, could be one of the reasons for their lack of success at school.... By not having their topics accepted in classroom discursive practices, learners are learning to use language in contexts where their contribution to meaning is not taken into account, and therefore, in the last analysis, they may be learning to discount their own political effectiveness. This point becomes even more crucial when we consider that the pupils participating in this research belong to the oppressed social classes: the possibility of social transformation may be annihilated in schools through the interactional roles played by the teacher and the pupils.

FOR DISCUSSION

Here is a nonexhaustive list of ways that a lesson can be opened:

1. review
2. elicitation of student knowledge or opinion concerning topic of the lesson or teaching point
3. statement of topic

4. motivational remark
5. simple directive to continue with material studied from previous lesson
6. worked example without statement of topic (inductive approach)

Have you seen any of these recently? Which do you find yourself using most often?/least often? What others have you seen or used?

YOU TRY IT ...

Collect (by audiotaping or making notes) a few lesson openings and closings from lessons you have observed recently, or from your own teaching. Did they conform to the suggestions made in the above section? Drawing on them, can you give examples of how students contribute to the opening or closing of lessons?

Pace

Pace is the rate at which a lesson progresses through its component parts, and in particular those parts which have major instructional functions. It is clearly related to how much time is available overall for a course of instruction and the amount of material that must be covered or that a teacher judges is appropriate. It also reflects teacher judgment about the complexity of particular activities in terms of the abilities of the group of students being taught.

Successful pacing decisions are widely agreed to be important for the overall success of a lesson, yet some have questioned whether pace can be taught (e.g., Cripwell, 1979). Insofar as effective pacing depends on, for example, being able to predict how a particular group of students will cope with a specific learning task, some aspects of pacing indeed cannot be taught, and are a direct reflection of teacher familiarity with a given teaching context. This is pointed out by a less experienced EFL teacher, part of a study of lesson planning in Hong Kong (Richards, 1998, p. 114), who when asked about aspects of pace and time in a class, commented:

The students finished quicker than I thought they would, so I kind of filled in a little at the end. . . . I think sometimes you can prepare a lesson plan but you don't know often how fast or slow it will go in the classroom. Perhaps with time or maybe when you are into a course or a term you will be able to predict more accurately either how much or how fast they will catch on.

Pacing will also benefit from the teacher's ability to depart, in a controlled manner, from a preexisting teaching plan (see following chapter).

Despite the importance of context familiarity in pacing, an analysis of the topic can still assist the development of skill in this area. "Pacing decisions can be considered . . . as described by three questions: Who decides? For whom is the decision made? On what basis is the decision made?" (Posner, 1987, p. 266).

In a teacher-fronted model of the classroom, the teacher is assumed to have the major responsibility for, and power to make pacing decisions. However, those decisions may be the result of a compromise, on several levels. For example, pacing decisions may reflect an overall "attempt by the teacher to solve partially the unavoidable coverage/mastery dilemma" (Posner, 1987, p. 266). When syllabus design decisions are not in a teacher's hands, s/he may feel pressure to "cover" the material, even at the risk of some students not learning it. Or, a teacher may be sensitive to the state of a particular subgroup of students:

A . . . group-based approach to pacing [can be] found. The teacher moves from one activity to the next when he or she believes that a sufficient number of learners have gained a sufficient grasp of the material. . . . [Some teachers] "identify a group of learners, termed the criterion steering group [Dahllöf, 1971], to whom the teachers refer when making pacing decisions" (Posner, 1987, p. 267).

Alternatively, a teacher may use a standard derived from outside the class – past classes, or an external exam for which the course is preparatory. The results can be problematic. Black (1998, p. 112) comments worriedly:

In a classroom, teachers are likely to look for feedback to confirm the success of their own performance. Their priority may be to keep the process going and the reaction of pupils is used to judge whether it is feasible to carry on. Teachers often choose a sub-group of only a few pupils, and it is their reactions and responses to questions which serve to justify proceeding. In an atmosphere where a fast pace is judged to be necessary, and particularly where a teacher is insecure, such practices serve the teacher's own purposes . . . and may say little about the real learning of pupils.

The extent to which decisions are in the teacher's hands alone becomes less obvious in group work. It may be true that even in a lesson in which there is a lot of group work, the amount of time spent on each activity is partly determined by the teachers' original selection of materials, as well as the extent to which s/he intervenes in such work. But when periods of group work alternate with teacher-fronted sessions, and especially if group tasks form the prerequisites for succeeding segments of the lesson, then matters of pacing become more difficult, because they are less directly under the control of the teacher.

In my experience, pacing is a term that is often applied by experienced classroom observers as a way of judging at an initial level the likely success of a lesson. The ability to pace a lesson effectively is a commonplace basis for assessing a practitioner's skill. However, empirically-based treatments of the topic, particularly in ELT-related contexts, are rare.[2] Marshall (1998) is a very brief though helpful piece of teacher research. An exploration of the moment-to-moment aspects of teacher decision making in the area of pacing is provided by Ulichny (1996), who draws on her (1989) dissertation study of an experienced ESL teacher, Wendy Schoener. It provides a rare glimpse of pacing decisions under successive phases of reconsideration.

Wendy's class was a U.S. university-based content ESL class, with some EAP characteristics. Ulichny (1996, p. 181) says that Wendy's "philosophy of teaching included [the] belief that . . . [a]ttention must be paid to all learners in the class, not just the ones who understand and seem to follow the lesson. The lowest-level students serve as the barometer of where to engage the class." In a segment of one of Wendy's ESL classes that Ulichny analyzed, at a point two weeks into the semester, she begins with a minilecture based on a sociology text. This she then changes to "a dictation more than a college lecture, as she responds to student pleas to change her pace"; Wendy then asks the students "to rephrase the five main points from their notes." The students are almost completely unable to do this, and what was originally planned as a short segment is radically altered; repaced, one might say. The intent of this phase of the lesson, which was to have students demonstrate comprehension of the minilecture, remains the same, but the teacher shifts her approach radically. She ends up by constructing a sentence on the board addressing a single point of the minilecture from students' contributions, although she had intended to solicit their complete oral comments on the full range of content. Ulichny comments,

I believe that this episode represents a familiar moment in ESL teaching practice: trying to coordinate comprehension and task completion simultaneously. . . . The art of making the lesson comprehensible *is* the art and the method of ESL teaching. Particularly when the background knowledge of students and teacher differ and English as the language of instruction is not shared equally among participants, cues of student comprehension, or lack of it, guide the teacher in mediating the talk and the task to meet students' performance and abilities (p. 193).

FOR DISCUSSION

1. How does the topic of pacing apply to your own classes, or classes you have observed recently? If you are presently (or recently) teaching, what principles do you use in pacing your class?

2. Here are some possible factors affecting pacing: coverage, understanding, performance, interest, variety. Do they include factors you have been using or responding to, and/or can you suggest additional ones?
3. Here are some pacing problems that Marshall (1998) reports:
   • allowing an activity that is working well to take extra time
   • the teacher provides too many examples to illustrate a teaching point
   • extensive use of black/whiteboard slows exposition
   • homework reviewed in a nonselective manner in class
   • teacher tries to teach for mastery of each point
   • teacher addresses a single student's question at length
   • student groups in class repeatedly diverge from the group-work assignment

   Should these be avoided, in your opinion, and if so how? If not, what should be done to prevent them becoming serious problems for pacing?
4. Would you (do you) involve students actively in pacing decisions? When, how, and why?
5. Coverage versus mastery: Do you ever find yourself pressed to cover more than you think is pedagogically desirable? If so, how does this affect your pacing? (In what other ways do you respond?)

Nonverbal aspects of S/FL teaching

Earlier, I drew on a conception of teaching as something with dramatic aspects, and as any actor would acknowledge, the nonverbal aspects of performance are as important as the verbal aspects for engaging the audience, and for aiding and strengthening communication. Space, movement, and tone of voice are used by humans as systems for modifying or commenting on messages transmitted by the words used themselves. The body itself, including its clothing, sends a message too, of course; and this is all within systems of expectations which are cultural. We expect speech to have a volume appropriate to mutual interpersonal distance, as culturally defined, for example; and when such expectations are not met – when, for example, what we interpret as "shouting" takes place at close range, or when whispering takes place at a distance – the strict content intended by the words alone may be overridden by the implication drawn by the listener as to what the speaker really means by behaving in this unusual way.

The problem for us as cross-cultural teachers is that we do not always have full conscious active control of these domains and systems of communication as speakers; and also, sometimes, we are not fully aware of the interpretations that can be drawn, across cultural differences. For myself, as an ES/FL teacher educator, I was always aware of the power of the non-verbal, but it wasn't until I saw it as a set of systems for *meta*communication that I realized why these matters seemed important and powerful, and why I had been right in asking my teachers-in-training to concern themselves so much with aspects of language that didn't seem to reside within our familiar grammar books, let alone our SLA manuals.

The topic seems unduly neglected by teacher educators both in our field and generally.[3] In the following discussion I draw on Bowers and Flinders' (1990) treatment of the classroom as ecological system, which reflects the classic research of Bateson (1972) and Hall (e.g., 1959), to briefly review nonverbal communication under the headings of proxemics, kinesics, and prosody.[4]

Proxemics: Space and its use

At its simplest, proxemics refers to cultural rules concerning proximity, which are stereotypically "close" for some cultures, including those in Southern Europe, and "far" for others, such as, stereotypically, the Germans and British. At the level of individual student-to-teacher interaction, teachers working across a cultural difference must be sensitive and informed about these conventions. In classroom terms, we also need to know, and work with, whatever is the normal distance between teacher and student when in a formal teaching mode. We also need to have an awareness of the extent to which this is modifiable without breaking any "rules" or making anyone uncomfortable. My most frequent observation in this area is that both teachers and students will sometimes allow themselves to be at the mercy of furniture, sitting or standing simply where a seat or space has been left by the set of previous occupants of a room. Instead, I would urge the teacher to be reflective and proactive about how this space can be used. While not breaking rules, there is a range within which one can be closer or farther away. Students may wish for simple reasons (insecurity, work not done) to be farther away; teachers for other equally simple reasons (greater impact, better chance to relate to students) may wish to be closer.

The classroom is a political place in which unevenly distributed resources are allocated according to power, and this applies to space and movement before any more physical possessions or attributes. In the orthodox Western high school classroom of the early twenty-first century, it is usually the teacher, not the student, who controls space and moves. Furthermore, in a teacher-fronted classroom, a proscenium arch format is to be found, with the front one-eighth of the room being mostly free from furniture, and constituting a horizontal space within which the teacher has freedom to move easily, and in which students do not move unless given special reason.

Having registered this as a conventional structuring of space by way of rules incorporating the construction or reinforcing of social roles through restrictions upon movement, the teacher in development can begin to extend her or his use of space beyond this. For that matter, many of us working in secondary and tertiary education could benefit from considering the use of space in many elementary classrooms, which is far more varied.

Kinesics, including eye contact

In the area of non-verbal communication it is recognized that we send messages by the way we hold or move our bodies, by how we sit and stand, and this is the area of "kinesics." I think that there is plenty of room for individual differences and personal variation here, not to mention cultural difference. Thus the following set of points has to be hedged around with caveats. Overall, in line with a general advocacy of teacher reflection, along with the idea that posture transmits both a message and a commentary on any verbal utterances, I think that ES/FL teachers should regularly consider any possible impediments to communication their posture might constitute; or any unwanted messages it might be sending.

For example, one simple "impediment" sometimes faced by teachers of children results from the height differential: Jackson (1986, p. 76), speaking of when he was a new nursery-school teacher, comments:

When I myself spoke or listened to a child I tended to bend at the waist rather than at the knees. As a result I hovered about the tyke like some huge crane, causing him or her to gaze skyward and, if out of doors on a bright day, to shade the eyes while doing so.

And Ashton-Warner (1958, p. 22), speaking of a six-year-old notes: "I kneel to her level; it's the least of courtesies." But those of us working across cultural boundaries know also to think about or check for expectations concerning relative head height and status (in some SE Asian and Pacific cultures, for example).

To the beginning teacher who is unsure how to handle themselves in this area, I have often said, in the past, "first, transmit relaxed confidence, and second, transmit enthusiasm for the material, lesson, or students." But is one culture's relaxed confidence another's sloppy exuberance? The ESL teacher working with a culturally-diverse group has greater justification for falling back on her home culture norms than the expatriate EFL teacher who may have some ethnopedagogical research to do. That is to say: if you are teaching English in the United States, Australia, or Canada, to a class of students with individuals coming from a wide range of different countries, you may wish to recognize and try to be accepting of different student understandings of what is acceptable movement in a classroom; but at the same time, you may have a responsibility to explain what the host culture takes as "normal," and in the end you may even choose to insist on that. On the other hand, if you are teaching English in a culture you do not know well, where all your students have a particular expectation of appropriate and inappropriate teacher behavior use of classroom space, which may be different from your own, you are the individual who may have to make compromises, and it will be your responsibility to find out what normally goes on in the classrooms of the host culture.

The orientation of the body while in communication with others sends further metamessages. In Anglo culture, it is generally considered correct to face those being addressed, particularly in a one-to-many setting. This is not *always* the case for one-to-one communication, and may also not be true for non-Anglo individuals (men in certain Pacific cultures, for example; Miller Retwaiut, 1994). Beginning teachers are sometimes found to favor one or other side of the class in physical orientation. This sort of thing needs to be watched for and corrected.

An important range of metalevel messages are sent via something known as "eye contact." This is found to be important in many Western cultures, but it has a more ambiguous status in certain other cultures, including some of South America, as well as of East Asia, for example. Why does my own "Anglo" culture find it important? Because eye contact is taken to symbolize, and directly manifest, that lines of communication are open; but this is obviously culture-specific and merely a convention. The negative effects that arise when teachers and students have different rules about eye contact have often been commented on. But as an observer of beginning teachers, I have occasionally noticed problems where it is the *teacher* who fails to make eye contact with the students. For the absolute newcomer to teaching, this may be a manifestation of a lack of confidence. In other cases, the cognitive demands of teaching produce forms of eye contact behavior which interfere with the use of the eyes to support communication and rapport: a teacher is "glued" to the lesson plan, or consults the window or ceiling in the course of explaining material, and the like.

Finally, dress is a matter that generations of young teachers have been cautioned about, and the matter seems, on the one hand prosaic and on the other something perhaps unworthy of comment because it falls into an area seen as private. However, as the social body has become more an object of theory and research, so too has dress, and with once again our concern for boundary crossing and the cross-cultural, S/FL teachers can consider this as an area in which they can choose consciously, though in which they will also be the subject of scrutiny and duress.[5]

The voice itself

There are regularly teachers who need to give attention, often just a small amount, to improving their performance in regard to the voice. Consequently, at an elementary level of discussion, projection, use of intonation, and even volume, need to be mentioned.

In language teaching, within the conventional technology that a classroom represents, students must be able to hear the teacher well. A key factor is the ability of the teacher to use the human vocal apparatus effectively for communicating over distances. A large classroom might be at least 30 feet (10 meters) in length, and a lecture hall might involve distances of 50 feet (about 15 meters). Even small classrooms can be noisy, in all too many ES/FL contexts. It sometimes needs to be pointed out that most of us can and do actually amplify our voices easily by the use of vocal resonators within our body that we are not even conscious of most of the time. Singers do this, and anyone who has had training in public speaking can do it. Of concern is the fact that, many ES/FL teachers have never had training in public speaking and aren't even conscious that there is a source of information and technique to be drawn upon (cf. Donaldson, 1995). So my duty initially is to alert the teacher in development to this information and request that the teacher check their ability to be heard easily. If this is problematic, we need then to consider the difference between projection and shouting, and develop techniques for projection.

The next point concerns *appropriate* use of the voice, primarily at the level of volume. For most of us, this again comes as a natural side-effect of being adequate communicators in daily life, though on occasion one finds even language teachers who are not always good communicators. A lack of variety in use of the voice seems to be the most common problem, which may result from the press of the classroom overwhelming normal decision making. For example, I have encountered teachers who failed to switch to a volume appropriate to relaxed one-to-one chat from a volume appropriate to addressing the whole class despite actually moving to address a single student at close range. Naturally, the message transmitted becomes altered as a result.

An aspect of the voice that is a concern to inexperienced teachers is its traitorous tendency to transmit the emotional state of the speaker. Cohen,

Manion, and Morrison (1996, p. 347) remark:

The student teacher's voice is of considerable importance in establishing emotional tone in a classroom. If it is relaxed, natural and mainly conversational in manner, it will assist in creating a relaxed, tension-free atmosphere favourable to interaction and learning. Further, the students' voices will in turn tend to reflect similar qualities. Conversely, the emotional tone will be adversely affected by an anxious, high-pitched voice which will tend to generate a correspondingly tense atmosphere.

These authors leave the topic with the remark that

it is mainly the non-verbal aspects of speech – timbre, pitch, manner and speed of delivery, smoothness and flow – which contribute for good or ill to the classroom atmosphere.

As second and foreign language specialists, however, we know that these things vary considerably across cultures, and can by no means be taken for granted. The norms for such things as "timbre" are culture-specific; consequently, we may be sending a message when we use what for us is an unmarked timbre, but which for speakers from a different culture is unusual. The work on cross-cultural understanding, or misunderstanding, of intonation patterns indicates this, and reminds us to check our own practices. Gumperz's (1977) study (involving a West Indian speaker of English) of how falling intonation patterns signal authority in one culture but not necessarily in another is widely cited, for example. But native speaker patterns cannot be taken as the absolute uncriticizable standard in these matters; even if a language lesson is involved, the instructor needs to be certain that her/his way of speaking is not being misinterpreted via paralinguistic patterns that convey a particular message, probably affective, to the students.

FOR DISCUSSION

1. In all areas of teaching techniques (such as those covered above), shared teacher review of current practices and the exchange of experiences are valuable in aiding teacher development. If you are using this book in a group, pick one or two and explain to the rest of the group your practices or ideas in that area.
2. Do you have any experiences of problems caused by misinterpretations of intonation patterns? Are these more likely, or less likely, to occur in classroom instructional situations, than others, do you think?

YOU TRY IT ...

Have a colleague or friend observe a class you teach or a presentation you might give, simply focusing on use of space, body movements, and voice, and give you feedback. Share with your teacher development group members, if possible.

ES/FL teacher talk and teacherese

Applied linguistics has given a great deal of attention to the talk of learners in the classroom; Barnes's concept of "talking to learn" (1971) was influential in the growth of early SLA research and CLT methodology, and as a result ES/FL is far ahead of most other subject domains in recognizing the need for students to talk, and that it is through talking that they learn. ES/FL teacher talk has received attention too. Indeed, the term "teacher talk" is often used negatively, to characterize teacher speech to language students that seems to underestimate their capacity for understanding, or is exaggeratedly clearly articulated, or on the other hand syntactically simplistic. This certainly needs to be avoided. Research attention to teacher talk has seen it primarily as a source of input for SL learners – that is, SL samples or models that can be acquired (see Chaudron, 1988, for review). What I include here under this heading is a little wider than is usually implied by the term, but I will begin with these two senses. In these terms, S/FL teachers' talk needs to be comprehensible, and in some sense authentic, or at least not markedly nonnative. So an aspect of teacher expertise in this area is the teacher's ability to judge the comprehensibility of her/his remarks, and pitch the overall linguistic demand in accordance with students' knowledge of English, and of particular registers or domains of English, *without* going too far in the direction of simplicity or overclarity.

In addition, we can give attention to the topic of teacher talk, conceived positively, as an aspect of discourse that a teacher needs to master. Hodge (1993) calls it "teacherese – knowledge arranged for others" – and comments that "it needs to be taught to teachers because it is in many ways so unnatural" (p. 118). He continues,

Teacherese . . . is most dominant at points of exposition, especially at the beginning and end of a lesson or theme. . . . The aim in teacherese is to be clear and explicit, but also stimulating and seductive. The information structure (Halliday, 1985) must be linear and legible, a hypotactic structure in which the whole and the parts are clearly divided into "given" (elements already known and taken for granted) and "new" (elements to be introduced). The "given" elements should be explicit (so that connections can be made by the pupils, not just guessed at) but brief (so that the new learning has time to happen). The "new" should be expansive (so that pupils have the chance to grasp its novelty) but focused (so that they always know what is the point of the lesson). The overall lesson must be cohesive, with clear indicators at the beginning ("advance organizers") to show how the lesson will progress. Summaries at the end should state what ought to have been understood, with markers along the way to indicate stages in the lesson.

And indeed, we don't usually talk like that. Yet most regular students trying to learn unfamiliar material will welcome language that is structured in this way, at least from time to time. It might be argued that S/FL learners, if learning the target language through formal instruction alone, have a particular need for forms of language that will aid comprehension in two key areas: (a) "procedural explanations" or "the structuring of lesson activities" and (b) explanations concerning the language itself (cf. Chaudron, 1988). How can this clarity in these areas be assured? That is, how can we teachers assist students by being clear as we produce utterances with these functions?

Surveying the state of S/FL classroom research some years ago, Chaudron (1988) observed that teacher explanation, despite its obvious importance, had been "surprisingly little investigated" (p. 86). For both categories of explanation Chaudron distinguished ("procedural" and "language-related"), the S/FL classroom research simply provided some description, and little guide to clarity or effectiveness. The situation has not changed greatly. There continue to be many descriptions of English intended to aid ES/FL teachers' explanations of problematic areas (e.g., Yule, 1998). There are some accounts of how teachers explain language (e.g., Donato & Adair-Hauck, 1992), or in general (Book et al., 1985),[6] and reviews of explanation within the discipline of communication (Brown & Atkins, 1997) can be consulted; but on the admittedly narrow matter of procedural explanations in cross-linguistic or L2 classrooms, the research record is scanty. In the absence of such work, I will draw on mainstream educational research (particularly Cruickshank & Metcalf, 1995; see also Sánchez, Rosales, & Cañedo, 1999) and my own S/FL classroom observation and experience.

A first approach to seeking clarity in explanations is to recognize that on the one hand there are prepared explanations, and on the other there are those one must deliver impromptu, in response to relatively unpredictable student questions or matters arising in the course of the lesson. The latter are probably a bit more demanding. Initially, at the moment one contemplates responding to, say, a student question with an impromptu explanation, at that point there is already a teacher decision to be made. One has the option, usually, of deciding almost unilaterally whether or not to commence an improvised explanation; key points obviously being whether the matter in question is relevant to the main point of the lesson, interesting to all, needs to be addressed immediately and can be encompassed within the time frame of the lesson without disrupting it. Sometimes (and with hindsight) one may realize that it might have been better to say "I'll address that next time/after class." Explanations of the language itself obviously require a command of sometimes quite complex and detailed information; the astute teacher may defer till next class, allowing time to consult a reference work or source; or even assign the inquiry back to the students for next time. (*Repeated* use of the latter strategy may be counter-productive.)

It may not be really necessary (or best) to use words at all. A gesture, a quick sketch on the blackboard, mime, or modeling/demonstrating/showing what is required may be better. The possibility of modeling, perhaps with a student, is a particularly appropriate substitute for complex explanations of classroom procedures to be followed in doing, say, the next task or activity. There is also the possibility of providing a partial explanation to the whole class, and following up with detailed explanations, possibly individualized, once the main class activity has begun.

If we have committed to actually doing a verbal explanation, other matters are relevant. The earliest findings of research on teacher talk in S/FL classrooms suggested that there is probably too much talk by teachers, and not enough by students. Occasionally S/FL teachers may need to engage in longer explanations or expositions of material, which presumably should have the best teacher talk characteristics. On the one hand, for teachers who feel their skills are not adequate in this domain, the discipline of Speech Communication has much to offer (e.g., Klopf & Cambra, 1983). On the other hand, there is always the question, in a S/FL class, whether perhaps the students need time to actually use the language, rather than the teacher needing time to explain the language. The next question (after deciding in favor of a verbal explanation of some kind) is whether it needs to be done totally by yourself as teacher, or whether the students can be involved. Allowing or encouraging a dialogical structure to an explanation may allow for immediate negotiation of meaning (and real communication) which will be much easier for all concerned than if students have to wait until the end of something long and complicated. Then, in addition, "explanations . . . must be psychologically appropriate. Among other things, this is accomplished by centering on the learner's frame of reference, providing only enough information that can be assimilated, and using techniques to enhance clarity and emphasis" (Cruickshank & Kennedy, 1995 p. 235).

Some related matters in this sort of teacher language are to be found in Land (1987; a review of mostly older quantitative classroom research on non-S/FL classrooms). First, English has a wide variety of terms which we make use of when we are thinking on our feet, admitting uncertainty (or bluffing ineffectively), or when we are being ambiguous or unclear. They're kind of, sort of, well, let me put it this way, in a nutshell what I'm trying to say is – Land calls them "vagueness terms," and their overuse by teachers may be connected with student comprehension or learning problems.[7] Second, teachers (and other speakers) may sometimes produce "verbal mazes," which include false starts, self-interruptions, and redundant words in reformulations. In at least one study (cited by Land) these were found to be more distracting to students than vagueness terms. Finally, and most simply, the actual length of an utterance or sentence is itself an indicator of comprehensibility, other things being equal; and one to which I myself as an academic have had my attention drawn, as I expostulate at great length apparently without pausing for breath on matters of enormous interest and lifelong concern to me but not necessarily so to my students.

YOU TRY IT ...

1. In small groups, prepare a list of simple items of machinery or processes, like "using a stapler" or "washing clothes." Select an item at random, and explain to your group members how to use the item or do the process. Peers can assess the clarity of your explanation and give each other feedback.
2. More seriously: audiotape a class in which you do have to provide "teacher talk." Analyze it for clarity of explanations and make an estimate of the amount of time you spend talking, overall. Are you satisfied with the proportion of class time you "took the floor," given your teaching goals for the lesson?

The nonverbally enhanced ES/FL teacher

As language teachers, we work with students who, though they sometimes speak more languages than we do, have less in the one that is the subject of instruction. Accordingly, we must ask ourselves, are we doing enough to use other nonverbal/nonlinguistic communication systems as auxiliary systems to aid comprehension and uptake of the one that is the subject of instruction? I have briefly considered the human versions of these nonverbal auxiliary systems (space, movement, intonation, gaze, etc.), but what about the *technological* auxiliary communication systems that teachers can employ? This is not the place for an extended exposition of educational technology, but it is in line with the general intent of this book to identify areas in which S/FL teachers in development may wish to reflect on their practice (see Hodge, 1993, p. 119).

At least for the less experienced teacher, I do not think a practicum is the time to focus on developing advanced competence in the more specialized dimensions of ES/FL educational technology, such as use of the language laboratory or web-based distance education. What then would be reasonable? Given our classroom focus, one might expect teachers-in-development to consider their use of the main educational aids that are generally in play in classrooms in their immediate vicinity. Usually this would be various low- to medium-tech display systems, such as chalkboard/whiteboard or overhead projector (OHP). And why do we need to consider them at all? Because they are so ubiquitous that they rarely have their use thought through; and they are so elementary that they are generally used adequately, so reflection about them won't occur until problems arise.

When these are used as the main tool of instruction, they replace the textbook as a primary delivery system for content. At that point, criteria for their use overlap with a textbook at the level of legibility. Whoever regularly uses chalkboard, whiteboard, or OHP – generally the instructor, but if you have students using them regularly this applies to them, too – must exert efforts to make their writing legible and not block the view of others. This much is obvious.

We can also consider these aids as allowing us the possibility of using the written modality as a supplementary communication system which assists the comprehension of oral instruction. What are the ways of using OHPs, chalkboard, etc., simultaneous with and auxiliary to the oral modality? The most commonplace and least needing of treatment here is when a teacher uses them to support the teaching of specific lesson points, explanations, vocabulary items, etc., writing them out, diagramming them, and so on. Conceptually more important is when a teacher uses them to state the overall goal of the day/class/activity, to provide the topic for the day/class/activity, or to provide an agenda, list of activities, or phases of the lesson. It is this latter function that I feel is often overlooked, and which I therefore wish to draw to your attention. The basic question, as Lewis and Hill (1985, p. 52) mention, is "would what you can see help anybody?" And, one might add, is it well-organized and legible?

Given the apparently elementary nature of the topic, not surprisingly it is to the older pedagogical literature of ES/FL one must turn (e.g., Hubbard et al., 1983; Wright, 1976). These sources draw our attention to the availability of other matters to aid comprehension or supplement communication. Realia, pictures (sketched by instructor or brought in from magazines, etc.), and wall charts all fall into a basic low-tech category of things that even the experienced teacher should not overlook, and should be able to use effectively.

YOU TRY IT ...

At the beginning of this section I wrote "for EFL teachers, the extent to which [aspects of classroom communication] may be somewhat culture-specific has not been adequately scrutinized." I think this area is a clear case of a job for the teacher-researcher. First, in collaboration with a sympathetic partner or supervisor, teachers using this book could check basic aspects of their verbal and non-verbal performance when in a "traditional" teacher-fronted information presentation mode. Second, reflective and exploratory discussion among teachers, drawing on their somewhat tacit knowledge of acceptable or desirable performance of the role of teacher in their classroom culture is needed, to establish on a surer footing which of these techniques or procedures are most important for them in their circumstances.

5 Doing the Right Thing: Moral, Ethical, and Political Issues

- Does teaching well mean teaching efficiently, or is there more to it than that?
- What does it mean to say that an ES/FL teacher has moral responsibilities?

Warm-up

Think, not of a specific decision, but of a general pattern of behavior that you manifest, as a teacher, which you think is called for. (For example, "As a teacher, I should usually. . . .") And then, think of some thing that you, when you are a student, consistently *don't* do, because it is wrong or inappropriate for you in that role. In each case, what guidelines, rules, maxims, or principles are you referring to when you take the view that these things should or shouldn't be done?

In going on to discuss and review material in this chapter, I am continuing (I hope) to assist the development or reconstruction of your teaching philosophies. Moral, ethical, and political matters play a part here. Most teachers want to manifest the teacher role correctly because we feel a responsibility to students (among other reasons). As we have been students ourselves, we know the teacher has a duty to perform the role properly, that is, in a way that aids students' learning. Even when we were students, we understood this. Thus, we might say that we recognize the moral responsibilities of this role right from the beginning, or even before we step into it. It does not require a long experience of teaching to encounter moral and ethical concerns or challenges; these are there on the first day of teaching. And in addition, because of the international power and potential influence of English within both English-speaking and non–English-speaking countries' school curricula, and because of its influence on the life-courses of many students, teachers of English find themselves acted upon by political forces and sometimes find they are (minor) political actors themselves.

Much of the academic literature on ES/FL instruction does not engage with those political and ethical dimensions.[1] However, in the last decade, debates in applied linguistics particularly in the area of language policy have alerted EFL professionals to the need to think carefully about their role in promoting English internationally, on grounds other than those of efficiency (cf. Alatis & Straehle, 1997; Phillipson, 1992; inter alia). Similarly, within English-speaking countries, ESL teachers working with immigrants and bilingual programs have increasingly to deal in an active way with the policy and personal implications of their governments' support, or lack of it, in providing for the language needs of ESL students.

It is necessary for both would-be and established teachers of ES/FL to have some familiarity with systems of thought which will help them to address the moral and ethical issues that they face, and see their work as having dimensions that legitimately have a political character. The sections which follow simply provide brief introductions to systems of thought and analyses which support this goal. These sets of ideas, when integrated with teachers' own experience, provide some help when we ask ourselves difficult questions, like, what is the right way to do this? Am I really helping here? Should I be doing this at all?

Such discussions as do exist on this topic in our field tend to focus on the macro-level dimensions of moral and ethical concerns – that is, concerns at the national and international level. The chapter begins, however (following definitional work) with matters at the individual oriented microlevel, closer to the teacher-student interaction.

Definitions of the political

Let me explain why I have attached the word "political" to "moral" and "ethical" in this chapter. It is because some of the time when we are faced with trying to decide if we are doing the right thing, we are faced with this problem because of the political dimension of our work, or the impact on our work of the political world. The political dimensions of ES/FL may be particularly obvious to those teachers who have to concern themselves with the immediate effects of government policy in matters of language. One notable trend is that state education systems around the world are coming under increasing pressure for funds. Consequently, more ES/FL teachers will have to learn from their fellow-workers in the adult education sector of ESL, who like others working in support of marginal groups (such as refugees or immigrants) have become accustomed to working with communities and power-brokers to organize support and raise funds for their programs – a distinctly political enterprise (cf. Kaplan, 1995).

This connects us to one of the conventional understandings of the world of politics – that politics is concerned with who gets what, when, and how (Lasswell, 1936).[2] A second related understanding that most people working in education recognize occurs when the term "politics" refers to aspects of their working conditions. In these contexts it does not refer to views about the governance of societies, but concerns the use or command of power in their immediate vicinity, often related to getting, keeping, or losing a job (sometimes known as "clientelistic politics"). This is an important and valid sense of the term. Academic study of the distribution of resources and power at the interpersonal level now sometimes comes under the heading "micropolitics" which continues to be an expanding area of debate and research increasingly applied to the work of teachers (e.g., Blase & Anderson, 1995). The power imbalances within the classroom itself, across teachers and students, or among students, directly relate to or determine the allocation of resources, including even such things as turns at talk, so important for S/FL learning. Given these common and meaningful senses of the word, it simply is not the case that one can separate teaching, or teachers, from the conceptual area of politics.

FOR DISCUSSION

1. Use Lasswell's definition of politics to analyze your own teaching (if you are presently teaching). How is what you are doing aiding the life-chances of your students? Is it helping some achieve a certain amount of extra wealth or resources? Do you think all students have an equal chance of arriving in the class you are teaching?
2. If you are presently passing through a period of study toward a qualification which will assist your teaching career, can you expect to continue in your present position or find a new one easily when you finish your study? What political structures support your employment in English teaching? What political actions would be necessary to improve the status or continuity of programs or institutions in your vicinity which teach English?

Definitions of the moral

There may be considerable differences in the prominence of moral aspects of ES/FL teaching across age ranges taught, and across cultural differences. Teachers of elementary students are not usually solely language teachers, and often have responsibilities right across the curriculum, including in the area of morals or moral education. Teachers of high school students, though more likely to be subject area specialists, are probably still aware that they have some general responsibilities in the area of morals, at least, let us say, in the area of interpersonal interaction in the classroom. Teachers of adults, whether in university or in other forms of postsecondary education in the West, are less likely to have a specific concern in this area; but in other cultures this is not seen as something the adult educator can avoid (see, for example, the student comment on Korea, at the end of the chapter).

Here is a statement from an experienced secondary school teacher addressing the moral-ethical area. For Griffin (1993), morals are a category of values, and ethics is a code of conduct related to them:

The way I see it, values are a person's (a) fundamental preferences and commitments, (b) standards for determining worth or merit, and (c) basic concepts of goodness, rightness, and fairness. Values serve as criteria that guide three kinds of choices an individual makes: What is preferable here? What is of highest quality? and, What is right?

A similar perspective is outlined by Tom (1984, pp. 78–79), who provides a "working definition of moral":

I do not want to restrict *moral* to questions of right and wrong actions or behaviors. In addition to right conduct – a conception of moral that frequently involves measuring behavior against a personal or social code of ethics – I am using *moral* to refer to more general questions of valuation: What really matters during one's life? During one's career? . . .

The key that distinguishes valuational concerns from those that are not is the implicit or explicit introduction of desirable ends. Such desirable ends may involve explicit criteria by which behavior is judged to be right or wrong, or may be implicit in the choice of one position or course of action instead of another. Each of us comes to terms with countless moral situations in a lifetime, though we frequently choose to leave unexplored the desirable ends latent in those situations. . . .

But when we move to moral situations involved in teaching, the case for carefully analyzing and reflecting on desirable ends is considerably more persuasive. Teaching, after all, is a social act involving at least two people and usually carrying the sanction of a public institution. While much is in dispute concerning what it means to act in a moral way, there is widespread agreement that we need to take great care when our actions affect other people.

It can be argued that all situations involving humans are at least potentially moral. . . . But moral valuations are not the only possible valuations in a social setting. For instance, besides a moral point of view focusing on desirable ends, a person in a social setting may adopt a legal, an aesthetic, or an economic point of view. While nonmoral perspectives may be somewhat related to certain desirable ends – as when the legal perspective implies the importance of obeying the law – our awareness of these varied social valuational perspectives helps demarcate moral from nonmoral valuations.

To summarize, by *moral* I mean both a concern for the rightness of conduct and a broader concern for what is deemed important or valuable, provided that these valuational situations clearly entail desirable ends. While the desirable ends related to personal moral situations may justifiably remain latent, the ends related to social moral situations – for example, teaching – are legitimately subject to public scrutiny, especially when these situations occur in officially recognized institutions.

Act morally locally

I think it follows from the foregoing that even when morals are not being taught explicitly, schools and teachers are generally trying to do the right thing by their students, and thus they have (in a technical sense) a moral life, and may, like it or not, be seen as exemplifying one (cf. Jackson, Boostrom, & Hansen, 1993). Within this context, some of the more complex aspects of being a professional arise when a decision must be made in which there is a tension or conflict between different aspects of one's professional practice. As one teacher put it, "Well you know, morality and everyday actions get pretty tied together when you're teaching. There are very few situations where there's a clear right way and a wrong way, or the shadings are very simple" (Lyons, 1990, p. 168). This is most obvious when primary ethical considerations, such as the intent to do good or care for someone, and the intent to be just or fair, appear to be about to come into conflict.

At the classroom or even at the interteacher level, perhaps ES/FL teachers have neither more nor less moral worries, no greater difficulties to face in making moral decisions, than teachers in any other subject domain. But because of the role of language in matters such as cultural and even national identity – that is, precisely because there are aspects of their profession that pass across cultural and national boundaries, I think they may have knottier issues to deal with than teachers who work in other areas. In addition, there is some risk that because entry to ES/FL teaching (not to mention teacher education) is often by way of qualifications in applied linguistics or second language studies, some specialists in the area have received no formal orientation to the moral dimensions of their work.[3] It is important for the ES/FL teacher to recognize that there are ethical systems that can be used as a basis to support our "commonsense" judgments. Unfortunately, different ethical systems sometimes provide better support for some cases rather than others, and may also provide conflicting advice.

Sources of guidance (1): ethical systems

At least two preliminary ways of categorizing ethical systems present themselves: those based on religions ("fideist"), and those based on philosophies. Compressed presentations on this topic immediately abstract from the range of ethics in world history (Confucian, Buddhist, animist; hedonist, cynicist, stoic, etc; Kantian, utilitarian), to the following major positions.

First, one of the oldest ways of approaching this topic emphasizes the importance of personal virtues. In this line of thinking, ethical decision-making is likely to be effective when an individual has been trained to be of good character and accordingly manifests a variety of positive virtues. This tradition appears in both the Western tradition (e.g., Aristotle) and in Eastern thought – Confucian ethics is an ethics of virtue (Cua, 1998). With its emphasis on good upbringing, this has implications for the function of schooling and the content of curriculum. Broadly it suggests that teachers should act so as to be good models, though it leaves to tradition any argument as to which specific virtues should be striven for. Some of the virtues, such as justice and responsibility, also appear in general professional guidelines (discussed in the next subsection).

Second, there is a pair of related traditions that date from the period in European history known as the Enlightenment. These have been termed "consequentialist" and "non-consequentialist" (e.g., Strike & Soltis, 1992). They refer, respectively, to (a) systems in which we are advised to take into account the consequences of our actions, and (b) systems which propose that we decide simply according to rules and duties.

The former are particularly associated with the system known as utilitarianism – the greatest good for the greatest number. This line of thought is heavily involved in the political philosophy that went into the building of the liberal state or systems of government, and is a common heuristic for decision-making in many contexts.

The latter rules and duties-based system is also part of many readers' heritages: the primary rule being "do unto others as you would have them do unto you." In one formulation this appears also in the Confucian tradition, as well as in many religions; substantially reworked during the Enlightenment it became the Kantian "categorical imperative": "so act that the maxim of your will could always hold at the same time as a principle establishing universal law." Following it, one might decide not to lie, because one could imagine that a rule such as "do not lie" could be a good universal law.

(Another well-known rule is "always treat a person as an end, never as a means only.") This area, more formally known as deontological ethics, also encompasses the concept that humans inherently have "rights." The idea that teachers should act toward their students (and each other) in ways which respect human rights clearly has basic implications for our instructional and classroom management practices.

Some say that much of the time we act (as teachers) in accordance with the ethical traditions just sketched, and experience no difficulties. We only have to concern ourselves consciously with them when they don't work (or, as in the case of a practicum, when bringing the tacit to consciousness is essential). Instances in which it could be said that they don't work are those where it becomes clear that assiduously applying one or the other position alone will lead to what intuitively seems to be bad things. Illustrative cases have been constructed. Take the rule "do not lie." It can be justified because if it were universally applied there would be widely positive effects. However, suppose a potential murderer comes in search of his victim whose hiding place we know, and asks us where the victim is. In this case, we would probably be reluctant to be guided by the general rule "do not lie."

The fact that ethical systems do not help us make decisions easily in all cases doesn't mean we should give up on them. It does suggest, however, that trying to constitute a moral realm (the world of teaching) in the midst of the day-to-day world of popular life at the beginning of the twenty-first century is not necessarily easy. Perhaps these older traditions need to be extended, critiqued, or supplemented.

Indeed, the recognition that both utilitarian and deontological approaches date from the seventeenth century in Europe (at least) can be recast as indicating that they draw on introspective data from the dominant group of that period: well-to-do European males. Unless the perspectives of those individuals are universal, this, together with the fact that they are not even supplemented with empirical data, could be seen as a potential weakness. The cultural and partial inheritance (and implied non-universality) of the virtue tradition is equally clear. This is the view of moral psychology (cf. Rest & Narváez, 1994). Recently within this field, investigations of female or feminist perspectives have become important.

For feminist developments of ethics, the moral philosophy of Iris Murdoch (1970) and Blum (1980) is one starting point, and the empirical work of Carol Gilligan (1982) critiquing earlier moral development theories is another. These lines are unified by Lyons (1983, 1990) and join forces with the philosophy of Noddings (1984) in promoting "an ethic of care." The basic position here is that adults' ethical systems may reflect a concern with values such as justice, fairness, and reciprocity, probably associated with a view of people as isolated individuals; or they may reflect a concern with, or value for relationships, particularly "a response to others in their terms ... mediated through the activity of care, and grounded in interdependence" (Lyons, 1983, p. 134). It has been suggested, though also disputed, that men tend to use the former of these two systems, women the latter.[4] It would follow from this work that it is much harder to sustain a position in favor of a universal ethic; in making an ethical decision one needs to be clear about what system one is adhering to in making it, and the full range of options available.

As teachers, we make many day-to-day decisions which are of a moral character almost without noticing. However, we experience ethical or moral dilemmas when a problem in our work with our colleagues, students, or other community members, does not resolve itself whichever approach we apply, or particularly when one approach seems to conflict with another. A concern for justice (whether consequentialist or rule-based) may seem to indicate one way to proceed, while a concern for care may suggest another. Under these conditions we are advised to proceed cautiously, to make the most of our limited human faculties. Indeed, a useful part of thinking in this area concerns not so much the ethical systems themselves, but the day-to-day procedures we should use in order to help make our decisions as good as possible, particularly when faced with difficult cases or instances. Due process, deliberation, and consultation with others, are essential. A final point is that some recent work in this area (Lyons, 1990) suggests that many of the ethical dilemmas we encounter as teachers are not immediately solved, but are grappled with, deferred, or develop towards a solution over an extended period of time.

FOR DISCUSSION

1. Share a case of an ethical dilemma you have faced as a ES/FL teacher or as a student. How did you solve it (Did you solve it?) What use, if any, did you make of principles from ethical systems? Or, if you have a cooperating teacher, pose this question to him/her and report the results to your peers.
2. If you are aware of ethical principles besides the handful that have been alluded to in the preceding section, particularly those from non-Western cultures, share these with your colleagues and discuss how they might apply to your day-to-day practice as a teacher, or to any of the dilemmas you have discussed.
3. Here are some extracts from a published account (Peterman, 1997) of how a teacher in post-secondary education developed a philosophy of

teaching. "At the end of my first year, I participated in a workshop in which I developed a professional teaching portfolio. To do so, I was asked to write my teaching philosophy. Writing this philosophy synthesized the new ways of understanding learning and teaching I developed as a graduate student at a large research institution in the Southwest. Several key words framed my philosophy: academic task, constructivism, caring, and studenting. In my teaching portfolio I wrote, 'the following principles guide my teaching':

1. *Promoting good studenting is more important than promoting good students....* To me, while a good student has learned the rules and means that lead to good grades and the teacher's approval, good studenting involves the students in a critical analysis of what is important to know and how they come to know it....
2. *Knowledge is socially constructed....*
3. *An ethic of caring guides a good teacher's actions, encouraging good studenting and learning....* An ethic of caring requires that the teacher engage in knowing the student from the students' perspective and without judgment. It results in affirmations of the students' self, mutual respect, and an open classroom environment ...."

What general labels would you provide for the three areas of this teacher's principles? What statements of principle can you make for yourself in these areas?

4. Look again at the gloss provided for an ethic of care in Question 3 above. Our student body may include minorities who are oppressed or discriminated against. One example is gay, lesbian, or bisexual students. What implications does an ethic of care have for our professional practice with this group of students?[5]

YOU TRY IT ...

This will take a little more time. Go through an ES/FL textbook and try to identify its political and ethical assumptions, and share your analysis with your peers. (It may be easier to do this with an older textbook or one you are not in sympathy with!) What would you do if you were obliged to use this textbook to teach?

Sources of guidance (2): professional codes

Besides drawing on broad ethical systems and principles of philosophy (not to mention politics and religion), one's decisions and behavior as a professional may also be aided by reference to a professional code of ethics. Many professional organizations do have a code of conduct which they expect their members to follow.[6] State codes of ethics for teachers in the United States first appeared at the very end of the nineteenth century, and were actively disseminated, particularly by the U.S. National Educational Association, from the 1920s on. As recently as 1984 Rich was able to find little evidence for instruction in these matters as a part of teacher pre- and in-service education in the United States. However, there has been considerable increase in interest in the general area of applied ethics in the last decade.

Codes of ethics tend to be pitched at a level of abstraction below that covered in the previous section, though they can still be rather general. The NEA code of ethics, for example (see Appendix B), is based on two principles: a commitment to the student, and a commitment to the profession. Both of these manifest in statements that it would be hard to disagree with, and which are hedged around with words like "unreasonably," "intentionally," and so on, which may not help us when it comes to the hard parts of applying such codes at times when they seem to have been breached. ("Yes, but did s/he do it *intentionally?*") They are also, necessarily, of their times, of their culture, and may bear the hallmarks of development-by-committee. But I believe that they are certainly useful for the teacher-in-development, as they can provide useful input in asking the question, "What am I, as a teacher, trying to do?"

The main sanction applied following a demonstrated failure to follow the relevant professional code of ethics is expulsion from the professional organization. In the traditional professions of law and medicine, the legal right to practice the profession in a particular area is usually connected with professional membership, so sanctions for demonstrated failures to abide by the code are powerful. Membership in a professional educational organization, however, rarely is directly attached to certification, so there is little equivalent power, and breaches of ethics in state systems are handled by state authorities (such as boards of education). In the case of TESOL, no code of ethics exists as yet.

Finally, it should not be overlooked that codes of ethics are themselves (even when they exist) relatively brief, and may even offer advice which conflicts with that from more wider ranging ethical systems in the most difficult circumstances. The importance of the individual's own personal judgment cannot be subordinated to such systems, though they may sometimes be an aid. All the more need, it might be argued, therefore, for professional training in this area (Ozar, 1993).

FOR DISCUSSION

1. Refer to Appendix B – What are some of the implications of the introductory section of Principle II of the NEA code? What do you think about point 5?

2. At the time of writing, the TESOL organization provides guidelines for professional practice in terms of employment issues and student attainment but TESOL does not present a code of ethics along the lines of the ones mentioned in this section. Why do you think that might be? As a teacher of English to Speakers of Other Languages, to what sources would you turn for guidance in matters of professional practice?

A STUDENT TEACHER COMMENTS ...

In Korea, teachers are considered a role-model for the students [who] learn ... not only knowledge but also morals, that are certainly related to how to become an acceptable person in society. This may be the reason that we usually remember bad teachers for a long time, since our expectation of teachers is not only related to learning ... knowledge. We also expect teachers to be our moral source, so if we find a teacher [who is] not ... we get hurt and it remains as an awful memory for a long time.

When many teachers were advocating a teachers' union and its positive aspects on education, the government did not allow teachers to have their own union. In addition, it stated that it shouldn't have been allowed because teachers were social service people who should not care so much about their own profit. It also emphasized that teacher was such a noble job that God bestowed [it] only on specific people who deserved [it] ... Many people still say and believe that teaching is not a mundane job, and hence, teachers are not mundane workers, either. Teaching is a process of making people as people. The government opposition to establishing a teacher's union was very successful since many people still agreed with the above idea as to teaching. ... No one mentions how teachers feel about the disparity between the present poor working conditions and people's expectations as a moral barrier.

Act morally, nationally, and globally?

The domestic scene, and sources of guidance (3)

All teachers, but particularly those who work in state systems, are involved in implementing or resisting national educational policy, and are contributing, in a small way, to the reproduction of society or to changes in society. However, in countries where English is a second language for various cultural groups, the ESL teacher is likely to find themselves closer to issues of national identity and cultural preservation or change than, say, the average math teacher.

In ESL countries such as Australia, Canada, the United States, and the UK, governments have taken a special interest in the provision of English instruction to the various non–English-speaking cultural groups in those countries, both indigenous[7] and those that migrated into those countries in the period after World War II. Until recently, these governments' language policies were assimilationist, but more recently, cultural groups have increasingly pressed for preservation of their cultural identity through support for instruction in their first languages, as well as English. The ESL specialist in these circumstances is often also a specialist in multicultural and bilingual education, may indeed often be a first language speaker of a nondominant language, and is faced with having to support or grapple with the implications of government language policy that s/he may see as threatening the cultural identity, or survival, of his/her fellows.

If members of this category of ESL specialists consider the ethics of their professional behavior, besides addressing the interpersonal or classroom instructional behaviors, they may be forced to consider the domain of political morality, and themselves as actors (with small parts) in the political realm. In supporting, resisting, or going along with educational language policy, they may need to ask themselves, "what sort of society or nation do I want?" and "what understandings of nation and politics subserve these educational and language policies?" These questions, and the implications of their answers, are explored by Bull, et al. (1992) in much more detail than we have space for here. Let me highlight some of their key points, however.

First, it is worth recognizing that political systems have a morality. That is, they are attempts to say what one *should* do, within a system of governance, if one has certain beliefs. This puts them firmly within the ambit of this chapter. Because of the national and international aspects of ESL teaching, it turns out that, for ESL teachers, what form they believe a country's government should take might have implications for their actions as ESL professionals; if not immediately in the classroom then at the level of curriculum and with regard to, say, professional activity within a professional organization (touched on in the next subsection).

Within the governance systems of most ESL countries, at least three approaches coexist. Following Bull et al., I will refer to these as liberal, democratic, and communitarian. The liberal tradition emphasizes personal rights, justice, and individualism, in attempting to specify a way that society can be governed and organized fairly. The democratic tradition emphasizes *process* as the way that a fairly governed society can be arrived at: in this case, if everyone has an equal share in the discussion and voice in the governing process, a fair society will be arrived at. The communitarian approach, as suggested by the name, gives greatest attention to communities, including their competing claims to and understandings of, fairness. It is from the first two traditions that the common descriptor "liberal-democratic" arises. The term "communitarian" is less well known, but has become very popular among political scientists (and some activist groups) in the last ten years (cf. Tam, 1998). It incorporates some aspects of welfare state traditions, with its concern for community, as well as being responsive more explicitly than the other two to the make-up of the modern nation-state, which often has many different cultures contained within it. Arguably, a teacher whose sympathies lie with the liberal tradition, with its emphasis on individual rights and responsibilities, is less likely to see the wisdom in professional organizations acting to support minority community language needs, than is a teacher in accord with a communitarian perspective. For informed teacher decision-making, it may be that all three of these broad political traditions will need to be called upon by ESL specialists engaging with the development or implications of national language policies. And in my view, this need for informed decision-making is great even at the "low" level of classroom delivery of curriculum.

TESOL, etc., as INGO

Professional organizations in our field, such as TESOL and IATEFL, as organizations fall into the nongovernmental category: they are non-governmental organizations (NGOs). But by the nature of ES/FL teaching, they have an international orientation, and are thus in an increasingly large and influential subcategory – they are international nongovernmental organizations (INGOs). International as well as domestic nongovernmental organizations have existed, in a sense, just as long as there have been governmental organizations, but their rise to present-day prominence can be seen as taking off from the rapid growth of international professional associations in science and education in the middle nineteenth century, with extra impetus coming from the establishment of international governmental organizations (IGOs), most obviously the United Nations, in the post–WW II period (Chiang, 1981; Chatfield, 1997; cf. Boli & Thomas, 1999). Recent rapid changes in the international political scene associated with the demise of the USSR has given further prominence to them, including the involvement in international English teaching of, for example, the Soros Foundation.

We have seen that as professionals, we are subject to codes of professional ethics.[8] Since one of the defining characteristics of a profession is that it monitors and checks the behavior of its members itself (Middlehurst & Kennie, 1997), it is highly desirable that individuals calling themselves professionals should be members of their professional organization, and preferably active ones. The largest professional organization of teachers of English to speakers of other languages is TESOL. Presidents of TESOL, past and present, have often articulated an international perspective on our professional responsibilities.[9] In one such appeal, past TESOL president Mary Ashworth (1991) asks us to consider ourselves as teachers within an international "family." She argues that we should consider what it is we want our professional organizations to do, recognizing that they are actors, or potential actors, on the national and international stages. In particular, she points out that the TESOL organization has influence:

TESOL can act as an advocate . . . by supporting global rather than particular issues: that is, TESOL will have more impact by seeking to improve literacy worldwide . . . by identify[ing] those global issues, about which, because of its specific expertise in second language learning and teaching, it has the right to speak out upon and to act upon in a way that will neither offend nor alarm various authorities, but will help to put right what may be wrong. What might some of those issues be? (p. 234).

Ashworth identifies the following: Peace, Literacy, Language Rights, and Education, and she goes on,

Does TESOL have a responsibility to listen and to speak, to inform, to enlighten, and to a certain extent, to guide public opinion, as well as to make itself accountable to it? Yes, I think it does if it is to fulfill those two attributes of a profession set out by Peter Strevens – international interdependence and social responsibility – but it must be prepared to listen to all its members, those near and those far away, those rich and those poor (p. 238).

A somewhat similar viewpoint is found in a special interest group of the other major international professional organization for ES/FL teachers, IATEFL, whose Global Issues Special Interest Group

was set up to encourage EFL teachers to debate and take appropriate action, both as individuals and as professional educators, on world issues such as poverty, war, hunger, oppression, racism, sexism and environmental damage, and to explore the place of such concerns in the sometimes cloistered world of EFL teaching. www.iatefl.org/iatefl.html

This orientation to issues broadly intended to help rather than hinder the planet is in line with much academic discussion of the role of NGOs (e.g., Boulding, 1988, esp. Ch. 3).[10]

1. For those engaged in ESL, rather than EFL: what do you think about the remarks made above, about the likely orientation of the ESL teacher toward particular approaches to the governance of the nation-state of which you are a political member, and in which you are potentially a political actor? Does being a professional imply a duty to be civically engaged on matters touching the profession?
2. Are you presently a member of either an international professional organization (such as TESOL, or IATEFL) or a similar domestic organization (such as JALT – the Japan Association of Language Teachers)? Why/why not? Does your organization exercise any of the attributes Ashworth describes? If you wished to encourage it to do so, what would you have to do?

EFL as foreign policy and cultural intervention

This international, emancipatory intent for TESOL (espoused by some presidents of the organization, rather than the organization itself), contrasts interestingly with the historical international dimensions of EFL as outlined by Phillipson (e.g., 1992) in recent work on the promotion of English by British and U.S. governments. My personal view of this work is that it facilitates the expatriate sector of the EFL community taking a reflective look at their moral responsibilities, whether or not present-day situations are consistent with the historical circumstances Phillipson discusses.

On the basis of historical research, Phillipson argued that U.S. and UK governments had actively supported the teaching of English as a tool of foreign policy. This conclusion would hardly have come as a surprise had it referred to efforts made at the height of the colonial efforts of the English-speaking countries in the first half of the twentieth century, but Phillipson's documentary and interview evidence mainly concerns British government efforts during the period from the end of World War II up until the 1960s. I assume that a key point here is not that a country shouldn't have a foreign policy; nor that language shouldn't be a part of a foreign policy; but that the teachers teaching English and the students learning English may not have understood what larger aims their efforts were supposed to serve.

Unfortunately, the already complex matter does not end here. At the more sociocultural and pedagogical side, there are other concerns. Julian Edge, in what was originally a plenary address to the TESOL Convention, suggests a dilemma for ES/FL specialists – that their work inevitably involves cultural intervention:

The TESOL professional abroad who is deliberately moving away from a teacher-centred style of teaching is seen as threatening the position of colleagues in that country for whom the centrality of the teacher is the culturally sanctioned basis of their teaching. The TESOL professional is introducing a lack of proper respect for teachers and by extension for elders in general. The TESOL professional who insists on peer correction in order to foster student autonomy is from another perspective, demonstrating a lax and self-indulgent lack of real interest in whether the students' work is correct or not. If the teacher doesn't care, why should the learner? . . . If what we (and particularly we who live in or draw on such centres of TESOL as the U.S. or Britain) have to offer is essentially methodological, and if those methods are subversive and inappropriate, how exactly do we justify our activities? (Edge, 1996, p. 17).

FOR DISCUSSION

1. Do you agree or disagree with Edge's position above? On what grounds?
2. Find a written syllabus – if you are teaching, one of your own; otherwise, one from a class you are quite familiar with – and examine it for indications of a teaching philosophy. Is there much there? If it is your own syllabus, explain the presence or absence in the syllabus of statements which are indicative of your philosophy of teaching.
3. Share a story which involves some aspect of your philosophy of teaching.[11]
4. For the EFL teacher: As an EFL teacher, whether a native or an expatriate, are there circumstances where you are more, or less, likely to be part of your government's domestic or foreign policy?

YOU TRY IT ...

1. Try to write down your philosophy of teaching, as it is in its present state of development, and share with your peers.
2. Search for sources (like the newspaper *The EL Gazette*) which provide some indication of current international developments in ES/FL teaching. Do any current trends suggest, or call into question, the position that EFL instruction continues to be a tool of foreign policy?

6 Lesson Planning, Improvising, and Reflective Teaching

- I'm a beginning teacher – how should I approach a lesson plan?
- I'm an experienced teacher – do I still need to worry much about lesson plans anymore?
- What *is* happening when we diverge from our lesson plans?

Warm-up
What kind of planning do you do before teaching a class? If you have a cooperating teacher, what kind of planning does s/he do?

Discussions of lesson planning are common in ES/FL teacher education programs. They tend, unfortunately, only to target the beginning teacher and also often reflect a simplistic model of lesson planning which does not reflect the practices of the more experienced teacher. However, explorations of the topic based on a realistic, empirically-based understanding of what teachers actually do, or can do, in planning at the lesson or unit level, can contribute to the development of the practice of teachers, both novice and expert.

The discussions of past chapters apply to this chapter also. What a teacher knows, in terms of views about technique or content, as well as what a teacher believes, in terms of values, come in to play, consciously or unconsciously, as classes are planned. Of course, how you open the lesson, the approximate timing of activities – and thus the pacing of the lesson – and how you actually explain certain things, all must be planned for as well. If one plans in a particularly conscious and complete manner, one has a firm basis on which to reflect upon the lesson once it has actually taken place. For the experienced, as well as the beginning, teacher, planning is a substantial aid to reflection, and thus to development.

In this chapter, I first refer to some literature in our field that provides elementary advice to the beginner about lesson planning. Then I draw on selected discussions from within educational psychology, which put planning in a broader psychological context, including novice and expert teacher planning. Finally, I consider improvisation, as a necessary complement to planning and something again characteristic of the experienced teacher; and ask what is needed for successful improvisation. Throughout I will refer to Woods (1996), one of the more extensive, empirically-based studies in our area for which teacher planning is a concern.

Use of a lesson plan in a practicum

Many accounts exist which advise the less experienced ES/FL teacher about lesson plans and planning (e.g., Bechtold, 1983; Harmer, 1982/1991). While observing that a lesson plan should not be a straitjacket, they often present a list of items for which an entry in the lesson plan is desirable, commonly accompanied by a sample lesson plan format. Brown (1994), like many others, mentions goals, objectives, materials and equipment, procedures, and evaluation. A sample lesson plan format is often provided (e.g., Harmer, 1982/1991).

At the level of procedures, some standard features are advocated in this normative literature. The older British structural-situational tradition in ES/FL is associated with lesson planning involving "the three Ps": Presentation, Practice, and exPloitation/Production (Richards & Rodgers, 1986; derived originally from the Direct Method and the ideas of Herbart). Use of formulaic lesson planning is not confined to our field, though, as in mainstream education in the United States, the Madeline Hunter "Seven-step lesson plan," with its "anticipatory set, objective, input, modeling, checking for understanding, guided practice, and independent practice" has become common, or commonly advocated (Wolfe, 1987, p. 70).[1] The beginner may welcome such guidelines, but the more experienced teacher may find them constricting, deprofessionalizing, or inapplicable (cf. Maroncy & Scarcy, 1996).

In a practicum, following from its function, we can give attention to the lesson plan and its associated cognitive processes, as a way of fostering teacher development. Even teachers with relatively little classroom experience may have moved away from writing detailed lesson plans, particularly if they have available textbook material that is either adequate or that they are required to use. But during a time of intensive practice and reflection, such as a practicum, a return to the making of detailed plans, both mentally and even on paper, may be desirable. Detailed planning provides a concretization of practice, or at least of intended practice, and as such is also a tool for distancing oneself from practice so as to reflect upon it (cf. Rule, 1994).

In addition, it is essential that in a practicum, the teacher-in-development will be observed, preferably not only by the practicum supervisor, but also by peers. Accordingly, under these circumstances, a lesson plan can and probably should be written as much more of a public document; it can be shared with the observer and a better kind of feedback obtained as a result. Harmer (1991), for example, provides a specimen lesson plan in which the teacher is supposed to have entered a few descriptive comments about the class ("students are generally enthusiastic, but often tired"), which are most unlikely to have been made by any teacher planning for themselves alone. This is not to say that such explicit description in a physical format is useless to the teacher outside of a period of practice teaching; in fact, it could be very valuable to set such matters down in writing in order to think about them. However, the teacher's journal may be the more likely location for this. Similarly, a teacher who is going to be absent may provide a substitute with a lesson plan for the future classes.

Perhaps we should pause for a moment to ask what teachers do really plan about, then. Researchers in ES/FL (e.g., Crookes, 1986) have regularly drawn on Shavelson and Stern's (1981) review, which suggests that teacher planning is primarily concerned with the activities, or tasks, that will be used in a classroom; and thus, by implication, they do not follow the Tylerian model in lesson design and begin with goals. This would still appear to be correct: Burns (1996, p. 167), in a study of six experienced ESL teachers in Australia, cites with agreement the same review, and then writes:

> For all the teachers in the study, the lesson "task," the setting up and managing of the activities and the materials associated with the task, emerged as the major and focal unit of reference for classroom planning. Their thinking about lesson content and processes centered primarily on the tasks and activities considered appropriate, given their evaluations of the proficiency levels and learning strategies of the learners.

Woods (1996), drawing on his study of eight Canadian ESL teachers, comments that they first make decisions about what to do, and later rationalize them, though he emphasizes the complexity of the planning process.

Lesson plan, materials design, or curriculum planning?

Lesson planning, conceptually, shades into materials development and curriculum planning. Or, to put it the opposite way around, lesson planning is sometimes the final stage in curriculum design and implementation, particularly when these are functions performed by the same individual. They all deserve careful attention and could be focused on in a period of reflective practice.

For the less experienced teacher in a practicum, however, I am inclined to discourage teachers from placing too much of their planning energies in what we could call the "middle" of the planning dimension, on materials. I have observed student teachers place a large amount of time and energy into the development of creative materials for their practice teaching assignments.[2] In this, they are using time in a way they may not be able to when they have a regular placement or full-time position, as their teaching load will not permit it. In addition, the success of their lessons ceases to depend on their gradually improving ability to manage a class with existing materials, and turns on whether or not a set of new and untried materials will be effective in the hands of an inexperienced teacher. Any development involved comes not from reflection on teaching in the sense of immediate classroom practices, but from reflection and action in the area of materials adaptation and design.

However, having said this, let me concede that if handled carefully, attention to materials may be appropriate. This follows from my view that it is desirable that teachers consider goals more than usual in a practicum (along with values and relevant background knowledge). If one's goals lead one to be critical of existing material, then (with care not to overstretch resources of time and energy) even the student teacher can introduce additional material or activities (cf. McCall & Andringa, 1997). Alternatively, existing material can be adapted to compensate for its perceived weaknesses, while still providing a support for the beginning teacher (cf. Ball & Feiman-Nemser, 1988).

For the more experienced teacher, breaking away from existing materials and experimenting with new materials and activities, if they reflect different values or pedagogical philosophies, could be a useful means for professional development, particularly within a practicum (or teacher development group) context. However, experienced teachers also know that full-on materials writing is an extremely time-consuming process; setting new goals and exploring how to attain them pedagogically can be done without having to begin a major materials writing project, and indeed, perhaps the logical order of steps for the experienced teacher is to make the tentative shift to new goals, try them out, and only if satisfied complete the process by reworking sketchy experimental lesson plans into actual "materials."

Psychological aspects of the lesson plan

Within information processing models of cognition, planning has often been viewed as one of a small set of "executive processes" or aspects of "metacognition" – mental processes that control the operation of other mental processes. Planning is a practice essential when we humans, with our limited cognitive capacities, engage in new or difficult tasks. It is conceptually linked with monitoring; the execution of a complex task is problematic if we do not have a sense of the desired outcome and appearance of the tasks against which to judge performance and correct it as necessary; in addition, the execution of a complex task new to the performer is improved by mental rehearsal (Crookes, 1989; cf. Woods, 1996).

The physical lesson plan is simply a manifestation of one or more psychological processes engaged in before delivering a class. In addition, the lesson plan may well be consulted by the teacher during the class. In this role, it represents a memory tool, or cognitive aid. Though that point is obvious, it is worth considering the lowly lesson plan in this light simply so that it may not be dismissed as so elementary an aspect of practice as to be unneeded by the more experienced teacher. Why is an aide-mémoire needed on some occasions? Because teaching makes so many simultaneous demands on our cognitive resources that we may forget or poorly execute steps, or stumble over content, unless we have the psychological add-on that the plan represents. In regular teaching, we cope with the cognitive load by automatizing behaviors; in running new material or working in unfamiliar circumstances, and especially when we are being more reflective than usual (itself a demanding cognitive task), the humble lesson plan, in its psychological guise, should reappear.

Costa and Garmston (1985) are among those who have stressed the cognitive dimension of lesson planning.[3] They identify four aspects of this "design phase" of instruction:

- developing descriptions of student learning that are to result from instruction
- identifying the student's present capabilities or entry knowledge
- envisioning the characteristics of an instructional sequence or strategy that will most likely move students from their present capabilities toward immediate and long-range instructional outcomes
- anticipating a method of evaluating outcomes

They comment (p. 73) that

during the planning phase, the teacher can use a wealth of information because there is enough time to call it from memory. . . . Planning may be done in a formal setting – thinking, writing, and devoting attention to it – or informally – while driving to work, washing dishes, and so forth. This unpressured planning contrasts sharply with . . . teaching.

A more recent empirical study of teachers' planning recall protocols (So, 1997) surveys 26 previous investigations of lesson planning and identifies domains concerning which teachers plan: aims and objectives, subject matter, teaching approach, pupils, activities, theories/beliefs, and evaluation; So characterizes teachers' planning as at least recursive, and possibly "collaborative, dialogical, and non-sequential" in the face of the swiftly changing and somewhat unpredictable classroom context.

Background knowledge drawn on in planning

Within the overall context of lesson planning as a consciousness-raising tool, I am particularly interested in encouraging teachers-in-development to articulate the sources they draw on in lesson planning. Woods (1996, p.129) lists 31 factors mentioned by a teacher as affecting her planning, 10 of which she articulated before the lesson, and the remainder after reflecting upon the lesson. For present purposes, some were mundane ("how many students will turn up," "availability of photocopying"), but others were more significant; for example, "class dynamics and individual dynamics in a class," and in particular, "prior experience as a student" and "underlying beliefs and assumptions." The last may not be a common element of regular lesson plans, but may be appropriate for those used in a practicum. (In a recent practicum exercise, my students suggested including this on the lesson plans to be used in a "lesson plan exchange" activity.)

FOR DISCUSSION

1. What is the first thing you do in lesson planning? Do your practices match with those identified by Woods? How does goal setting appear in your lesson planning practices?
2. Compare your planning and your use of lesson plans with each other. Bring in a *real* lesson plan to share as the basis for this. (Do not create a lesson plan for this purpose.)
3. The normative literature on lesson plans advises beginners to include alternative activities or steps to be taken in case an activity doesn't work, or takes more or less time than the teacher had estimated. Under what circumstances, if any, do you do this?
4. Think back to Chapter 3; choose one of the more abstract aspects of your philosophy of teaching, and then review a past lesson plan with this added on. What changes, if any, do you need to make? How does Woods's factor "underlying beliefs and assumptions" show up in your lesson plans normally?

But sometimes it goes better when I don't plan

Many of us will have experienced success with lessons we didn't thoroughly plan; occasionally greater success than with those we prepared with great care. For us, on some occasions, improvising works. However, I sometimes feel that recognizing this, or admitting that one improvises, as a teacher, seems to be confessing to some sort of unprofessional practice[4]; yet it is an essential human attribute and potentially a manifestation of expertise. It also reflects a defining characteristic of the teaching situation: uncertainty, for which teachers should be prepared (Floden & Clark, 1988). Possibly my discomfort with recognizing the importance of improvisation stems from socialization into a Cartesian way of understanding human action: the highly rational individual thinks carefully, then applies that knowledge to action. The mind, to work best, must be separated from the messy influences of the body. Of course, this extreme position is more and more criticized these days because it is increasingly accepted that Cartesian dualism is not the only way to understand human rationality. One alternative but long-standing philosophical tradition that rejects the separation just mentioned is the phenomenological tradition. In education, one notable proponent of this is van Manen. According to Springer et al. (1997, p. 7, citing Brown, 1992):

Van Manen . . . conceptualized teaching in very different ways from those in much technically oriented literature. He suggested, for instance, the need for "pedagogical tact" – a sensitivity that enables a teacher to do the right pedagogical thing for a learner. Such tactfulness is not found in a body of knowledge, but in "a knowing body" – a way of being with students that incorporates an "improvisational thoughtfulness" and recognizes pedagogical actions appropriate in a given moment with a given learner.

Springer et al. (idem) comment that this perspective should be seen as complementary to "technical or functional viewpoints."

Part of our early socialization into the use of language collectively in peer groups may involve learning to improvise (Sawyer, 1997), and improvisation figures prominently in the skills of some of the more creative members of society (musicians being the paradigm example: cf. Sudnow, 1981). Within teaching, improvisation falls within the general area of teacher decision making or teacher thinking, and the term may cover a range of possibilities. A simple understanding of the term could be paraphrased as "thinking on one's feet," as in the account provided by Knezevic and Scholl (1996) of two novice Spanish as a SL teachers devising a filler activity when material for a prepared activity was lost. This might also be called coplanning,[5] or planning while teaching (Woods, 1996). A more complex understanding is that used in a study by Borko and Livingston (1989) of novice and expert mathematics teachers. They remark that

an improvisational actor enters the stage with a definition of the general situation and a set of guidelines for performing his or her role, rather than working from a detailed written script. . . . [and similarly] when improvising, a teacher begins with an outline of the instructional activity. Details are filled in during the class session as the teacher responds to what the students know and can do. Preparation for such improvisation entails the creation of general guidelines for lessons that are designed to be responsive to the unpredictability of classroom events (pp. 476–477).

In this investigation, case studies of teachers that fell into the two categories were developed and compared. The three expert teachers did their planning outside of formal planning times – one is quoted as engaging in review or rehearsal of the anticipated lesson "spontaneously at odd moments throughout the day." These teachers (who had repeatedly taught the same material on previous occasions) did not write lesson plans for the material covered in the investigation, but were able to report plans containing "a general sequence of lesson components and content"; when these lessons were observed, the researchers write,

all three were very skillful at keeping the lesson on track and accomplishing their objectives, while also allowing students' questions to be springboards for discussion. When problems were needed to illustrate or reinforce concepts and skills, they successfully generated them on the spot or quickly located them [in material available to students] (p. 481).

How is it that these expert teachers can succeed? In this case, it is because their lesson plans can be constructed on the basis of what Borko and Livingston, drawing on terms from schema theory call scenes, scripts, and propositional structures. That is, the teachers have a number of overarching understandings (abstract cognitive structures, or schemata) of how a lesson can proceed. Borko and Livingston refer to them as "scenes for instructional formats such as whole-class or small-group instruction." Within these the expert teachers can embed "scripts for teaching activities such as explanation or discussion," in which in turn they can place "propositional structures for specific instructional content." Expert teachers have automatized the use of these elements over the years, and they have an extensive repertoire of them, which they can move flexibly among, particularly when an overall arrangement appropriate to a particular lesson has been settled upon and reviewed. Concluding their theoretical discussion, the two researchers remark that "successful improvisational teaching requires that the teacher have an extensive network of interconnected, easily accessible schemata" (ibid., p. 485; cf. Woods's [1996] "experienced structures").

Borko and Livingston go on to describe three novice teachers in similar circumstances, and to identify similarities, and more importantly differences in their planning, and in the execution of their plans, as well as occasions of improvisation. Their work helps us to understand the complex basis for skilled improvisation. It also helps us to recognize improvisation as an essential skill of the teacher. Good improvisation, it seems, is a difficult thing to do – a skill of the advanced practitioner, rather than something to be admitted to shamefacedly.[6]

A final comment on improvisation: it is probably impossible if planning is too firm; lesson plans which are "robust," because they can alter easily, because they allow flexibility, are needed (cf. Floden & Clark, 1988). Woods's (1996) investigation of ESL teacher planning considers the matter at levels ranging from moment-to-moment changes of plan all the way up to course planning. He observes (pp. 169–70) that at all levels there was a considerable degree of tentativeness.

Very often lessons were tentatively planned, with many choices and changes made as the lesson was unfolding (a frequent change for almost every teacher was to postpone or scrap the final part of the lesson when there was not enough time to complete). . . . This finding . . . seems to go counter to the traditional wisdom of teacher education programs of top-down setting of goals, of being organized and well planned. . . . [A] framework must be there to constrain current decisions, but there are new factors being considered on an on-going basis. So previous decisions must narrow and constrain current possibilities, but must allow the new factors to determine the final shape of the decisions. . . . Being organized means having a range of possibilities and an understanding of the criteria needed for reducing these to the final decision.

FOR DISCUSSION

What would you do if half-way through a lesson you realized that the material was inappropriate – too difficult or easy, or just boring for the students? Make a note of several options, then pool yours with those of other teachers. If your peers come up with options you would not have thought of, highlight them for discussion and for trying out in practice.

Development in planning

The question remains, how does one move from novice to expert in planning and improvising? My initial response to that question was "experience, reflected upon," which I recognize may not be a particularly stimulating or surprising one. A slightly more satisfactory answer would refer not only to experience but to having an understanding of what the point or intent of lesson planning is, and having an adequate conception of this process and its manifestations, which is why I have been reviewing different understandings here. But in addition, however, we may also refer to recent discussions of the conditions for professional growth that have arisen out of constructivist understandings of learning. Feiman-Nemser and Beasley (1997) describe mentoring as "joint participation in authentic activity" (p. 110), and apply social theories of learning, to professional and adult learning. In this descriptive study of a junior teacher working with one of the authors (Kathy Beasley), we are provided with an account of the planning of a unit in which two teachers work together, and in which the mentor teacher provides extensive modeling of the planning process, as well as direct instruction concerning how material is to be taught. The authors remark,

> Working alongside her mentor, Elaine [the junior teacher] has an opportunity to learn about planning and teaching from the inside. As she observes and participates in the design process, Elaine forms ideas about what planning entails while contributing what she can to the developing curriculum. As she attends to Kathy's demonstrations and advice, Elaine learns what to say and do in the lesson, while acquiring contextualized knowledge of students and pedagogy (p. 124).

Perhaps this understanding of how planning is learned provides a counterweight to the previous discussion of the nature of planning. The literature on teacher thinking of the late 1970s and 1980s, in which the work of Clark and Peterson, Yinger, Zahorik, or Costa and Garmston is to be found, was developed within the cognitive psychological tradition, as I mentioned – a rather individualist tradition. The coplanning study of Feiman-Nemser and Beasley, however, reflects a substantial shift within educational psychology as a whole to place greater emphasis on the social dimensions of learning.[7] In moving from the question of what is planning, to the question of how it might be acquired as a skill, it is appropriate that the emphasis on learning with and from others should reappear, given the collaborative thrust of the present work.

STUDENT TEACHERS COMMENT...

[a beginning teacher]
Many thoughts ran through my mind as I reflected upon my own experience with the process while teaching last semester. Though I loved my work, lesson planning was always difficult . . .

There were two problems that I regularly faced – weekly plans and daily plans. I would try to prepare basic lesson plans for the whole week so that I could know the direction I wanted to take. . . . But it was often so very difficult for me because while I wanted to maintain this basic "outline", sometimes I couldn't predict how the class would go. . . . Trying to predict the unpredictable every week was one of the difficulties I had . . .

And similarly, where daily plans were concerned, I had a hard time revising the night before what I had planned for each day of the week. Again, sometimes I felt very unassured about what or how much we would cover the following day. No matter how much I prepared, there was always a feeling of uncertainty lurking in the back of my mind. . . . In fact, I was so worried and afraid about extra time that I overprepared and overplanned. And quite honestly, I felt as though this overpreparation often hindered my teaching. . . . For this reason, I was too afraid to be open to the idea of improvisation.

[a U.S. teacher]:
Although [improvisation] is widely acceptable and accepted in American education, this may not be the case in Asian education systems [so Asian ESL students in the U.S.] might perceive the freedom and openness of the lesson to be an indication that the teacher is unprepared or unorganized. . . . I've often asked myself, if the students don't realize or understand what a teacher is doing or where the teacher is coming from in an approach or idea or practice, can the intended learning truly occur?

[a Japanese teacher]:
I agree that it is necessary to have a specific goal and plan before starting the class, but I also feel it's very important to have some "room" for unexpected events that may occur during the class. I've heard somewhere before that the original meaning of "educated" is "to draw out." The teacher should not just transmit information and knowledge but try to discover the students' potentialities by interacting with them. If we think about this in terms of goal, we must be aware of the fact that a goal is usually what the teacher sets, not what the students establish by themselves of the teacher draws out from the students. It is almost impossible to predict what s/he can draw out from the students before the teaching takes place, because what can be drawn out is entirely dependent on the context. Therefore, I believe that a good teaching is possible without achieving the goal thoroughly that the teacher sets beforehand. The teacher should not hinder the students' unfolding their ability just by trying to fulfill the goal.

When I was in Japan, few professors provided a precise syllabus with a specific goal of the course. Some of them didn't even seem to have an idea about what they were going to do in the class. It looked like there was too much "room" for improvisation and the students sometimes felt at a loss. Since it was usual, I had never thought it was bad or unkind of the professor.

FOR DISCUSSION

1. What do you think are the positive and negative aspects of improvisation? When, or under what conditions, do you improvise?

2. A number of authorities in this area suggest using the (physical) lesson plan as a means for teachers to reflect on whether they are providing sufficient variety in format or content to engage the students. How would you do this?

YOU TRY IT...

1. (a) Create a more formal lesson plan than normal; (b) teach the class, and either during it or after the class, annotate the lesson plan to record the extent you deviated from it when you gave the lesson – that is, document your improvisations and try to determine what things were causing you to change your plan. (c) Share your analysis with another teacher.
2. If circumstances permit (i.e., if you are working with a cooperating teacher or with a peer), try coplanning a lesson. What are some of the key differences between planning and coplanning, in your experience?

7 What (Else) Do You Know?

- How does what I know as a teacher match up with what the experts say?
- How can teachers' knowledge be labeled, or conceptualized?

Warm-up

Call to mind a principle, or a fact, about S/FL teaching. How does it feel when you do that? How do you feel about being *able* to do that? Now write down a metaphor or simile that describes your knowledge of S/FL teaching and learning.

In establishing a values-based approach to our practice it is important not to lose sight of what research-based knowledge has to contribute to our overall teaching philosophy. Many investigators have looked at a huge variety of issues in S/FL learning and teaching, but does this information get incorporated effectively into teachers' (reflective) practice? And if it does, is this possible without devaluing the knowledge that teachers independently develop through reflecting on their practice? In my opinion, we can be optimistic about the outcome if we emphasize "knowing what you know." Being clear on one's basis for action is a key aspect of professional practice, whatever the source of those views. I propose that we take a look at, first, how to conceptualize one's knowledge of ES/FL teaching (and learning), and second, what it is we actually know in that area. Let me explain a bit further...

Developing a sophisticated understanding of learning and teaching, the classroom, and students, is obviously an essential part of growing as a teacher and this is the rationale for exposing teachers to the best or the latest in academic research and theorizing about ES/FL learning and teaching. It is assumed that expert teachers draw on their preexisting views about instruction and language together with the results of their reflection on research and practice to guide their professional actions. A substantial research literature on teachers' "background knowledge and beliefs" (Woods, 1996) or their conceptual understandings of their practices has accumulated in recent decades (cf. Clark & Peterson, 1986), some of which has come specifically from studies of S/FL teachers (e.g. Cumming, 1989; or cf. Brown & Peterson, 1997, for a rigorous quantitative example). Considerable academic discussion has been directed to the matter of how much of this knowledge is conscious or articulable, the forms that it may take, as well as how new knowledge gets added to this body of information or conceptual structure in the mind of the developing teacher. Research on these topics draws from many areas, including education, cognitive psychology, and anthropology.

On the one hand, developing language teachers, even at the beginning of their career, are quite likely to have some conceptions of learning and teaching, particularly of S/FL learning and S/FL classroom instruction, which have arisen from their own experiences. On the other, they may quite possibly have been exposed to discussions (perhaps formulated rather academically) of what the S/FL research community has come up with in the last few decades. The material in this chapter is intended to help bring the former to consciousness, and aid the digestion and use of the latter.

Personal theories and conceptual frameworks

Teachers' development in the area of conceptual understanding of practice occurs through reflection and through various forms of consciousness-raising; the process has inter- as well as intrapersonal characteristics. Some distinctions can be made by considering the stimuli involved in this process: (a) We might draw on our own teaching practice directly – either our observations of it or our reflections on it. By trying to say what it is we should do, or "what works," we may be able to obtain general statements or principles. (b) Alternatively, we might work with other people's preexisting general statements about (ES/FL) teaching and learning, agreeing, disagreeing, or modifying them to construct our own. We can apparently do both (a) and (b) alone, to some extent; that is, this kind of teacher learning can be seen from an individual perspective; but also, like other aspects of teacher learning, "the process [can be seen as] a socially negotiated one, because teachers' knowledge ... is constructed through experience in and with students, parents, and administrators as well as other members of the teaching profession" (Freeman & Johnson, 1998, p. 401).

Definitions and taxonomies

The "general statements about ES/FL learning and teaching" just referred to can at least superficially be separated according to the prominence with which they do or do not relate to values. Those primarily concerned with values have been addressed, to some extent, in Chapters 3 and 5. The others, typically attempts to conceptualize generally "what works" in ELT, what is involved in ES/FL learning, and so on, have of course been very prominent in the literature of ELT and education in general; and these accounts are often assumed to be value-free. Because I think they have utility at least for reviewing (and digesting for future use) what teachers-under-construction have been exposed to in much of their formal education, I propose to bring in some of these general statements here – in due course. But first let me attempt to organize statements of this kind a different way, using two other categories.

The first are statements by individual teachers of their pedagogic understandings and teaching practice, whether broad or narrow of reference. These may be referred to as "teacher lore" (Schubert, 1991; Schubert & Ayers, 1992), and form an important part of the literature of teaching. They can take a relatively nonacademic, popular form, such as Sylvia Ashton-Warner's (1963) autobiographical work *Teacher*, or they can take a more focused and academic form: Borg (1998), for example, is a recent extensively theorized journal article account of practice in the teaching of grammar in TESOL. These statements are often called personal theories, practical theories (Marland, 1995), or subjective theories (Grotjahn, 1991). I will not draw on such statements heavily in this unit. They can be rather lengthy – too long to summarize in material of the present kind, unfortunately, and as Schubert (1991, p. 219) says, these "renditions lose their vigor when summarized." Some partial recent versions from our field are gathered in Richards and Freeman (1996), notably Burns (1996); see also Golombek (1998). Within this small literature, Woods (1996) stands out; he studied the ideas of eight ESL teachers to arrive at an understanding of these conceptual structures, and he refers to the entities involved as networks of beliefs, assumptions, and knowledge (BAK networks). He emphasizes the difficulty of distinguishing between those three terms; and also notes however that these networks can be reduced to (or inferred from) statements about relationships in the domain of S/FL learning/teaching (for example, the relationship between motivation and learning, or between learner independence and a teacher-conducted needs analysis). I will return to this literature toward the end of the chapter.

The second category consists of attempts by academics who were trying to present their understanding of a large body of research findings and general understandings of practice in an encapsulated form, either to teachers or to other researchers. Stern (1983) calls these "conceptual frameworks," and they usually constitute a concise structuring of a part of the professional and academic domains of ES/FL. I would also assert that they could be used to generate many statements in the professional language of our field. Incorporating and digesting this language until it becomes one's own has been identified as a notable aspect of teacher development (Freeman, 1993).

YOU TRY IT...

1. As a beginning, let's look at some general statements concerning the learning and teaching of a second or foreign languages. These (following) are admittedly a bit simplistic or overly general, but they will get us going.

   Annotate the statements according to the extent you agree or disagree with them (try "agree," "neutral," "disagree"). And/or, note "it depends" if you think that the truth of the statement depends very much on context. In addition, some statements may look more as though they derive from disciplinary knowledge, and some, you might think, would come under a heading like "teacher lore" or "rule of thumb" – mark the statements accordingly.

   1. All languages are equally capable of expressing complex meanings.
   2. Children learn a second/foreign language easier than adults.
   3. A standard language is neither more efficient nor morally preferable to a nonstandard language.
   4. It doesn't matter if students don't understand all target language utterances their teachers make.
   5. Teachers should only use the target language to teach with.
   6. Translation is a good way to learn vocabulary.
   7. A new teacher shouldn't smile until week six.
   8. Chinese students learn well through memorization.
   9. A learner's personal investment in what s/he is learning is crucial for success.
   10. A process approach to writing requires students who are willing to learn from each other.
   11. Pair work is a good way to maximize use of classroom time.
   12. Most cultures are multilingual.
   13. Rich people are more likely to successfully learn a second language at school than poor people.

14. Students usually cannot correct each others' errors effectively.
15. A positive attitude to the target language is essential for learning.
16. It is the teacher's responsibility to specify what topics, language items, functions, etc., will be taught and learned.
17. Some people have a natural aptitude for learning second/foreign languages.
18. Women are better second/foreign language learners than men.

2. Now add a few statements of your own to the list from (1) above. Share them with your peers. Do they agree with them, or find them provocative?

Sample conceptual frameworks

I present here three examples from older TESOL literature (see Figs. 7-1, 7-2, and 7-3), the work of Stern, Strevens, and Spolsky, respectively, prominent figures in ELT in the academic generation preceding my own. Synthesizing models of the sort displayed here seem to be less common in the professional literature of our field these days. (Perhaps this is a side effect of the criticism by postmodernists of "grand theory.") As I have become more aware of the differences among the teachers I have worked with, and know more about the cultures and nations in which they in turn work, the limitations of general theories and the difficulties with specifying apparently fixed domains of knowledge seems increasingly clear.[1] However, some simplification of the complexity of the domain we are working in is almost certainly necessary as one engages in conceptual development (cf. Evans & Dansereau, 1991), and I believe that these frameworks may have heuristic value – that is, they may stimulate the development or articulation of the readers' own frameworks.

There are distinct differences across these three. Stern is attempting to map the disciplinary domains relevant to ELT specialists' academic knowledge. Strevens's chart is an attempt to diagram a system of relationships important for professional practice by ELT specialists. Finally, Spolsky's is a visual representation of a "set of laws" theory of SLA. These three diagrams interlock, but also, they operate at different levels of abstraction over different topics or bodies of knowledge.[2]

Sample conceptual framework 1: Stern's "general model for second language teaching"

Working in Canada in the 1980s, H. H. Stern developed the framework of Strevens presented below, and also built on a conceptual framework

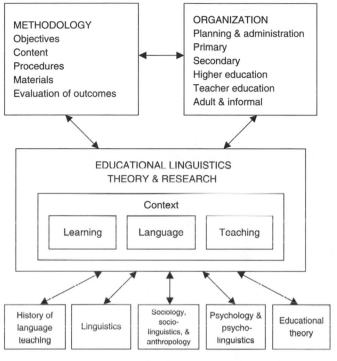

Fig. 7-1

of Spolsky (earlier than Spolsky's SLA work illustrated here), and a few other related frameworks to develop what he called a "general model for second language teaching." Spolsky's term for the area of applied linguistics concerned with education, that is, "educational linguistics," occupies a prominent place in it. At its core, it places an academic subdiscipline, then. At the bottom, four grander academic disciplines and a part of the discipline of history feed into this subdiscipline of educational linguistics. Educational Linguistics provides the metalevel understandings which inform teaching, in this model.

According to Stern (1983, pp. 44–45), the purpose of the model is (1) "to serve, above all, as an aid to teachers to develop their own 'theory' or a philosophy ... in answer to those questions: 'Where do you stand on basic issues?' 'How do you see your own teaching?' 'What needs to be done to teach language X or Y?' and so on; (2) It should help a teacher in analyzing, interpreting, and evaluating commonly held theories, views, or philosophies on the teaching of languages ...; (3) It should assist a teacher in analyzing a given teaching/learning situation so that he can cope with it more effectively."

FOR DISCUSSION

1. Try to narrate Stern's diagram – that is, say something about how the boxes are related one to another, as sources of knowledge and bases for planning and teaching decisions. Begin like this: "In making decisions in their teaching, ES/FL teachers draw on a number of areas. First, they may think about [insert name of box, or subheading from box here]. Then, [and continue]. . . . You might try this once confining yourself to Stern's framework, then another time while improvising, guessing, or drawing on your own experience and opinions.
2. If you are presently taking classes in a formal program of study related to TESOL, you may be able to use the classes themselves, perhaps in the form of a list or chart, as a way of organizing your growing knowledge base for teaching. List, then group together those courses. Which of the elements from Stern's diagram do they relate to?

    If you are not in such a situation, here is a sample list of courses offered (not every semester) from one large department to use instead:
    language concepts for second language learning and teaching
    second language testing
    second language acquisition
    sociolinguistics and second languages
    English syntax
    language and the law
    L2 literacy
    second language listening
    discourse processes
    second language ethnography
    universals and SLA
    critical SL pedagogy
    bilingual language attainment and attrition
    second language pragmatics
    task-based language learning
    bilingual education
    instructional media
    English phonology
    alternative approaches to second language teaching
    second language listening and speaking

second language writing
second language reading
second language program development
comparative grammar and SLA
second language quantitative research
research in language testing
applied psycholinguistics and SLA
second language interpretative qualitative research

Sample conceptual framework 2: Strevens' "learning/teaching theory"

Peter Strevens's (1976) framework reflects some of his professional concerns. As an academic active during the 1970s when applied linguistics was still a new field, he wanted to emphasize the professional character of S/FL teaching as well as its academic respectability. The various steps or elements in program design and implementation figure prominently, and we may notice that links to political and institutional entities at just one remove from the ELT professional are provided or implied in the diagram. (By "LL/LT types" – that is, "Language Learning/Language Teaching types," Strevens is referring to matters such as: kinds of learner, in terms of age range and proficiency, whether the program is, for example, English for general purposes or English for specific purposes, whether the students are required, or not, to attend, and whether it is in an EFL or an ESL context.)

For discussion

1. Try to narrate Strevens's diagram. The arrows in the diagram may be taken to stand for "influences," "determines," or "feeds into." With this in mind, try to put into words some of the claims the diagram seem to be making about S/FL teaching. Here is a framework to start: "Decision-making and professional ELT practice are influenced by many factors, and the success of the learner can be seen as affected by a whole series of choices. To start with, in any language teaching situation, we have to be aware of [say something about the first row of boxes here] ... In addition, the characteristics of the teaching and learning population will be important. For example, in my country we have [provide details pertinent to the second level box here]. ... Then if we actually look at the instructional program itself [insert comments about the central sections of the diagram here]. ...

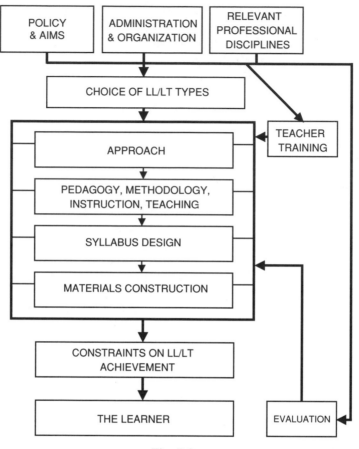

Fig. 7-2

2. In what ways, if any, would you alter or correct this model?
3. Which parts of Stern's diagram does Strevens's model overlap with?

Sample conceptual framework 3: Spolsky's model

Bernard Spolsky's model represents his theoretical model of second language learning (1989), and consequently does not directly address teaching. For present purposes, it has two virtues. First, even if you have not had a lot of experience teaching, you can try out this model against your own views and experiences as a S/FL learner as well as academic content you may

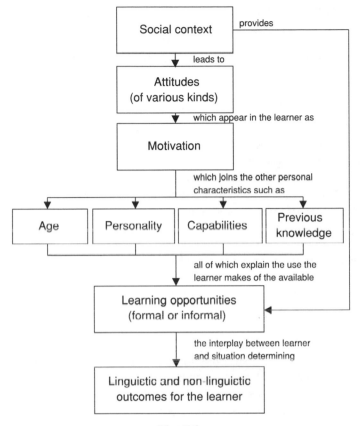

Fig. 7-3

have read or studied concerning learning a second or foreign language. And second, Spolsky's arrangement provides one influential way of looking at the field of SLA, knowledge of which in turn is assumed to have strong implications for the practice of any S/FL teacher.

For discussion

1. Try to provide statements concerning SL learning that reflect the structure of the diagram as well as your own beliefs or knowledge. For example, using the top box and the arrow at its side, we can make a statement beginning like this: "In general, Spolsky believes that social context provides SL learning opportunities, and I agree (or disagree).

For example, if a student is in a country where English is widely used, s/he can simply draw on the environment as a source for learning. In my own case ... [and continue]." Compare your statements with those of your peers, if possible. Are there any areas which promote disagreement? Are there areas for which you feel your knowledge is lacking?

2. Look again at the headings in Spolsky's diagram. Have you been exposed to lectures, coursework, or read studies in any of these areas which claim to be knowledge about S/FL learning, but about which you have reservations? (For example, claims that you think would not hold up in learning and teaching situations or conditions with which you are familiar.) If so, make a note of these areas and discuss how you might test these claims, in the course of your work as a teacher.

Methodology as conceptual framework

One also sometimes comes across discussions of Methods which are presented as a personal practical theory. Stern calls these T2 theories, and places them between a broad conceptual framework such as his own, set out earlier, and a scientific theory, a T3 in his terms, which is what Spolsky is aiming at. When trying to help student teachers articulate their views about teaching, I have discouraged them from simply restating a "Method," partly because I have felt that the statements that arise might duck broad important issues, moral issues, like the overall goal of teaching, or how one should treat students, and stay mainly (or apparently) at the level of technique ("drilling is good"). However, as some more recent Methods have become all-encompassing, they have sucked in moral, ethical, and philosophical positions as well; and looking at it from another point of view, many Methods that present themselves as purely technical conceal value judgments about the roles and relationships between teacher and student. So it may be worthwhile to engage with a recent example.

"Whole Language" is an approach that developed for the teaching of first language literacy, with a strong emphasis on the social dimensions of literacy and of learning. It was taken over into the domain of second language instruction over a period of at least ten years, and as this process took place, it incorporated broader perspectives. Its proponents are now extending it further to address the needs of EFL learners. Two prominent "Whole Language" theorists (Freeman & Freeman, 1998, pp. xvii–xviii) couch their views as a series of "should" statements (with one exception), which is partly what makes them of interest to me. Here they are:

Learning proceeds from whole to part.
Lessons should be learner-centred.
Lessons should have meaning and purpose for students now.
Lessons should engage students in social interaction.
Lessons should develop both oral and written language.
Lessons should support students' first languages and cultures.
Lessons should show faith in the learner to expand students' potential.

You might like to try using them as statements to test against your own thinking.

YOU TRY IT...

Here is another opportunity to produce some writing that could contribute to a philosophy of teaching. Use the "should" statements of the Freemans as models for your own. You could extend or modify them, if you disagree with those statements, or replace them completely with other "should" statements that make use of some of the same central terms, like "learners," "meaning," "language," and so on. Are there things that lessons should be that in your view the Freemans completely overlook? You might also try replacing the words "Lessons should . . ." that they use with your own "Teachers should . . ." or "I as an ES/FL teacher should. . . ."

Personal practical theories again

In my work as a teacher educator and SL researcher, I have for a number of years been advocating teacher research, and arguing against the hierarchization of knowledge in our field. I am, like many others, worried about the separation of theory and practice in TESOL. So it would be contradictory for me to prioritize conceptual models just of academic researchers over those of teachers, in material intended to help teachers work out their own views and perspectives. I agree with the following remarks of Golombek (1998, p. 447; made in introduction to a study of teachers' practical theories):

L2 teachers' knowledge is, in part, experiential and constructed by teachers themselves as they respond to the contexts of their classrooms. However, research in teacher education has largely focused on developing an empirically grounded knowledge-base to be given to teachers rather than on examining what teachers' experiential knowledge is and how they use that knowledge (Carter, 1990). Imposing a codified knowledge on teachers and separating them from their experiential knowledge "may lead to closed worlds of meaning rather than opening windows on possibilities" (Harrington, 1994, p. 190).

Golombek's boiling-down of the teachers' personal practical knowledge is presented in narrative form (hence problems in summarizing it concisely) but a key point is that in it, teachers

revealed that their moral and affective ways of knowing in relation to themselves and others were permeated with the consequences of the strategies they used to deal with the tensions they experienced in the classroom. What these teachers knew was clearly woven together so that they used this knowledge in a holistic way.... The way L2 teachers understand and respond to their classrooms is mediated by their experiences as teachers, learners, and persons outside the classroom: personal and interpersonal factors and values, as well as their professional knowledge (Golombek, 1998, p. 400).[3]

There are good historical reasons, and even good practical reasons why one might wish to consider professional knowledge at varying levels of abstraction and with varying degrees of context, but I would not wish to suggest that the depersonalized perspectives of Stern, Strevens, or Spolsky, should be taken as a model for or be seen as equivalent to teachers' knowledge. They are just one part of a broader picture, important details of which are being filled in by more recent research and theorizing. As will be seen in the extracts from student teacher theorizing that follow, for some past students of mine it has indeed seemed difficult to separate these domains of knowledge. Nevertheless, they (and I) have been following the advice of Golombek, who says,

the way to acknowledge teachers' personal practical knowledge is for teacher educators ... to link participants' personal practical knowledge with the empirically grounded knowledge generally presented in teacher education coursework.... [T]eacher educators should provide teachers with opportunities to make sense of theory by filtering it through experiential knowledge gained as teachers and learners (p. 461).

For discussion

In a discussion of teacher beliefs and intentions, Woods (1996) refers to "hotspots" – that is, areas where a teacher's intentions or beliefs about ES/FL teaching don't fully match their actions. Do you have any such? Try using the following frameworks to make your own hot spot statements . . .

- "I'm pretty sure that ___ would be a good thing to try, but I haven't figured out how to work it into my teaching yet."
- "I've read research which states that ___ is beneficial, but I know I'm still doing ___."
- "I really believe in the value of ___, and I'd like to incorporate it in the curriculum, but if I did so I'm afraid I'd lose my job/get into trouble/meet resistance from parents or students."

STUDENT TEACHERS COMMENT . . .

Fredericka
I was toying with the diagram by Strevens of his "learning/teaching theory." I began with a needs analysis for a population of learners undertaken by teachers and others in the education domain. This analysis is done by assessing both learner and community/governmental needs. This umbrella is then connected to the following three areas: Policy and Aims; Administration and Organization; Relevant Professional Disciplines. Each of these areas filter into the middle block and impact these: Choice of LL/LT types; Pedagogy, Methodology, Instruction and Teaching. They also connect to a box labeled Evaluation of Teaching so that there is a means of monitoring if learning is going on in the classroom. The middle block also contains a means for evaluating the three areas directly above it and for evaluating the learners. Below this middle block is a block containing the heading Constraints on Individual LL/LT achievement and directly after this comes the block containing the heading Individual Learner. This last box is also connected to the box labeled Evaluation of Teaching, so that learner input is considered. One cannot emphasize enough the recursive nature of this type of framework. I feel it is incredibly important to put both teachers and learners at the top of any framework of this type.

Angelo
My model for teaching and learning in the L2 . . . is as follows:

Society/Institution
Learner
Teacher
Methodology/Pedagogy
Syllabus
Activities
Assessment

I can explain my model by emphasizing that the goals and aims of education begin with the society and/or institution providing the services. The society's values and beliefs determines what is important for their members to know and the institution provides instruction that cultivates these traits and skills accordingly. Then the learner influences how these values are applied academically by personal factors like personality, capability, and motivation. The teacher's goals and philosophies are governed by the learner and the society and/or institution. The teacher's methodology and pedagogical philosophies are influenced by research in the field and knowledge from other disciplines (psychology, anthropology, linguistics, etc.). Then the syllabus, activities, and assessment are adapted by the knowledge garnered from these aspects of the teacher's training. Assessment is conducted by the institution/society, the learner, and the teacher. I think assessment should be the responsibility of all these parties.

Marlene

It is very difficult for me to visually express my conscious knowledge of SL learning/teaching, and how it relates to me and my practice as a teacher. I have attempted to sketch out a (tentative??) model [see Fig. 7-4] of my beliefs, but perhaps with time it will change . . . I think it looks rather simple – but I'm comfortable with this . . . My boundaries are marked by dotted lines instead of straight lines – this reflects my belief that nothing is really fixed in life . . . It is only because our boundaries are open and flexible that we can grow in knowledge and practice as both students and educators.

At the heart of my model is a box containing student-teacher and student-student relationships. Essentially, the relationship is triadic, with bidirectional arrows to indicate that learning and teaching is not a one-way process, but rather reciprocal. Teacher learns from students . . . as he/she teaches them, and students teach their teacher . . . Likewise, each student also learns from and teaches their fellow classmates, just as fellow classmates teach and learn from individual students. . . . There is an additional necessary element if education is to occur: personal reflection by each individual or group of individuals. For this reason, there is a "mirror" box under/above each of the three participants in the triad, again with bidirectional arrows to indicate the reciprocal nature of the relationship. Here, I want to say that there must be a relating between "self" through reflection. We can absorb knowledge, but we must also process it . . . for it to be meaningful in our lives. This kind of intrarelating within the self complements the interrelating among participants. Thus, individual and group relating between/among teacher and students are at the heart of language education.

Immediately outside of this box is another box signifying the various outside influences that affect teacher-student and student-student relationships. These can be any and all factors that surround language learning and teaching, including – but not limited to – methodology, organization, research, theory, (national/local) political policy, economic resources, and population. In my view, each of these factors shape the relationships among students and teachers in the classroom, and certainly the kind of education that takes place is highly dependent on these outside influences.

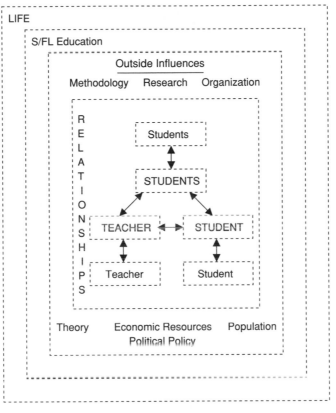

Fig. 7-4

Both classroom relationships as well as outside influences are informed by the third box in my model, namely S/FL education. Essentially, S/FL education (or the lack of it!) shapes the kinds of factors that affect learning and teaching, as it does classroom interaction. Also quite conversely, classroom interaction and outside influences affect, or at least form a substantial part of, S/FL education. It is a space of analysis and reflection of philosophy, theory, content, research, and practice.

8 Motivation and ES/FL Teachers' Practice

- Is it my responsibility to motivate my students?
- If so, what are my options?

Warm-up

Make two lists: What conditions motivate you when you are learning a new language? What things seem to motivate your students? Compare your lists with another person, and try to put the entries in categories.

Following on from the earlier review of planning and improvisation, I want to introduce the matter of motivation – something that certainly is important enough to deserve to be planned for. Motivational considerations apply across all skill areas or content in ES/FL teaching.[1] Motivational concerns will also drive several aspects of the nonverbal aspects of teacher-student interaction discussed earlier, and will be served by good interpersonal relations, a matter addressed in the immediately following chapter. It seems quite likely that there is a connection between successful performance of the verbal and nonverbal demands of the teacher role, and student motivation; though the extent to which a teacher feels responsible for motivating students, and how s/he does so, is likely also to reflect the teacher's values, as well as what research may say.[2]

The older literature in our field addressing the topic of motivation in S/FL contexts concentrated on the attitudes of individual S/FL learners to the target language. Much was made, and still is, of a distinction between students whose reasons for learning a second language relate to a desire to "integrate" with its culture, and those whose reasons relate to the utility of the language, the "instrumental" use to which they could put it. I would not wish to suggest that these are unimportant understandings of students' motives for S/FL learning, but I am more concerned with what we as teachers can do to induce and sustain relevant action in groups of learners, within and in immediate connection with the classroom. I have preferred to concern myself with how *teachers* use the word "motivation"[3] than with how SLA researchers use it, when trying to make use of research on the topic of motivation in SLT contexts (Crookes & Schmidt, 1991). However, we should not lose sight of the possibility that our students have different motivational characteristics outside of the language domain as well, a point I will take up toward the end of this section. But first, what are some ways of defining this term?

FOR DISCUSSION

Share an incident where you had a problem with motivation, whether as a student or as a teacher. Did the problem get solved? If so, how?

Definitional

A definition of motivation that I have found helpful is as follows:

Motivation refers to the choices people make as to what experiences or goals they will approach or avoid, and the degree of effort they will exert in that respect (Keller, 1983, p. 389).

(Note that this goes a long way beyond "attitudes to the target language," the sense used in the older SLA work referred to above.) We can extend or amplify this definition by focusing on how motivation manifests itself behaviorally (following Maehr & Archer, 1987). Motivation has directional or choice aspects, appearing when a person selects and carries out one among a set of activities, or attends to one thing and not another, or chooses one activity over another. Persistence can be easily recognized as a manifestation of motivation, occurring when a person concentrates attention or action on the same thing for an extended duration. Closely related to this is continuing motivation: returning to previously interrupted action without being obliged to do so by outside pressures. Finally we may note that an elevated activity level, that is, a high degree of effort, or intensity of application, would often be seen as indicating motivation.

The definition I use here is taken from Keller's (1983) theory of motivation, work located within the discipline of educational psychology. Like most older work in that field, it seeks to generalize across cultures, and across many other diverse aspects of human existence that teachers and researchers might want to pay more explicit attention to these days. I recommend its use only as a tentative guide for practice, and we should be on the alert for alternative conceptions of motivation arising from different contexts (e.g., Pierce, 1995; cf. Nicholls & Thorkildsen, 1995).

Keller identifies four major determinants of motivation: interest, relevance, expectancy, and outcomes. The first of these, interest, in cognitive terms is a positive response to stimuli as a result of which learners' curiosity is aroused and sustained. The second, relevance, is a prerequisite for "sustained motivation [and] requires the learner to perceive that important personal needs are being met by the learning situation" (Keller, 1983, p. 406). The most basic of these personal needs Keller calls "instrumental needs," which are served when the content of a lesson or course matches what students believe they need to learn. Relevance arises also out of the way human beings need to learn (and how they need to behave in social situations in general). Keller observes that humans have needs for achievement, for affiliation, and for power. That is to say, people generally like to be successful, and we usually find activities in which we can achieve success pleasurably. We like to establish ties with people – solitary activities being often less valued – and adults are accustomed to and desire a measure of control over the situations in which they find themselves. The third heading, expectancy, subsumes a claim that learners who think that they are likely to succeed are more highly motivated than those who expect to fail; those who think that they control their own learning and attribute success or failure to their own efforts are more motivated than those who attribute outcomes to external causes such as luck, a teacher's moods, or the difficulty of a task. Finally, there is that all-too-familiar determinant of motivation: reward or punishment, which can be labeled "outcomes." Activities for which the motivating forces are outcomes have been referred to as extrinsically motivated, as opposed to those which are intrinsically motivated, where the inherent characteristics of the task are what engage and motivate the learner. Intrinsic motivation can also be closely related to expectancy; in this case it is said to arise when individuals subjectively estimate that their skill level is equal to the challenge level, and both are relatively high. This may be clearer if we think about the cases where tasks do not match ability or challenge. When the level of challenge is perceived as higher than the level of ability, the result is anxiety, and when the level of challenge is perceived as lower than the individual's ability, the result is boredom (cf. Csikszentmihalyi & Nakamura, 1989).

Motivation and the S/FL classroom

What use might teachers make of these and related ideas if working on the motivational aspects of their classroom practices? One way to answer the question is to think through the successive stages of our instructional efforts with them in mind. I will tackle the in-class aspects first, then consider broader matters, like needs/interests analyses and their input to syllabus design.

Lesson openings

At the opening stage of a lesson, or equivalently, a unit of material, Keller's factor of "interest" may have particular implications for classroom practice. That is to say, this is one obvious point in a lesson at which the teacher might explain or remind students that what is coming will actually be interesting to them, and thereby engage the power of students' motivation. This would be an improvement on the fairly routine openings that apparently prevail. The small amount of research that exists on this point, done on mainstream elementary and secondary schools in the United States, is surprisingly negative; it would seem that teachers do not take this opportunity. Indeed, according to Brophy and Kerr (1986) teachers rarely bring such considerations in at all:

If the students we have been studying are typical . . . then it appears that there will continue to be little evidence of student motivation to learn in the typical classroom until teachers are trained to socialize such motivation in their students (Brophy & Kerr, 1986, p. 285).

The point is, however, that even the straightforward framing remarks initiating an activity or the presentation stage of a lesson deserve to be assessed in the light of motivational considerations (see Chapter 9, on "framing").

Activities

Turning now to the activities of a lesson, the matter of interest as related to curiosity can be addressed. The teacher who attempts to develop or act on students' curiosity may have to depart from the mainstream of S/FL teaching techniques and/or materials, and make an effort to find out what students are really interested in, and then supplement materials accordingly.[4] Change is also an essential part of maintaining attention, since otherwise habituation will set in. Therefore, a too-regular pattern of classroom routine (as may be produced by adherence to the many traditional ES/FL texts which use the same format for each unit) should probably be avoided.

As mentioned, Keller's second factor of "relevance," deals not only with instrumental needs (often ascertained in ES/FL course design through needs analysis; see below) but also "personal-motive needs" such as our needs for power, affiliation and achievement – considerations that don't usually appear in S/FL syllabus design or even activity choice as an explicit concern. Before considering the implications of this position for ES/FL classroom activities, let us note, however that different cultures differently value needs for power, affiliation, and achievement (Cooper & Tom, 1984; Sloggett, Gallimore, & Kubany, 1970; see also Hawkins, 1994; Markus & Kitayama, 1991). Some cultures allow for individual excellence, with toleration of competition (sometimes intense) whereas others strive mainly for group excellence (Brislin, Chushner, Cherrie, & Young, 1986), though we should recognize that these patterns may not be consistent across contexts even within a single culture. One very simple example of exploiting cultural values in this area is provided by Iseno's teacher research study (1998): one of the factors she used to improve her (Japanese) students' motivation was to apply grades to pairs of students (not individuals). This tapped the "sense of responsibility that the Japanese people share" (p. 141), and students attended better and prepared more thoroughly.

The need for affiliation has some straightforward implications: communicative approaches, in particular, are characterized by a fairly extensive use of group work, which has been said to result in greater motivation among students (Long & Porter, 1985). Group work allows students to influence both each other, and also, for example, the sequence of activities followed by a group (Littlejohn, 1983). Collaborative group effort serves the need for affiliation, and makes it easier for a feeling of achievement to be attained, since it removes to some extent the need for one individual's achievement to be attained at the expense of another's – the condition which would obtain in more competitive arrangements. One example of recent teacher-research in this area supplements this take on group work. In more structured group work, particularly that advocated under the heading of "cooperative learning" (at least since Johnson & Johnson, 1975, and repeatedly since then) students are assigned roles in working groups, usually by the teacher. Thorkildsen & Johnson (1995) found that a U.S. classroom of fourth and fifth graders had very clear preferences about their need to choose their fellow group members, and both resisted and produced poor learning when they were assigned to groups by the teacher.[5]

FOR DISCUSSION

1. Do you find Keller's assertions about the key needs we have as humans plausible? To the extent that you do, does your selection of classroom

activities, or their structure and presentation, address these needs? If not, what alterations are you in a position to make?

2. Are your motivational practices adequate? Take our first subheading first: lesson openings. Can you do anything, and *do* you do anything, to justify the material or content you are working with when you begin it?

Feedback

An intriguing aspect of educational research on motivation is the apparent weakness of extrinsic rewards (those imposed or provided from outside). While an emphasis on external evaluation may momentarily enhance performance, it may negatively affect continuing motivation by ruling out the establishment of more intrinsic, task-related goals (Maehr & Archer, 1987). The classic study of Lepper, Greene, and Nisbett (1973) dealt with preschoolers who were offered an opportunity to draw pictures with materials familiar to them from an art class (an activity previously established to be intrinsically motivating). One group got no reward for the activity, one got a surprise reward, and one was shown a reward and told they could win it by performing the activity. Subsequent observation of the children found that those who had experienced the last condition then chose the activity less when it was freely available without any reward. This finding has been extensively investigated: Lepper (1983) cites 47 studies covering all age ranges from preschool to college that bear out the original results.

A related issue concerns the effect of performance goals on behavior. Some research suggests that if the goal of individuals is to achieve positive judgments concerning their behavior (i.e., good grades), they will wait until certain that their ability is high before displaying it, and will otherwise avoid behavior that could expose them to evaluation (Dweck, 1986). If students actually have learning as an objective, they are more likely to engage in challenging tasks and activities where errors may be made. That is to say, in some ES/FL classrooms, teachers may need to discourage a concern with grades because otherwise unsolicited participation and risk taking will be low.

According to Keller (1983), for teacher feedback to be most efficiently utilized, it needs to be provided not only at the end of an activity, but also at the onset of a similar, subsequent activity. In addition, teachers' feedback should be informational, directing the student's attention to what s/he did that resulted in success. In providing feedback, instructors need also to take into account the cultural variation in acceptability of praise or criticism of individuals.

1. Does your own experience as a student and as a teacher bear out the claim that provision of extrinsic rewards diminishes the effectiveness of intrinsic reward of activities?
2. Have you ever had to take a class, as a student, the material of which you were not particularly interested in? What modified your initial motivational state? Do you think your answers would be different depending on whether you were an adult as opposed to a child when you took this class?
3. Can a task be inherently intrinsically interesting (independent of context) for a given individual? What effect does your overall state of mind, or pressures in other parts of your life, have on your approach to learning tasks?
4. When learning something new, do you like to wait until you are sure of yourself before trying it out, or are you willing to make errors in the process of learning? How does the presence of an audience of your peers affect this?
5. Do you think you are similar to students you teach in your response to extrinsic motivation and to the motivational effect of feedback, or different?

Materials and testing in classroom practice

I have deliberately not treated materials and testing much in these chapters. Though they have many nonskill – area-specific aspects, the most important tests and materials in many curricula are not selected by teachers at all; being so little under the control of regular teachers, and hardly part of day-to-day classroom practice, it is unlikely that they can be worked on much in a teaching practicum. However, for completeness in the present discussion, here are just a few points.

First, on materials: When planning to maximize motivation, if a teacher has the authority to choose materials, or design supplementary materials, it is desirable to act with an awareness of the motivational importance of appearance and content (cf. Peacock, 1997), not to mention (once again) students' *real* interests.

Second, on testing: Setting aside government or state-mandated tests, the teacher still often makes and uses informal classroom tests. Murphey (1994; cf. discussion of his work in Brown, 1994) comments that "In the old, traditional view of testing, there was surely no such thing as an 'enjoyable test' ... but an intrinsically motivating test is not at all unrealistic, especially within classroom ... settings" (Brown, 1994, p. 382). Tests that Murphey has implemented (in Japanese EFL contexts) include cooperative item construction, student pair work to test each other, and use of self-evaluation; procedures that once again involve personal control and interaction as means of motivation. The interested reader may also want to explore the area of "authentic" or alternative assessment (cf. Huerta-Macias, 1995) from a motivational point of view. Among the range of alternatives to multiple choice tests encompassed under this heading are many forms of student assessment that have greater visible connection to the actual use of a S/FL in real contexts. Among these, the idea of "portfolio-based assessment," in which testing relates to a set of products that a student puts together that reflect or indicate their S/FL-learning in a class, is becoming well-known. Some students may find putting together a portfolio of work during a semester as a basis for assessment much more motivating than taking a test, both because of the personal relevance of the products, their clear relationship to S/FL use and production, as well as the probably less intense pressure that this process has compared with a single "sit-down" test.

FOR DISCUSSION

Are you satisfied with the amount of variety you are presently getting in to your lessons? What factors hinder your pursuit of variety? How does your present situation with respect to your control over materials and testing help or hinder your ability to motivate your students?

The syllabus/curriculum level

The original proponents of needs analysis in our field made little or no explicit reference to motivational research but took for granted the importance of the matter (see, e.g., Wilkins, 1976; cf. Brindley, 1989; Richterich, 1972; Robinson, 1987). They assumed, reasonably, that a program which appears to meet the students' own expressed needs (or whatever their supervisors believe to be their needs) will be more motivating, thus more efficient and successful.

However, ES/FL teachers are very often not in control of a program or course to the extent of being able to conduct a needs analysis or redesign an existing course before being required to teach it. Yet every teacher is familiar with the ease of working with students for whom the material and course content is stimulating, as opposed to the struggle or lack of energy that comes from students who find little or no relevance or purpose to their classes. Some attempt to assess attitudes to the material or the structure of the course would be advisable particularly if the teacher is at the same time trying to work on his/her own skills. It is difficult, and possibly counterproductive, to be trying new and not fully automatized behaviors with a group of students who have no desire to be learning anything the teacher is trying to teach. Even when a needs analysis is out of the question, and when there are no obvious real needs for the language being taught, the possibility and potential utility of an "interests analysis" still exists (cf. Swaffar, Arens, & Byrnes, 1991, pp. 208–11).

FOR DISCUSSION

If you are currently teaching, to what extent was the syllabus (or syllabi) you are working with designed with your students' needs or interests in mind? Do you need to modify it to deal with motivational problems; or what other techniques are you using to ensure adequate motivation?

Students' self-perceptions and self-conceptions

The way students think of themselves, of their abilities, and latterly their identities, has played an important role in discussions of motivation. As a result of their experiences, some students develop the impression that events are under their control, and that effort will lead to academic success. That is, they have an interior "locus of control," and they have a high degree of "self-efficacy." Others, through repeated failures or through being in situations where they cannot influence reward or punishment by their behavior, have learned that they cannot bring about comfort or success through their actions; they have "learned helplessness." (These three terms are from Bandura, 1982; deCharms; 1984, and Weiner; 1984, respectively.) It seems likely that students who have experienced failure in ES/FL learning (arguably a large proportion of learners – Gatenby, 1948; Ingram, 1982) and attribute this to their own inabilities rather than problems with the course or text, are likely to have a low estimate of their future success in language learning, which may in turn lead to low risk-taking, low acceptance of ambiguity, and other behaviors which are probably negatively correlated with success in S/FL learning. Obviously, we should try to avoid these sort of perceptions developing in the first place, but if they have already been developed, some possibilities for modification nevertheless exist. One means is the use of cooperative, rather than competitive goal structures (Ames, 1984, 1986). In cooperative learning (e.g., Slavin, 1983), groups of students work on learning activities structured so that there is positive interdependence – typically, all parties have information or a specific role, and for success to be achieved all must collaborate; in addition, often the reward or grade for the work is assigned on the basis of the overall group performance. Work done by Ames indicates that, whereas in a competitive learning situation (typical of most schools) self-perceptions following success or failure are based on how a student performed relative to his/her fellow students, cooperative learning situations may "alleviate the otherwise negative self-perceptions that evolve from poor individual performances" (Ames, 1984, p. 182). Under these circumstances, the underachiever (or the previously unsuccessful S/FL learner) can begin to change self-perceptions and develop the feeling that for him or her, success is in fact possible.

Other, perhaps more challenging initiatives teachers might consider in this area would be allowing a measure of flexibility in the curriculum, so that students could contract for a particular grade in accordance with a particular level of performance if they feel demotivated by the challenge of the course; another possibility might be allowing a gradual approximation to a particular level of work through repeated revision of initially ungraded assignments. For such demotivated students, the work of McCombs (1984, 1988, 1994; McCombs & Whisler, 1997) suggests the possibility of adding instruction in self-management strategies (which contribute to motivational self-control and facilitate change in locus of control) and other metacognitive strategies to ES/FL syllabus content.

The idea of self-perception with regard to achievement in learning as important in motivation can be extended to self-perception with regard to identity – the self itself. This has become a growth area for research involving language and identity in recent years. For our field, Pierce's (1995) study of the self-conceptions, or social identity, of Canadian immigrant learners of English emphasizes that "a [second] language learner's motivation to speak is mediated by investments that may conflict with the desire to speak" (1995, pp. 19–20), and whether such investments result in action, in use of the language, depends on context and shifts in identity. Whether you can really conceptualize yourself as a real user of English would then have motivational effects.

Besides being aware of research findings in this area it will be particularly important for us as teachers to find out what our students' past experiences with ES/FL learning are, why they are studying, what the respective roles of grades and interest are for them, and discover if possible their self-concepts as English speakers. And if, upon gathering this information, we conclude that some (or all!) of our students have already developed negative views of their ability to learn English, or have a self-image or an identity which precludes being a speaker or user of English, presumably we should try to modify them.[6]

YOU TRY IT

Construct a questionnaire to investigate your students' past S/FL learning from a motivational point of view. You will need to ask about their actual classroom and out-of-class language learning situations; whether they believe they were or were not successful, and why; whether they have positive or negative attitudes to being (somewhat) bilingual; whether they have techniques they use to motivate themselves, mitigate frustration, and so on. If possible, share drafts of your questionnaire with peers, then actually implement them. (This exercise is more appropriate for diverse groups of older learners.)

Motivation as interactive, located, and sociocultural

Looking back, Rueda and Moll (1994) see a steady progress in the dominant orientation to motivation. In behaviorist days, they say, it was thought of in terms of drives (for example, hunger); later, it was thought of mainly as largely immutable traits of individuals (e.g., need for achievement), and presently, it is being seen to a greater extent than before as contextually driven, or "located." In a similar review, Paris and Turner (1994) agree with this depiction, except to point to a long-standing line of research which has always considered the interaction between individual and context as important. They comment,

We believe that some situations have prototypical characteristics that are generally more motivating than other situations but we hasten to add that the person by situation interaction provides greater information about who is motivated by different situations and why. The tensions between generalizable claims about motivation and idiosyncratic claims about a contextualist view of motivation can be reconciled when the different levels of analysis are considered. Therefore, a focus on task features or situational characteristics is not contrary to a person by environment perspective as long as both levels of analysis are pursued (p. 222).

We can expect the balance of interest to shift in the sociocultural direction advocated by Rueda and Moll (see e.g. Pedraza & Ayala, 1996, for another example in this line), but Paris and Turner's point is useful in bringing together the various emphases on differing aspects of motivation, which will certainly continue as research (and publication) continues in this area at an increasing rate. For most recent developments in S/FL contexts, besides the work of Pierce (mentioned earlier), see especially Oxford (1996), Syed (2001), and Dörnyei and Schmidt (2001).

FOR DISCUSSION

1. Are student self-perceptions a motivational concern in your teaching circumstances?
2. I prefer to distinguish between motivation and affect. By affect I mean positive and negative emotions. One negative emotion that has been studied in connection with S/FL learning is anxiety. Is this a factor affecting your students, and if so how do you address it? What other elements of the affective domain are important in your teaching?

YOU TRY IT...

1. Observe a class, with the following questions in front of you.
   • What techniques and approaches, if any, did the teacher use at the outset of the lesson to engage the class's interest?
   • How did s/he sustain the interest, once aroused?
   • How did s/he deal with the problem of flagging motivation?
   • In what ways did the teacher capitalize on the students' own interests?
   • Could any parts of the lesson be explained in terms of the concepts of intrinsic and extrinsic motivation? (Was there any use of e.g., curiosity, challenge, or reward?)
   • What part did feedback play in the lesson? How was it conveyed? What were its effects?
   • What effect did the personality of the teacher appear to have on the overall success or failure of the lesson?
   • How would you describe the teacher's attitudes to the class, and his/her expectations of their performance? Could either of these be seen to affect the class's motivation?
   Which forms of motivation did the class appear to respond to best? (from Cohen, Manion, & Morrison, 1996, with some modification).
2. Most of my discussion places in the teacher's hands the responsibility for fostering motivation in her/his students. Only indirectly do I allude

to the role that students might play in motivational matters (for example, through contracting for a grade). However, a collaborative action research perspective would imply that teachers worried about their practices in this area should investigate them jointly with their students. What possibilities do you have for investigating students' motivation in your class? How might students have input into motivational matters?

9 Classroom Management in ES/FL Contexts

> - What strategies can be used to manage a class?
> - Are these workable and appropriate in all contexts?
> - How do my values and beliefs as an ES/FL teacher come out in my approach to classroom management?
> - Now that I'm more experienced, should I reevaluate my procedures in this area?

Warm-up
List some typical signs of a classroom management problem (and compare with peers). Have you ever had a problem managing a class? Or, have you been a student in a class that wasn't managed well? What happened? Did the problem get solved? How?

Classroom management issues are certainly a high-priority concern of many a beginning teacher (cf. Fuller & Bown, 1975) and, for these individuals, becoming skilled in running a classroom smoothly seems a particularly relevant aspect of developing one's teaching technique. On the other hand, even slightly experienced teachers, particularly those who have acquired their experience in well-supported schools, with well-motivated students, and have remained in one cultural context, will perhaps consider attention to this topic beneath them now they are beyond the absolute beginner stage.

In addressing the latter group, I would make the following argument. Some aspects of classroom management may be quite culture-dependent, so if one is a member of the culture one is teaching in, there are known and accepted ways of behaving as a teacher, which will be used under favorable conditions unconsciously, and only come to consciousness in a crisis. However, insofar as ES/FL teachers are sometimes cultural boundary crossers (more so than teachers of other subjects, perhaps), they may find that sometimes their expectations about classroom behavior break down completely. Some in this group may find a need to reevaluate their skills once they begin to deal with groups of students who are new to them: of different age ranges, different levels of motivation, different cultural backgrounds, and so on. Perhaps therefore, even the experienced ES/FL teacher needs a thorough understanding of this area. Clearly, classroom management has an intimate connection with classroom practice, so a practicum should be a good opportunity to work out or further develop this understanding.

In my experience, for some sectors of ES/FL instruction, classroom management is hardly a problem at all, whereas for others it is often a challenge. On the one hand, there are teachers who will be (or have already been) working with elementary- and secondary-school age children. Many of their students are under a legal requirement to attend school. Some of these students, particularly in EFL contexts, have no immediate communicative need to motivate their learning of English, and this together with the compulsory nature of their education can present real classroom management challenges. And on the other hand, there are teachers working in the adult sector, both state and private, where student attendance is usually voluntary. For these teachers, "maintaining discipline" is usually not a problem, although they may be interested in understanding how classrooms in varying cultures are orderly places and the means teachers have at their disposal to ensure this. This group's most serious managerial concerns may arise from class size, as some university EFL classes can be extremely large, or from nonhomogenous classes (as in many ESL contexts), or come from classroom manifestations of students' personal problems. Some management problems here may also arise due to classroom expectations from the students' culture being unfulfilled in the host (ESL) culture.

Thus far I have introduced the area from the point of view of practical problems or challenges to technical pedagogical skill. Now let me approach the topic from a values or philosophy of teaching perspective. Classroom management may be an area where difficulties surface when one is trying to make one's practice as a teacher match one's values. In a traditional model of the classroom (with which many of us grew up, and which is thus hard to shake off, even if one wants to), it seems that the teacher has primary responsibility for ensuring, or shall I say, "enforcing" order. But cultures and classroom expectations are no longer as homogenous as they once were, and teachers' autonomy in this area has been greatly diminished. When a plurality of values and expectations about behavior coexist in one culture or one school, here it seems the possibility of ethical and moral concerns might easily arise. What are a teacher's rights and responsibilities in this area, and how might they be justified; and what additional problems does the teacher teaching across cultural and language boundaries face in this area? Since there is comparatively little literature on the topic of classroom management addressed specifically to ES/FL teachers (Wadden & McGovern, 1991), I initially draw from mainstream educational literature resources.

Definitional: Elements of an orderly classroom

I will begin with a general claim that classroom management involves issues of power and control in small group interaction, and it has the aim of ensuring order. (This assumes that instruction and learning can better take place in orderly circumstances, though leaves open the matter of what counts as "order.") Doyle (1986, p. 393) says, "order is a property of a social system and thus needs to be framed in a language of group processes."[1] Reflecting this sort of conception, the early disciplinary homes of investigations of classroom management include ecological psychology (Gump, 1975), the social psychology of education (Bar-Tal & Bar-Tal, 1986), and educational anthropology. In addition, as handbooks like Wolfgang (1995) or Charles (1992) make clear, psychiatry has also had a hand in how research and prescription on this topic has developed. Closer to our own disciplinary homes, a search for literature on order in ES/FL classrooms might take us to those fields of study that emphasize investigating at a fine-grained level of detail the language and culture of the classroom, such as the microethnography of classrooms (Cazden, 1981; Mehan, 1979; cf. also Sinclair & Coulthard, 1975). Similarly, order under conditions of face-to-face interaction is often the result of language in action, so we may also turn to the fields related to microethnography, such as sociolinguistics and discourse studies, for input (Hodge, 1993). (Of course, besides these more abstract sources, reports of actual classroom practice and cases, cited later in the chapter, are vital.)

An initial approach to this topic I have found useful is Doyle (1986), whose conception of classroom management sees the classroom as a sequence of tasks or activities, and thus is at one level congruent with a prominent view of ES/FL curriculum (e.g., Long & Crookes, 1992). Doyle takes the view that teachers concerned with classroom management tend to have a crisis or problem orientation, but that before we as teachers can understand how to handle problems we must first understand their opposite, which is the normal condition of classrooms: order.

Order in a classroom simply means that within acceptable limits the students are following the program of action necessary for a particular classroom event to be realized in the situation (Doyle, 1986, p. 396).

Note that Doyle does not say who is responsible for this; in some sense, order, or organization, in any social grouping can be jointly achieved, though in cases of power imbalance, those holding the power do most of the explicit "ordering." In most classrooms, it is surely the teacher who most visibly, at least, performs this function. Classroom management is then "the provisions and procedures necessary to establish an environment in which instruction and learning can occur" (Doyle, ibid.), which is to say, a relatively orderly one, or at least one in which whatever superficial manifestations of disorder may occur either do not prevent instruction and learning, or actually support them. I add this latter formulation because for many EFL teachers, classrooms which their home or host culture perceives as disorderly may actually be necessary if language learning (particularly in the oral modality) is to occur.

Two terms shared by ES/FL and mainstream education relevant to this discussion are "task" and "activity." Writers on classroom management such as Doyle take a work-oriented view of the classroom. Classrooms are places where (academic) work is done; in which tasks are done. Syllabus and materials design specialists in ES/FL have in the last 15 years increasingly emphasized the task as a unit of analysis or design in our classrooms. The related term "activity" (sometimes seen as broader than task) is also used.[2] An "activity" is a segment of classroom life that can be separated from others in terms of four features: temporal boundaries, physical milieux, program of action, and content (Burnett, 1973). Since the term "activity" in this usage is intended to cover all distinguishable behavioral segments in a classroom, it includes matters like transitions from one segment with a specific learning objective to another.

The simplest common or conventional tasks and activities in classrooms may be seen as defined by rules for social behavior, and students are socialized into them as they learn to "do school" – to carry out the roles and practices implicit in being a student – in their home cultures. Different academic subjects may have their own characteristic activity types, for which additional explanation may be necessary upon first exposure. Doyle and others echo many teachers when they observe that order in classrooms does not have to be repeatedly imposed or enforced if students are actually engaged in classroom activities. Indeed, it is central to Doyle's view that the tasks themselves will serve to order the classroom. Even if they are relatively uninteresting, they provide a structure to which action, energy, and activity is to be directed. And of course, if they are actually interesting in themselves or seen as needful, no additional teacher effort will be needed to orient student energies to classroom tasks – perhaps the ideal and final target of any classroom manager. Doyle points out that "the nature of academic work influences the probability of student cooperation and involvement in a lesson" (p. 406), which obviously in turn impacts the teacher's management skills. This may manifest itself simply, as when work which is too difficult leads to trouble, or more complexly, when the work does not lend itself to being broken down into elements which fit easily in the class period, or which are completed at markedly different rates by different students. Order is also known to break down at "transition points," where one activity is concluded and another begun. The "continuity" of a lesson may be related and minimizes this problem. Continuity is high if there is a single external impetus (such as a teacher lecture) carrying the lesson along, or if tasks (of appropriate difficulty) are clearly linked one to another, and feed in to each other.

FOR DISCUSSION

Think of a smoothly-running classroom you are familiar with. What makes it run well?

Rules: Instrumental and constitutive

Among the most obvious "provisions and procedures" involved in having an orderly classroom and a program of action are the setting of rules for classroom activities. To a greater or lesser extent it is the individual teacher who determines what is acceptable or unacceptable behavior for a given activity (within the overall context of school and culture). Recognizing this allows us to put a conception of classroom management in terms of orderly engagement in tasks in a perspective better suited to our ES/FL classrooms with their potential for cross-cultural problems. Whose order, whose "acceptable limits" are going to be involved in establishing the rather anonymous "program of action" Doyle mentions? As cultural boundary crossers, we cannot without reflection assume that our own understandings of classrooms will be the only ones in play in an ES/FL classroom. To continue this topic, we need to consider the conventional, rather than given, nature of classrooms, as follows.

Understandings of classrooms in terms of the rules that are involved were studied by Boostrom (1991), based on an extended program of observation in U.S. classrooms. He begins from the position that many classroom "rules are generally arbitrary, not in the sense that they are capricious, but in the sense that they express a choice that could just as easily prescribe one way of proceeding as another" (p. 198). He goes on to identify four somewhat overlapping categories of rule (1991, p. 194):

- rules about nonacademic procedures ("stay in your seat while you eat lunch")
- rules about doing classroom work ("read the directions carefully")
- rules about relationships with others in the classroom ("don't be rude")
- rules embedded in the subject matter ("begin your sentences with a capital letter").

If, like me, drawing on your own experiences as student and teacher, you accept Boostrom's assertion as to the arbitrariness of some rules, this shifts them from a purely instrumental to a constitutive status. That is, it is no longer the case that specific rules follow without question from the need for order, which will inevitably be a particular person's, or possibly a particular subculture's understanding of order. Instead, the rules become the means by which behavior is recognized by the authorities and the participants as constituting order, that is, by which inchoate behavior is transmuted into recognizable "activities."[3]

Why might it be important to emphasize the conventional nature of classroom rules? As busy teachers we all recognize the difficulty of finding time to be sufficiently reflective on what we are doing. (I have emphasized, however, the particular importance of heightened reflection during a practicum.) Boostrom's view is that "believing their rules to be only the tools for establishing orderliness, teachers can separate within themselves the means of their teaching from the ends of their teaching," a recipe like any means-ends separation, for abuse. And when rules cease to be spoken anew every semester but are simply those things that one knows, unconsciously, and which "everybody" follows, they are hard to rerecognize as rules, being instead the constitutive traditions that make up a culture, or subculture. Which is all very well if you belong to that culture and have been adequately socialized into it – but not if you are an outsider learning it, in which case you do not have the "cultural capital" (Bourdieu, 1977) necessary to work with it or enter it. What I am suggesting here, then, is that sometimes to understand classroom management in ES/FL contexts we need to see the classroom from the perspective of our students, a place in which unfamiliar, arbitrary, and sometimes totally unknown, invisible rules are determining behavior.

FOR DISCUSSION

What are some explicit rules in the classroom you teach in or observe? What are some inexplicit ones? How were the former set up, and how have the latter arisen? How do they contribute to order in this classroom?

Rules for classroom rule?

Besides rules, providing resources and specifying tasks complete the provisions that primarily establish order, or a well-managed classroom. But what distinguishes the successful classroom manager from the unsuccessful one? In a range of U.S. studies by Emmer and colleagues (e.g., Emmer, et al., 1980) it became clear that clarity and thoroughness of rule presentation and enforcement had long-term benefits. "Successful managers anticipated problem areas, communicated expectations clearly, watched students closely, intervened promptly, and invoked consequences for behavior" (remarks Doyle, 1986, p. 411, in summary). Attentiveness to student behavior and the ability to anticipate problems are requirements on top of the ability to actually teach the content of the lesson. They are thus aspects of teaching that are facilitated by having freed up cognitive resources through automatizing some teaching behaviors. That is to say, they may not be easily available to the beginning teacher, or to the teacher who is beginning to work with a previously unfamiliar group or level of students.

Though it results in a depiction of the classroom which is worryingly factorylike, the idea that a "work system" in which students know what they have to do and are enabled to get on with it is apparently one thing which distinguishes successful classroom managers, particularly when working under challenging professional circumstances or with uncooperative students. When routinized, "the work system itself seems to be carrying the burden of order" (Doyle, 1986, p. 411) freeing the teacher to attend to individual students or other demands.

The communication of expectations, intervention when they are not met, and so on, that are referred to in the Emmer et al. studies, are very much part of the stereotypical aspects of classroom management, indeed, of "discipline." Authors who emphasize the term "discipline" over the term "management" call the area we have been reviewing thus far "preventative discipline." A recent review of this area (based on experience in Australian classrooms: Rogers, 1998) provides a useful taxonomy:

Preventative discipline
clear rules and routines established with the class
clear expectations about learning, tasks, etc.
attractive environment
well-planned room organisation . . .
setting up of time-out area . . . (age-appropriate)
adequate resources
organizing curriculum to cater for mixed abilities

When these provisions fail, we have arrived in the domain more generally understood as "discipline," the crisis or problem response referred to earlier (as only one, perhaps subordinate part of the whole domain of classroom management) by Doyle. Clearly, when faced with these difficult circumstances a teacher needs good techniques to prevent problems from escalating. Here is Rogers' (1998) summary of headings under corrective discipline.

Corrective discipline (What we say and do, when a student is disruptive or off-task.)
tactical ignoring of some behaviors
reminding or restating classroom rules
simple behavioural directions or warnings
casual or direct questioning
defusing or redirecting potential conflict
giving simple choices
directing students away from the group using time-out in class and out of
    class if necessary

We may also conceptualize a broader, supporting set of techniques, probably driven by higher level, philosophical or values commitments on the part of the teacher. Rogers calls this area supportive discipline:

Supportive discipline
developing and maintaining a climate of respect
building a positive classroom "tone"
following up disruptions later when the initial "interpersonal heat" has
    subsided
reestablishing working relationships with a "disciplined" student
encouraging students wherever possible
developing behavior agreements with a student
applying a team approach to solving discipline problems

FOR DISCUSSION

1. The differences in the area of classroom management between what can be suggested to teachers of children as opposed to teachers of adults are considerable. If you are working with adults, consider which aspects of this chapter are problematic for you. If your classroom is "orderly," why is that, and how does it relate to your working conditions? Are the managerial problems you face (if any) group-level problems, or individual and interpersonal in nature? Is your understanding of the

nature of an orderly classroom keyed to a culture-specific conception of "order," do you think? Or of "school"? Do elementary classrooms, in your culture, manifest a different conception of order from high school classrooms?

2. Do the ends in your classroom (e.g., learning English) justify the means (the classroom rules and associated order, not to mention possible stresses and strains on teacher and student participants)? Have you ever been in or read of classrooms whose ends did not justify their means?

ES/FL classrooms and their classroom management challenges

ES/FL teachers share many basic aspects of classroom management with teachers in other subject matter domains, as well as being faced with their own special problems. Three broad causes of problems that may be more marked in some ES/FL contexts come to mind: heterogeneity of students' linguistic proficiency, class size, and cross-cultural concerns.

First, in many ESL programs for migrants, limitations on finances and administration lead to continuous entry classes. The teacher may be faced, as a result, with markedly nonhomogenous classes, in which age, motivation, culture, social background, and goals, not to mention English proficiency and command of the material previously covered in a course, vary wildly (see e.g., La Fontaine, 1998; Lewis, 1998).

Second, in many EFL contexts, including even those of relatively rich countries like Korea or Japan, English is taught in very large classes. At high school these may approach 50, and some university "conversation" classes may be 100 or more in size. We may be grateful to the handful of specialists who have addressed these matters in print (e.g., Bell, 1988; Burns & Hood, 1998; Nolasco & Arthur, 1994; Mutoh, 1998 [on record-keeping]; Shawar, 1991), though this work does not of itself solve the classroom management challenges such contexts present. I will just highlight one beneficial, if small study in this area: McMurray (1998) reports how, faced with the problem of managing a class of 70 undergraduate Japanese students, she addressed the problem in a way that combined reflection on values as well as on desired outcomes. She writes,

I asked myself a few key questions and answered them as follows:

1. What are my values about authority and discipline?
   I want to assert my authority in a way that feels right to me, keeping in mind that I want to help my students make the most of their time in class.

2. What do I want to see happening in my class?
   I want to foster a secure environment by providing my students with a structure to work and grow in. All of us feel secure because the learning process and results are clear. I want to get to know the people in my class and give them an opportunity to know me.
3. What kind of results do I want and why?
   I want to show students that I value what they do in class. . . . I would like to see the results of my teaching and their learning. Because all these dynamics are interconnected, I will address my personal views on authority and discipline in the classroom, fostering a learning atmosphere leading to learning and assessment (p. 214).

A key point was McMurray's finding a way to "meet the students halfway" by sharing authority with them (even though they expected the authority figure to be the teacher). In this, she provided very clear rules and structure to the classroom, but delegated some responsibilities for attendance and discipline to group leaders. In concluding her report, she remarked, "I would like to stress the need for teacher self-reflection. . . . Only after examining my needs, wants, and assumptions am I able to see the adjustments I need to make because of class size and culture" (p. 216).

In a third category I would place the more ES/FL-specific management concerns. Often these arise when there are differing expectations about participation structures (the rules governing speaking, listening, turn-taking, etc. in particular activities) associated with culturally-distinct student or teacher populations. That is, what the teacher thinks is or should be going on is not what the students think is or should be going on. The teacher may feel a need, accordingly, to introduce unfamiliar forms of classroom interaction, and may experience accompanying classroom difficulties (cf. Bassano, 1986). This group of concerns has slightly different characteristics depending on whether it is in an EFL context or an ESL context; is the teacher a host, or is it the students who are guests? Let us take the EFL context first.

Scattered allusions in the literature of our field, and my own personal observations and experiences suggest that ES/FL professionals have been faced with these problems for a long time. From the early 1980s on (Rogers, 1982; Valdes, 1986; cf. Abbott, 1992), discussions of EFL classrooms and pedagogy which took an anthropological and culturally-relativistic perspective began increasingly to appear; however, a focused attention to these and related matters which draws on classroom management literature is almost non-existent. In the present section, I will draw primarily on a single recent collection (Coleman, 1996a, one of very few book-length treatments in this area) to exemplify these sort of concerns. The work of Coleman and associates, as well as of a variety of precursors (notably Holliday, 1992), arises from the recognition that attempts to transfer "the latest" S/FL-related pedagogical concepts from internationally influential development sites such as U.S. and UK universities, to countries which apparently simply need the most efficient EFL teaching techniques, are actually a confrontation of cultures and nations, rather than a neutral transmission of information. This does not necessarily mean that we should avoid such attempts; in fact, it is probably impossible, since a foreign teacher even if somewhat bicultural cannot usually alter her/his teaching style completely in a short period of time. And teachers who see their values as embodied in their classroom management practices are likely to be reluctant to abandon them completely.

In one study in this category, Chick (1996) describes EFL classrooms in rural South Africa under past White-minority governments, which he found dominated by choral repetition or choral sentence completion (which he came to term "safe-talk"). At one time, faced with a classroom of this kind, the visiting applied linguistics expert or INGO volunteer might have simply dismissed the established classroom routine as ineffective and moved to try to establish a better, probably more communicative one. Rather than that, or at the very least, prior to that, these days the culturally-sensitive visitor would want to understand the behavior, and a typical hypothesis would be to wonder if the behavior is a transfer of otherwise culturally-appropriate behavior into the more-or-less "Western" classroom setting, as did Chick initially. But, he explains, he finally concluded there was more to it than that:

The "safe-talk" which I had identified . . . does not represent the inappropriate use of culturally-specific Zulu-English interactional styles. Rather, it represents styles which the participants interactionally developed and constituted as a means of coping with the overwhelming odds they faced in their segregated schools. I suggest that these styles enabled them to collude in hiding unpleasant realities. Thus, for example, the rhythmically co-ordinated chorusing prompts and responses enabled the teacher and students in the episode to hide their poor command of English; to obscure their inadequate understanding of academic content; and to maintain a facade of effective learning taking place (p. 36).

Let's take another example from the same collection. LoCastro (1996) provides an overview of the problems facing English teaching in Japan. Her description of the typical classroom, like Chick's, at first seems to refer to a kind of classroom behavior that might also have been found in European classrooms somewhat earlier in time (cf. e.g., Duff, 1995).

A typical class in Japan will start and end with one student calling the others to order; all stand to bow and formally greet the teacher, who also usually bows, standing. Many classrooms maintain the practice that the student who is responding to a teacher's solicit or is asking a question must stand to do so. In general, however, an overwhelming proportion of class time is composed of teacher talk. . . .

I have noted that at least some teachers adopt what I will call pseudointeractional language. The teacher asks a question, apparently addressing it to a student, but then answers it, makes an assessment or comment on the answer, and then gives an acknowledgment . . . One interpretation of the teacher's behavior is that, due to the hierarchical nature of Japanese society, student-teacher interactions are not expected in classrooms. . . . Japanese students will commonly wait until after class to talk with the teacher, if they have questions.

LoCastro concludes (p. 53) that it should be obvious that the typical ELT classroom in Japan precludes CLT:

- The target language is not used in general, either by the teacher or the learners, except perhaps for greetings and some fixed expressions. Thus the comprehensible input is inadequate, coming mostly from non-authentic written texts.
- Interactions which would permit or require language use for negotiation of meaning tend not to occur in the classroom, *even in Japanese*, due to expectations of what constitutes permissible behavior in that environment.

And yet again, consider university ELT classes in Indonesia. According to Coleman (1996b, p. 73), classes he observed were as follows:

One participant, the teacher, stood and read aloud from a textbook in a manner which may or may not have been audible to other participants. Other participants, the students, spent most of the lesson sitting in front of the teacher, possibly paying attention but possibly engaged in activities which had no bearing on the subject being "taught." With very few exceptions, therefore, English lessons involved one person who talked, and a large number of observers who were free to move around the classroom, talk to their friends, write letters, pay attention to the teacher, or day-dream, as they wished. The performer did not hope for absolute attention to every word which was uttered, and the audience did not expect to be called upon to give that attention. Yet the audience which behaved in this way was not being disrespectful.

Descriptions of classrooms almost as "unusual" in terms of behavior are also to be found in nominally ESL contexts, when classrooms in North America in Native American settings are described (e.g., Philips, 1983).

We may take the descriptions of classrooms collected by Coleman and others and compare them with, for example, Rogers' (1998) set of basic needs for classroom management. The accounting is demoralizing, of course, because none of them are met. Resources are not adequate, mixed abilities are not catered for, and very often resources are extremely limited. But even more important, I think, there *are* "clear rules and routines established with the class, clear expectations about learning, tasks, etc." – it's just that these are not shared between the students and the teacher from a foreign culture. Holliday (1996) is one of a number of scholars who have documented the sort of "tissue rejection" that takes place when there are attempts to transplant CLT or other nonindigenous approaches to classrooms or education systems that already have a functional (but notably different) organization. It is not surprising, then, that Coleman (1996b) dismisses attempts to improve the teaching in the Indonesian example (by managing the class and activities differently) as likely to be failures, because participants are too constrained by the existence of well-established participation structures and interactional routines ingrained and definitional of the lesson as they jointly construe it. Instead he advocates working with whatever aspects of the *existing* "classroom rules" can be utilized to move the overall activity in a direction that would lead to potentially more useful English language use. He says,

We went about this by exploiting both the students' apparent lack of inhibition about moving around the classroom and their custom of working in small peer groups. So English lectures became highly interactive task-based events during which students exchanged, manipulated, and interpreted ... English. Teachers, meanwhile, took on consultative and inconspicuously managerial roles (p. 81).

Coleman is cautious, however, that such changes may have negative repercussions elsewhere in the social system if the original classroom practices are, or were, functional.

The discussion by Holliday (1996) of his extensive research on contact between indigenous and Anglo-American English teaching styles enables us to take Coleman's "build on existing strengths" position a little further. Holliday's work on ELT in Egypt leads him to conclude that indigenous Egyptian teachers, though not necessarily using activities or classroom interaction patterns thought most desirable by SLA or CLT theorists, probably did better than foreign instructors; but that the large class contexts that were new to the Egyptian education system (though not unusual around the world) were a challenge better met by the visitors. However, the techniques used by visitors to manage these challenges, Holliday suggests, would be unlikely to have positive long-term effects because they did not build on indigenous interaction patterns and preferences. His conclusion, and I think it is an important one (though obviously not definitive), is that

only a new, rationalized – yet traditional – approach, could be fully effective in the . . . culture of Egyptian university large classes. . . . Exceptions apart, *only* local lecturers would be able fully to achieve this, because it would require a rationalized building and re-allocation [of ideas and resources] on an existing traditional basis (p. 100).

While putting most faith in the local teacher, Holliday allows for the possibility that the expatriate with "an unusual gift in cultural sensitivity" may be of use. But more importantly, he asserts that it is not simply being a member of the culture that will be sufficient. Fauzia Shamim's (1996) honest account of her failure, despite being a Pakistani working in Pakistan, to introduce a change in classroom interaction patterns is a vivid illustration of this. Even local teachers will need to think carefully about classroom patterns, and possibly engage in ethnographic explorations of them, if they are to make effective changes at the curriculum or activity level, and, I would add, if they are to cope with some of the more basic challenges in the field of ES/FL classroom management as well.

Now, what about when the teacher is at home in an English-speaking country, and the students are guests? This situation appears both in language schools and in university-based Intensive English Programs (IEPs). It may be exacerbated if a particular classroom is made up mainly of students with the same cultural background. Many accounts exist of classroom management problems that have arisen under these conditions, though the advantage appears to lie with the language teacher, who can claim that his/her classroom not only teaches the language but in its activities exemplifies the culture that is also to be learned. But unless the teacher sees him/herself as a teacher of culture and not just of language, I fear that solutions of such classroom management problems will come because of power imbalances, not as a result of dialogue or explication. Happily, there are success stories. For example, Rilling and Pratt (1998) initially experienced classroom management problems with a a group of young adult international students visiting the United States. Providing these second language learners with the chance to actually *observe* classes at a U.S. college turned out to be important in addressing classroom conduct problems. Explicit statements of teacher expectations were also used but coupled with an effort to get the students themselves to develop a code of conduct partly reflecting their observations, and as a result classroom management problems were solved.

Changing classroom management

ES/FL appears to have a vested interest in calling into question established patterns of classroom interaction, classroom activities, and how they are organized and managed; at the same time not wishing to simply move from the patterns of one culture to those of another. The questioning of, for example, traditional management arrangements in non-Western classrooms means we should also be prepared to question management arrangements in Western classrooms too. For the absolute beginner teacher, managing the classroom, in the sense of being able to discharge the social function of the teacher as typically presented, is indeed often the first worry. Though for some beginning teachers, command of subject matter is also a worry; and yet, one cannot "deliver" subject matter unless classroom management is not too great a problem. But are we, and are the teachers-in-development reading this, satisfied with the interactional, managerial aspects of classrooms they see? Grossman (1992), criticizing a model of teacher development which puts classroom management first, has this to say:

Management is not neutral but carries within it its own implicit theories of instruction (Edelsky, Draper, & Smith, 1983) as well as assumptions about schooling as a form of social control (Britzman, 1986).

In their study of teaching advanced skills to children of poverty, Knapp and his colleagues investigated the relationship between classroom management and the kinds of instruction children received in math and literacy. They concluded,

"Ultimately, choices about management approach affect the kind of academic learning experience available to children ... On the whole we were struck by how often the academic learning environment was set by management choices made with little thought to academics, rather than vice versa" (Knapp et al., 1991, p. 41).

Grossman (1992, p. 176) in turn concludes that:

In the final analysis, it comes down to what we want and expect of future teachers. If we want future teachers to reproduce the schools we have now, if we want them to replicate existing models of teaching and learning ... then teacher educators can prepare future teachers to get along and survive in schools as they are and to acquire routines for managing classroom activity without questioning their implications for learning. In doing so, teacher preparation will continue to contribute to the inherent conservatism of schooling.

If, however, we ... want to change prevailing practices, to challenge the lessons learned during prospective teachers' apprenticeships of observation, then ... "to place the emphasis ... upon the securing of proficiency in teaching and discipline puts the attention of the student-teacher in the wrong place, and tends to fix it in the wrong direction" (Dewey, 1904/1965, p. 147).

And yet order is still required. Alternatively, since what order is is specific to culture, class, time, and even task, we may simply need a different kind of order, one differently constituted. Attention to the matter is still needed, but it must be that of an inquiring and exploratory teacher, rather than one simply apprenticed to a master.

FOR DISCUSSION

1. Which of your problems in classroom management can be traced to the S/FL aspects of your classroom, and which not?
2. How would you go about introducing changes in classroom rules or expectations? How would you do this differently, depending on whether you were teaching within your home culture, or as a visitor or sojourner in another culture?

STUDENT TEACHERS COMMENT ...

(1) On cultural differences.   [This teacher is a United States national, teaching a group of foreign adult students at a United States university. Her students mostly come from a wide range of countries, with East Asians the dominant group.]

I would like to ponder (in written form) the problems associated with cultural differences in the classroom. This is an interesting and relevant issue for most, if not all, ESL or EFL professionals because of the problems that arise when different cultural expectations are in competition in the classroom. Specifically, I would like to address my own ruminations and difficulties with cross-cultural communication in a language classroom and ways to overcome this barrier.

If two or more cultures are in conflict in a given situation, whose cultural style is the norm and therefore the culture that is adhered to in the situation? I suppose the PC answer would be to say, "well everyone needs to respect each other and their cultural differences [so] as to have a fair and even playing field for all." However, I do not see how this can truly happen in a situation where there is a power difference among the participants. For example, in my class, I am the instructor; I plan the lessons, I write the syllabus, I grade the papers, and perform all other class management duties. Therefore, shouldn't students adapt to me, especially if I represent the dominant culture being a native speaker and American? This assertion may sound horrible to some, perhaps most, people but there are expected behaviors from students participating in the U.S. educational system and there are expected behaviors from the instructors. If I am adhering to these behaviors, such as asking students to volunteer answers, expecting students to ask questions if they don't understand, and participate fully in class discussion, shouldn't the students be able to fulfill the expectations I have of students studying in the U.S.? The class and all instructional value crumbles if I am coming from a tradition where this type of participation is expected and the students do not adapt to this tradition. My position on this matter is that in these cases, there is no room for cultural compromise. To clarify, I can respect that my students come from different educational traditions and therefore have different expectations when they are in my class. However, if I begin to bend and break with regards to whose culture gets to "dominate" in the classroom, then nothing will get done. I won't be happy because my lessons, which are dependent upon participation, break down and the students won't be happy because their inability to participate prevents them from getting any instructional value from the lesson. . . . The ESL classroom is often multi-cultural and multi-ethnic. Therefore, if the instructor's educational culture is not dominant, whose will become dominant? The ethnicity that has the greatest representatives? Is that fair to the other students? An example of this type of culture bias that occurs in the classroom is the fact that there is not a lot of literature about different educational styles. For example, since I am in a department with many Japanese students and I have been exposed to many studies involving Japanese students, I know quite a bit about the Japanese educational culture. However, the same can not be said about my knowledge of Chinese, Indonesian, Thai, or Vietnamese educational traditions. If the instructor tries to assimilate to a Japanese style of learning, he/she will inevitably leave the other students out and will again defeat the purpose of education, which is to provide equal educational opportunities for everyone. Maybe I come from too populist of a background, but if one group of students are going to be disadvantaged, everyone in the class should be disadvantaged. It's only fair.

I also argue this assimilation stance based on the fact that the ESL classroom is not an independent institution apart from the rest of the U.S. educational system or from society. Most of these students interact in society outside of the classroom where the same norms and expectations exist. I think it would be a disservice to accommodate to the student too much. What I mean is that, why give the student an unrealistic view of the U.S.? Many people in the U.S. are unsympathetic to plights of immigrants or foreign visitors . . . Therefore, I almost see it as my duty as an ESL instructor to raise the students' awareness of what is expected in educational settings and to ask them to practice these behaviors in my class. So, I guess, my main point is that I expect students to adhere to my culture in the classroom because ultimately, in the real world this will help and benefit them the most. As far as when the instructor is in an EFL situation, this is a completely different situation and one I'm not sure I'll find myself in so I will neglect addressing it for now.

Reflecting on what I have just written, I believe the burning issue I want to have addressed is how to raise student awareness of the educational culture in the U.S. What ways should I go about encouraging Western style participation in class? Should I be very explicit about what I expect, will that work? Should I penalize students? If they know that 40% of their grade depends on how much they participate in class, will my classes run smoother or will they hate me because my expectations are so different than what they are used to? I honestly don't think it would be that difficult for students embrace Western style educational practices once they know what these behaviors are.

[The teacher whose words follow is a Korean teacher of English. At the time of writing he was teaching Korean-American students Korean and had been in the United States one year.]

There are several different age groups in my class. The youngest [student] is 6th grade and the oldest one is 11th grade, which means, even though linguistically they may have the same ability . . . they may also have some different interest or purpose of learning Korean. Meeting all of their interests or considering all of their needs is not easy at all. Here, the biggest concern, classroom management, comes out.

In Korea, classroom management is closely related to the concern of managing a big class which usually consists of more than 50 students. Naturally, students' academic ability is too various for teachers to focus on a specific level of students. Domestic Korean English teachers, therefore, claim that it is one of the reasons that they cannot approach their classes with a communicative teaching method. It could simply be said it is a methodological problem. However, it seems to me that the class size plays an important role in deciding not only what methodology a teacher chooses, but what teaching philosophy a teacher forms and pursues in a class.

When I started teaching Korean here, I had to consider how to manage my class seriously first, since the classroom situation or students' expectations here is completely different from that in Korea. For example, in classrooms in Korea, students are expected to give their full attention to the teachers. If a teacher finds one student doing something different from or which is not related to the class content, the teacher will consider it as a challenge to his/her authority as a teacher. Therefore, if a teacher experiences this kind of situation, while s/he is teaching, s/he might feel shameful to think that s/he lost her/his control of the class. Honestly, I also expected my students to follow all of my instructions without any exception in my class . . . [My principal] expected us to lead our classes with the same rules as domestic Korean teachers do in Korea. However, I couldn't compel my students to follow those kinds of rules, not because I thought it was not right, but I was not sure if it is really necessary for the students. I am not sure about this point, but I am getting more the sense, as time goes by, that they may be racially Korean, but their cultural identity is already decided as American individuals. If it is true, aren't we pushing our standard of how to behave in class on students (who are not motivated anyway at all)? In order to answer this question, I need more understanding about my students. But, without this understanding, I don't think I can be a good teacher who knows well how to deal with language classes . . . teachers cannot avoid dealing with cultural concerns.

FOR DISCUSSION

What do you think about the above two quotes? Are these aspects of class-room management, which obviously have arisen in specific, more-or-less second as opposed to foreign language contexts, relevant to your own situation?

STUDENT TEACHERS COMMENT...

(2) On issues of control.   [A North American teacher with a number of years experience; working with first-year undergraduate adult ESL students.]

I had an initial idea of having my students research what good writing is, such as: what are the components of good academic writing, what are the different types of writing one needs in academia, and what does good writing look like (finding specific examples of writing that they like)? I personally think this would be good for the students (and for me) but I haven't found a way to operationalize it efficiently. There are so many variables to consider in order to guide the students in the right direction. I think that is what is so scary for instructors, the releasing of control. As the instructor you're always supposed to have the right answers and be able to guide the student's progress in the class, step by step, at least this is the impression we receive through our experience as students and teachers-in-training. Therefore it is intimidating for the instructor to give that up, to let the student take over the task and interpret it for themselves. This takes practice for the teacher I think, it is definitely something I have not mastered.

[An American teacher with almost a decade of experience, much of it in Japan; working with university-bound adult ESL students]

The vocabulary component [of a course] lost steam a little before midway through the term, by my estimation. I attribute this to my own failure to consistently monitor their progress, or lack thereof, in this area. In other words, the lack of my controlling behavior in this area. To what extent would a perhaps firmer structuring of the vocabulary component have contributed to a more successful outcome? I think this is an important question, for I am beginning to see that the two things go hand-in-hand, or rather, they are mutually exclusive parts of the same whole. In other words, the more structure you have in the assignment, the less you need to control how the students act when carrying out the assignment, the more you can let them go about it on their own. And yet, now coming full circle, isn't structure the same as control? The more you structure something, the more you control it. The framework you set for the students to work within is, in effect, your control of the situation. They are no longer free to do as they please, but rather limited by the structure you have imposed on them. However this appears, perhaps, to allow them to go about the task on their own, without much teacher intervention I now realize this is not actually the case. . . . More structure provided, less control needed; less structure provided, more control needed. Proactive, reactive. Which should one be?

Adding to this topic later, he continued:

I chose to have my students keep dialogue journals this term, as a means of communication between teacher and student. This has allowed me to stay tuned to what my students feel they need to get from the course. And it is this input which has helped me to make the decisions I have made during the course of this term, regarding how much to "teach" them, and how much to let them "learn" . . . [This] helped me to see the imposition of structure/control as beneficial, when brought about by the needs of the learners, as expressed through dialogue with the teacher. And as a result of reflection and dialogue, I think I've finally put the learner in his/her proper place, as the driver of the educational process, and as an unequalled source of help in making classroom decisions.

FOR DISCUSSION

Have you ever tried to "loosen" control, as the above two teachers have? Why, and under what conditions, might this be appropriate in S/FL teaching, as opposed to other subjects, perhaps?

10 Social Skills and the Classroom Community

- How can we achieve good rapport with our students?
- What skills do we need to work well with our fellow teachers?

Warm-up

Do you make a conscious effort to get on well with your students or your fellow teachers? If so, what do you do?

In addressing the topic of "social skills," I am initially extending the discussion of classroom management from the previous chapter. Much in classroom management will go well if there are good teacher-student relationships, but we often need to take specific steps to establish and maintain them, the subject of the first part of this chapter. In the second and third parts of the chapter, I return to my concern that teachers be able to work with other teachers that underlay some of the material in Chapter 2. As any new teacher can attest, all the time you are in school, you are "on," you are a practitioner, whether inside the classroom or not. Even for the new teacher, plausibly carrying off the role of teacher when with other teachers, getting along with them, and so on, is almost as important as successfully playing that role with students; further along into one's professional career, teacher-teacher work and relationships continue to be vital. A teaching practicum is one place to work on skills and concepts for this domain of practice; indeed, for that matter, having a teaching practicum that is effective will also depend, to some extent, on good interprofessional relationships, not only among peer teachers, but as they involve any cooperating teacher or supervisor as well.

In emphasizing the importance of this area, I am making the claim that, despite traditional conceptions of teaching as a one-person operation, teachers cannot operate optimally alone, or in the face of colleagues with whom they cannot work. It is increasingly recognized (for example, in the school restructuring literature – see the following chapter) that the isolation of teachers must be broken down if schools are to improve, and throughout this book I have suggested that ES/FL teachers *can* work with each other to improve their own teaching. And in ESL contexts (especially in the elementary sector), it is common for an ESL teacher to work within the classroom of another, "content," teacher. Nevertheless, teachers face difficulties in working with teachers – sometimes it seems that a major obstacle to improving a program is one's fellow teachers ("Hell is other people," Sartre, 1947/1987[1]). Consequently, we need good interpersonal skills to persuade, negotiate, and collaborate with our colleagues.

Despite the importance of this area for teaching and teacher development, most teacher education programs in ES/FL devote little attention to it,[2] and the topic is not treated much in mainstream teacher education either. In what follows, I begin at the classroom level, tackling teacher-student followed by student-student relationships, and then move up to the interprofessional domain. I then briefly address an area where good interprofessional relationships may aid improvements – when we try to persuade our colleagues to change; and also allude to the social skills needed when such persuasion is ineffective. Finally, many ES/FL teachers' social skills will be particularly challenged by the added complexity of cross-cultural relationships, and advice (and research) on social and communication skills in teaching has not always been fully informed by a recognition of their cultural specificity. The concluding section will briefly refer to this problem.

Teacher-student relationships, or rapport

The importance of a supportive social environment both for informal ESL learning and in ELT generally has been repeatedly addressed by SL researchers. For example, Moscowitz (e.g., Moscowitz, Benevento, & Furst, 1973; Moscowitz & Hayman, 1974) became well known for introducing a humanistic concern with relationships into the literature of ES/FL. At a slightly more abstract level, theorists developed an early interest in the learner's relationship to the wider society as supporting SLA (Schumann, 1978), and a belief that affect supported acquisition (Krashen, 1977). Over the last decade, the academic fields surrounding ES/FL instruction have developed a greater concern for the importance of sociocultural forces supporting or opposing S/FL learning, and of the social dimensions of learning, thus continuing this interest.

Down at the more specific level of interpersonal social relationships, however, some TES/FL handbooks (e.g., Wallace, 1991; Woodward, T.,

1991) devote little, if any, space to the matter; older works of this sort gave it passing attention (Bailey & Celce-Murcia, 1979; Gower & Walters, 1983). This material is rather limited and does not take a research-based approach; indeed this is perhaps justifiable because so little research is available in this area in ES/FL (Bartu, 1991). It does, of course, provide plausible sets of tips for teachers; for example, Gower and Walters (1983) advised that teachers can promote teacher-student rapport by

showing personal interest in the students
being interested in their progress
asking for comments on the classes
having the right manner

They should also be sure to know all students' names, ensure that students know each other, allow plenty of group work, use activities that students enjoy, and let each class

develop its own atmosphere and encourage its own positive characteristics. If there are some students working against the interests of the group [teachers should] spend some time talking to them and sorting out their problems (p. 30).

Though the points above are useful, indeed almost indisputable, such treatments do not go far enough. A few more recent ES/FL-specific works extend these points a little. From a questionnaire surveying a group of British ESL teachers, Hadfield (1992) found that her teachers' most common concern was classroom atmosphere. Her book presents an extended series of activities teachers can use to develop student-student and teacher-student rapport.[3] Senior (1997) interviewed a group of Australian ES/FL language school teachers and found that group development was an objective for most of these teachers. "It seemed that the teachers had made the prior assumption that an atmosphere of classroom cohesion was a necessary precondition for the development of linguistic proficiency through oral practice" (p. 4).

On the other hand, a rather large body of relevant work is to be found in the mainstream education literature, and is summarized by Jones and Jones (1998; see also Lyons, 1990).[4] To make a very long story short, in this area substantial quantities of research strongly suggest a very important role for the establishment of good teacher-student relationships to ensure student retention, social and personal growth, and academic success at elementary and secondary school. At the same time however, according to Jones and Jones, teachers complain that they are not given adequate orientation to how this can be done in their pre-service training, and even experienced teachers may not be able adequately to mentor junior teachers in this area;

partly because past teacher education has led teachers to believe that it is not really their responsibility to foster such relationships (as opposed to delivering content instruction).[5]

Some authors and researchers place caring as central to this area. This concept has been taken up by moral philosophers in recent years, though as a central theme of human relations it is timeless. Gordon (1974) indicates that a caring relationship is one in which each one knows that the other values them. Additional descriptive terms for such a relationship, or orientation, could include "empathic" and "nurturant" (Kohn, 1991). Feminist philosopher of education Noddings suggests that for such relationships, modeling, dialogue, practice, and confirmation are needed: the first of these is simply the provision of adequate models in the environment, and the third similarly reminds us of the importance of ensuring that learners have the opportunity to practice engaging in such relationships (cf. Noddings, 1984; Katz, Noddings, & Strike, 1999). Such relationships need reinforcement, so words (not to mention time and space in the curriculum) must be found for confirming the existence of such relationships. Of the four, dialogue is to my mind the most important and difficult. It may also be the most historically or culturally limited of the four: not all cultures place the same emphasis on the maintenance of relationships through oral interaction.

Dialogue, if it means a true exchange of views, is difficult in school because of role expectations and power differentials (e.g., Sorensen & Christophel, 1992), not to mention time pressures. To have a true exchange of views requires openness, but sharing a full range of personal views and values may be a challenge, or quite undesirable, across a status or perhaps an age difference. It is likely to be seen as quite inappropriate to the role of the teacher in many cultures. However, some openness is valuable in supporting the dialogue generally necessary for establishing teacher-student relationships that go beyond the minimal. Jones and Jones (1990), who discuss teacher-student relationships of varying degrees of openness, specify a middle position as one concerning "openness related to our reactions to and feelings about the school environment, with limited sharing of aspects reflecting our out-of-school life" (p. 76). They go on to advocate use of three techniques to secure this: "(1) monitoring the quality of our relationships with students, with a focus on maintaining a high rate of positive statements, (2) creating opportunities for personal discussions with them, and (3) demonstrating our interest in activities that are important to them" (p. 78). The first of these may seem to have a behaviorist tinge, but might still warrant reflecting upon. The second need not involve class time, if adequate thought is given to the content of outside class interaction or homework; on the other hand, the assignment of in-class time to small-scale needs analyses, activities which capitalize on student backgrounds, or simply careful attention to students' work, is obviously in keeping with various aspects of common ES/FL procedures. And while teachers need not "gush" or overpraise – to turn around point 3, *dis*interest, or a teacher showing a lack of interest in their students, can be extremely discouraging.

Work in the area of "adult education" offers an additional perspective on teacher-student rapport. Adult education can be distinguished from tertiary or post–secondary education, or university education, though it obviously overlaps with this domain. At the same time, adult education is more likely to concern what has come to be called the nontraditional student, typically an adult returning to formal education after some time in regular employment; it potentially includes various aspects of in-service education.[6] The adult learner is generally seen as more independent than the child learner, and the teacher of adults is thus more often able to take a facilitator role (though as ever, cultural traditions and students' previous experience will modify such a claim). Since in adult education the learner's participation is often largely voluntary, the roles of motivation and supportive teacher-student relations in the classroom are accorded great importance, and not all adults, or adult learners of a second or foreign language, have had prior successes with school or with S/FL learning. This means that for some students, there are initial obstacles to rapport.

The prominent theorist and writer on adult education Brookfield has addressed the topic of the development of rapport in some detail (1990), though his work and advice should be seen as deriving mainly from U.S. and mainstream European experiences, and is not necessarily grounded in specific empirical studies.[7] Prior to establishing rapport, he proposes, is the prerequisite of addressing and if necessary modifying resistance to learning. In order to deal with resistance to learning, Brookfield points out that we must understand where it comes from, and treat it. Possible reasons for it are

learners' poor self-image as learners
their fear of the unknown
lack of clarity in teachers' instructions
students' personal dislike of teachers
disjunction of learning and teaching styles
apparent irrelevance (to learners) of the learning activity
learners' fear of looking foolish in public

danger of committing cultural suicide[8]
level of required learning is inappropriate

Possible responses are for teachers to

ask themselves whether the resistance is justified
try to sort out the causes of the resistance
research your students' backgrounds and cultures
involve students in educational planning
conduct regular formative evaluation sessions
explain your intentions clearly
justify why you think learning is important
involve former resisters
create situations in which students succeed
accentuate the positive
encourage peer learning and peer teaching
not push too fast
attend to the need to build trust
admit the normality of resistance
be wary of confrontational obsession
strike a bargain with total resisters
acknowledge students' right to resist

These initiatives, then, are the preliminaries to "building trust" and establishing rapport. Brookfield's suggestions for that are:

don't deny your credibility
be explicit about your organizing vision
make sure your words and actions are congruent
be ready to admit your errors
reveal aspects of yourself unrelated to teaching
show that you take students seriously
don't play favorites
realize the power of your own role modeling

These actions derive from two sources of rapport – that which derives from the teacher showing skill as a teacher to the student (credibility) and that which derives from the teacher showing trustworthiness as an individual ("authenticity," Moustakas, 1966; cf. Jones & Jones 1990, Chapter 3).[9]

The cultural dimensions of establishing rapport in classrooms are obviously important, particularly if teacher and student do not share the first culture. In drawing on past literature in this area, I have been concerned that while there is much in the way of plausible suggestion, one might be more confident of the prescriptions if we knew they were grounded in specific studies of specific ES/FL contexts. The suggestions, whether made by experts in adult education or ES/FL, are worth considering but we should recognize that they come out of specific cultural contexts, and what is more dangerous, those contexts are not always acknowledged or made manifest. As ES/FL specialists, we may have to be ethnographers of our own classrooms while using these suggestions primarily as heuristics to be tested in practice.

FOR DISCUSSION

1. Have you ever had students who were resistant? If so, were you able to lower their resistance, and how? Do you think you used any of Brookfield's tactics?
2. ES/FL teachers' behavior is constrained in most cases by the populations and cultures with which they work, as well as by their own status (adults and children, "traditional" and "modern" cultures, expatriate and indigenous). To what extent does your professional experience so far support the following statement: "In settings which require a more formal teacher-student relationship, rapport must be obtained primarily through demonstrating credibility. In others it can be obtained also through demonstrating authenticity"?
3. What do you understand of the term "self-disclosure"? What is its role in fostering relationships, in your experience, and how can teachers use it? Is this culturally-constrained, or culture-specific?

STUDENT TEACHERS COMMENT ...

[May is a beginning teacher. She thinks of herself as Western, though her ancestry is not; her students are mainly from East Asia, and they are temporarily residing in Hawai'i.]

As for my own efforts to develop rapport with students, I tried to treat them with respect and understanding. I tend to be more introverted at certain times, especially in situations that I am not too familiar with or around people that I don't know very well ... But in my own way, I try to care about my students as human beings and as people with different cultures. .... I think some of them felt comfortable enough with me because they asked me to meet with and help them with their conversation skills outside of class time, or called me on the phone to help them with an English problem, or emailed me messages of a less school-related nature, or even chatted with me outside of class. Or sometimes they would just simply bow to me with sincerity and express a cordial "good morning" or a cheerful "aloha" or even treat me with respect in the ways of their country, which I didn't feel I deserved but was touched that they extended their respect in such a way. . . .

But I also learned that rapport doesn't always lead to understanding in the classroom, and quite often the two are completely separated. . . . I would venture to say that maybe in some cultures (and/or even different individuals' minds) personal relationships and learning are two very separate things, and probably some students wouldn't care whether or not rapport was developed in the classroom because their primary concern is acquiring knowledge, and for them knowledge acquired in school has nothing to do with relationships of environment or anything else besides the teacher's knowledge, the textbook's information, and the student's brain. . . . I only wish to point out that sometimes a teacher . . . may value rapport more than students actually do, and may see rapport as an integral part of the education process whereas some student may not share this view; if the teacher is not aware of this, I think it is grounds for a misfortunate understanding.

[N is another beginning teacher. She is from Japan, but has lived abroad (outside Japan) extensively. At the time of writing, she was teaching English in Hawai'i to young adults who were college-bound.]

Showing personal interest in students and sharing emotions with students are crucial. Students will know that teachers are also human beings and they also have feelings and lives outside of the school. As a matter of fact, when I was in school, maybe up to when I was in junior high school, I could not see my teachers as ordinary human beings. Teachers were only teachers; not someone's sisters, mothers, brothers, or fathers. So, I would not have even known what I wanted to talk about with my teachers except something related to my school work. Realizing [the importance of] factors [fostering rapport] does not guarantee that they will be implemented. There could be many cases where teachers are aware of the importance of developing rapport with their students, but they are busy teaching the content of the class. Showing interest in the students, making sure that students know each other, and encouraging each class to develop its own atmosphere are important factors. They will help students feel comfortable in class and personalize the place where their learning occurs. However, carrying those out takes teachers extra time and effort. Some teachers may not be willing to work extra for things that may appear to be irrelevant to what they are teaching.

Another reason why teachers fail to develop a rapport with students can be their fear of giving students an opportunity to speak up and criticize them. For example, asking students for comments is one of the tips that are suggested for teachers to do. However, teachers can intentionally avoid this when they are afraid of getting negative comments. This is very easy especially when students do not know that they have a right to evaluate teachers or their class. Getting comments from students is crucial for the teacher and class to grow as a group. So, students first need to be instructed to speak up for themselves. Building rapport is absolutely necessary especially in a language class. Language is one of the fundamental needs in human life. In a beginning level class, sometimes we can say that language is missing when students are not feeling comfortable using it. In this kind of situation, establishing rapport should come before anything. Fortunately, I am promoting rapport with the students in the class I am teaching ... What I tried to do was remember the students' names and use them as often as possible, and before and after class, talk about their outside lives. I also tried to find out what they are interested in and talk about it. With the students in that class, I intended to treat them as I would new people who could be my friends. However, with much younger students, I think it is possible that teachers develop rapport by demonstrating credibility. Sometimes this can be expected by students in settings where more formal teacher-student relationship is required. This seems more reasonable with younger students. I think it makes it easier for students to know what kind of teacher-student relationship is expected.

Student-student relationships

Although individual teacher-student rapport can to some degree exist in an atmosphere of antagonistic student-student relationships, it is less likely to develop under such conditions. Teachers trying to foster good relations with students will also need to take steps to help students get along with their classmates. Mainstream education studies suggest the importance of student-student relationships in child learning (Jones and Jones, 1990). And, of course, there is a heavy emphasis in many ES/FL "communicative" class-rooms on learning activities which involve student-student interaction and the possibility of students learning from each other, within which context peer relations (whether of children or adults) are obviously important.

We cannot assume that satisfactory student-student relations will develop in the absence of intervention by the instructor, as both adults and children (cf. Yeates & Selman, 1989) are often not socially skillful. In a recent study of ESL teacher decision making, Smith (1996, p. 209) reports,

teachers did not consider ... social rapport as necessarily an "inherent feature" of the social context, but one that needed encouraging through various means. They therefore made particular decisions about the types of activities and materials they used and the student-teacher roles adopted in order to promote group cohesiveness.

In Chapter 9 we considered the role of the ES/FL teacher in providing, or negotiating, rules for classroom behavior, and these include guidance and directives concerning classroom interaction. Any teacher may in such directives specify interactions which will support rapport among students.

In addition, classroom activities can also facilitate the development of positive student-student relations. It is often recommended that teachers take a variety of simple actions to foster student-student rapport such as conducting "icebreaking" activities and ensuring that students know each others' names (e.g., Bailey & Celce-Murcia, 1979; Ji, 1997; Kuty, 1992; inter alia). Going beyond introductory icebreakers is often desirable, though ES/FL-targeted material in this area is rare (but see Birch, 1993). It is also hard to find efforts of this kind in ES/FL classes documented and evaluated for effectiveness, but Moscowitz (1981) reports that interstudent attitudes were improved following instruction in and use of humanistic exercises in FL classes:

after experiencing the humanistic techniques, [there was] a significant positive increase in the total attitudes students had toward the class and toward themselves and the perceptions they felt the class had of them . . . How students felt about their peers also improved significantly (p. 152).[10]

I alluded earlier to the possible connection between group work, so popular in "communicative approaches" to ELT, and positive student attitudes. But I doubt if there's any evidence that group work in communicative ELT classes fosters good relations between students. The area of "cooperative learning" is a source of insight here, however. This line of work developed independent of the developments in ES/FL that led to an increased emphasis on group work. It too involves extensive use of group activities, but differs from ES/FL's simple group emphasis. It uses highly structured groups, sometimes involves competition for grades between teams of students, and usually requires the grading of jointly produced work; it has become very popular in some areas of mainstream education. One of the forces behind its original development and use was a need to change negative interpersonal (racial) attitudes in students (Sharan, 1980). Early cooperative learning specialists found that simply putting students whose mutual attitudes were negative together in the same class produced no improvement in attitude, and it was only after ways were found to structure classwork so that there was mutual interdependence leading to shared outcomes in terms of work produced and graded that attitudes improved.[11]

The bulk of the literature on student-student relations concerns school students, but adult students' interpersonal relations also need attention. If adults find themselves in learning groups where they are ignored or feel they are disliked by their peers, they will describe such classes as "cold, hostile, and indifferent learning environments" (Kidd, 1973, in Wlodkowski, 1985, p. 197). Small-group research and intergroup relations (mainly involving adults) was an area of intensive research activity in the 1960s and 1970s. Relevant sections of this work for us have been usefully summarized in a number of sources. Wlodkowski (1985, pp. 198–199), for example, reports:

A positive emotional climate means members of a group like and are committed to the group. The most frequently used term to describe this state of affairs is cohesiveness (Johnson & Johnson, 1982). . . . There is enough research evidence available now to persuasively argue that the achievement of at least a minimal level of group cohesiveness can enhance learner motivation and performance, and that, therefore, our attempt as instructors to establish this condition is worth our effort, skill, and strategy (Schmuck & Schmuck, 1983).

Adult ESL teachers concur; from Smith's (1996) study again:

Teachers talked about fostering a classroom "dynamic" which not only motivated students to come to class but to participate when they were there. They also referred to "building a supportive climate" in which students were encouraged to get to know one another and would ideally continue this social relationship outside the classroom. A number of teachers commented specifically that their most successful classes were those in which there was a "social gathering atmosphere" in which students were friends as well as classmates. For example, one teacher commented: "Self-image and all those affective domain issues are priority in L2 acquisition or any kind of learning because if it's not in place, I don't see any kind of potential. I think that's why building a supportive group environment so they can connect with people and make friends is so important" (p. 209).

FOR DISCUSSION

1. As students, recently have you found yourselves in learning groups where you did not know your fellow students, or felt anxious about the situation? If so, did the instructor address the matter? How? If s/he did not, what did *you* do?
2. At present, as a teacher, what do you do to foster good student-student relationships in your classrooms?

Interprofessional relationships

Skills are needed

There seems to be little argument that certain skills are needed to foster good interprofessional relationships, or rapport, among teachers in general. I can think of two or three additional reasons that make them especially necessary for ES/FL teachers.

In English-speaking countries, the ESL teacher, along with others who teach students with special needs (cf. Conoley, 1989; Hudson, 1989), may often have to work in much closer collaboration with other teachers than is usual. Whereas in ESL countries school-age ESL students often used to spend a large portion of their day segregated from their native–English-speaking fellow students, this has increasingly been seen as undesirable; as a result ESL teachers, to a greater extent than other subject area teachers, may work on a team-teaching or collaborative and consultative basis with other non-ESL teachers. Consequently, they have heightened needs for communication skills for collaboration, consultation, student referrals, problem-solving, and for group process skills particularly as they apply in organizational development. Of course, these skills are also needed when ES/FL teachers are interacting among themselves, as well.

Also in English-speaking countries, ESL teaching is often less well-funded than instruction in other areas, and may even have a marginal status (cf. Auerbach, 1991). Accordingly, ESL teachers have a particular need to think of themselves as "change agents." So long as working conditions and the structure of ES/FL education are lacking, we must hope that ES/FL teachers will engage in the processes and tasks needed to improve working conditions, and the profession as a whole. On the basis of one empirical study in this area (Miles, Saxl, & Lieberman, 1988, pp. 157–158), teachers who are effective agents of change need

six general skills: interpersonal ease, group functioning, training/doing workshops, master teacher, educational content, and administrative/organizational ability. . . . In the "personal" area, the skill of initiative-taking was crucial. In the "socio-emotional process" area the skills were rapport-building, support, conflict mediation, collaboration, and confrontation. In the "task" area, the skills were individual diagnosis, organizational diagnosis, and managing/controlling. Finally, in the area of "educational content," the key skills were resource-bringing and demonstration.

Some of these "skills" are by no means narrow. Conflict mediation, for example, is more a domain of expertise that itself requires a variety of skills, or subskills. Many of these seem to be characteristic of responsibilities discharged by teachers in midcareer. On the other hand, many of them draw heavily on social, communicational, and interactional skills. The fact that Miles et al., in this three-year investigation of three New York school improvement programs, were able to identify these skills as critical for "successful change agent behavior" is a useful motivation for S/FL teachers to develop them. Until recently, however, such skills have been "generally ignored throughout professional education and training. Not only are they ignored but the methods of higher education foster attitudes and approaches that inhibit their development" (Cohen, 1982, p. 177; cf. Ryan, Jackson, & Levinson, 1986). A result of this absence is "the existence of tensions in staff groups that can lead to avoidance of staff or team meetings, lack of co-operation or outright war" (Cohen, 1982, p. 176). What, then, are some of these skills?

Listening and collaboration skills

There is a well-established tradition of research and training concerning communication skills, much of which is located in the discipline of counseling. Many specialists have seen this as applicable to communication between professionals (e.g., Brammer, 1985; Hobbs, 1992). In the specific context of interteacher communication, Conoley (1989) identifies five aspects of an interaction that particularly contribute to successful communication. During communication, it would seem that if an individual regularly repeats and paraphrases the other's message, does not fail to seek clarification where needed, and chooses appropriate moments to recapitulate the speaker's words, this should be facilitative. Throughout, culture-appropriate use of nonverbal signals of attention, concern, and support should be used. When the one who has been listening takes a turn, it is desirable that s/he should build on what the speaker has said, rather than ignore it in the interests of making his/her own points (a response stereotypic of masculine speech styles, in particular).

As obvious as these points may be, most of us can think of individuals in our own professional communities who consistently fail to consider them. Since these behaviors appear elementary, they would also seem to be amenable to simple training, yet as Kearney and McCroskey (1980, p. 533) remark, "teacher credentials traditionally emphasize content competencies to the exclusion of competencies applicable to the relational . . . communicative-exchange process."

A notable aspect of both teacher-student and teacher-teacher communication is the giving of feedback, particularly in the latter case where peer-peer professional development is the focus of interaction. ES/FL teachers may be familiar with this in the context of teacher education (e.g., Fanselow, 1988; Freeman, 1982; Gebhard, 1984). Some ES/FL teacher supervisors have been seen to have a quite directive supervisory style, in which their feedback to junior teachers is very much "on record," unhedged and evaluative, while others evince a more consultative style of feedback. The advice concerning teacher-teacher communication Conoley offers complements this. To ensure maximum utility or uptake of teacher-teacher feedback, we are advised that feedback should be

descriptive, not evaluative
aimed at behaviors that can be changed
based on a receiver's needs rather than sender hostility
timed to occur near the target behavior
checked to insure the receiver understands the giver's message and intent
    (1989, p. 252)

Conoley points out that it is desirable to hear feedback nondefensively, which may require an initial decision to relax and listen carefully, to overcome negative emotions induced by the message so as to be able to ask for clarification, and not to think of excuses or attacks (a common response to even constructive feedback, in my experience). Conoley comments (1989, p. 252) that

there is overwhelmingly positive evidence that communication skills are crucial to the success of interpersonal relationships. This evidence comes from the counseling psychology and teacher effectiveness literature. . . . Meta-analyses of therapy and training efforts consistently show communication training as having the greatest effect sizes of an array of outcome measures (Baker et al., 1984).

YOU TRY IT...

1. Conoley (1989) above identifies five strategies for listening. Use the following exercise to practice making conscious use of them. If possible, work in threes: a speaker, a listener, and an observer. The speaker can choose a topic for conversation (or you could negotiate one). A simple topic may be best, to start with. The listener should consciously try out all five strategies. After about 5 minutes, stop; the observer can give the listener feedback, and the speaker can perhaps contribute in this area as well. Then rotate roles and repeat twice more.

    Were you able to do all five? How natural or unnatural did it feel? Would all of these be applicable in your first culture? Do you think you usually do use them?

2. On a piece of paper, list Miles et al.'s "skills" needed by teacher change agents. Mark which of them you think are primarily social in nature. Now rate your competence in these areas. In which of them are you satisfied with or confident of your ability? In which of them would you like to develop? Compare with peers. Where one of you is confident or competent in an area another is not, try to have the more proficient individual explain how s/he came by this expertise. If the area is important to you, draw up a plan to become more competent in the area. What resources do you need, and how will you obtain them?

Going beyond interprofessional relationships

Changing attitudes and opinions

Having good relations with one's students, and particularly one's colleagues, can make a difficult job easier. But good relations with colleagues (or even students) can be difficult to maintain if there are differences of opinion on matters of professional practice, or educational theory. Teachers, like other professionals, are capable of holding on stubbornly to their opinions, and a positive interpersonal professional relationship can founder on a difference of opinion about matters of pedagogy, curriculum, or administration, unfortunately.

Few of us would say that the condition of ES/FL education anywhere is particularly satisfactory, and I have already alluded to the need for change and the role that the well-educated professional may play in it. The processes of personal and professional change and development that I hope readers of this book are engaging in, ideally are not intended simply for personal growth or even individual advantage. Many a teacher at workshops or on longer courses has said to me, "I agree with what you're saying. But what can I do about my colleagues?" By implication, the question being asked is, "how can I change *their* minds?" How, that is, can they be persuaded to change?

The study of persuasion has a long history. The academic study of persuasive discourse itself is located in areas ES/FL teachers may have some familiarity with: discourse linguistics (e.g., Mulholland, 1994) and the social psychology of language (Cody & McLaughlin, 1990; cf. Willing, 1992). The study of attitudes, attitude change, and what has been called persuasion theory (Perloff, 1993) is mainly to be found in general psychology (e.g., Newton & Burgoon, 1990; Storey, 1997; Tesser & Shaffer, 1990). For present purposes it may be sufficient to say that (unsurprisingly) there is no "magic bullet" – no one best way to persuade or change attitudes.[12] But research and personal experience do suggest that among potentially supporting factors is a good relationship.

We are just beginning to see the appearance of descriptive accounts of teacher change in our own specific area (cf. Bailey, 1992; Freeman, 1992). Pennington (1996a,b) documents movement of a group of eight Hong Kong English writing teachers in attitudes and understanding of process-based approaches to writing pedagogy. In this small group of teachers, it was true that the least positive about the approach before beginning a training program on process writing remained so at the end, but he did change somewhat. Another interesting point was that one individual who was, according to Pennington, "conflicted" about the approach, was the individual she identified as highly likely to experience attitude change, and was one of the two showing greatest attitude change (on a pre-post quantitative measure). Though the author does not draw on any of the academic literature on attitude change, she theorizes on the basis of the study that "teachers change in areas they are already primed to change, and this priming depends on their individual characteristics and prior experiences." She recognizes (with Freeman, 1989) that this change must also reflect the "attitudes and awareness of individual teachers towards their teaching contexts" (Pennington, 1996b, p. 340).

Conflict resolution, and conflict

Naturally, we wish to put our interpersonal skills, and even our attitude change skills to work within nonadversarial understandings of the desired goal – but this is not always possible. Interactions between teachers, or between teachers and administrators, not to mention between teachers and students, may at times be more oppositional. Here, work on communication in negotiation and bargaining, particularly in cross-cultural circumstances, is relevant (e.g. Gouran, 1991; Pruitt & Carnevale, 1993; Rojot, 1991; Womack, 1990). ES/FL teachers need to be aware that "conflict resolution" is an identifiable area of interaction with its own effective and ineffective ways of proceeding. For example, Johnson (1987) describes the steps to be taken if interpersonal, job-related conflicts are to be efficiently resolved. It is recommended that the individuals involved

define the conflict
label the problem, not each other
define areas of agreement as well as of disagreement
express their feelings but do not engage in threats
communicate cooperative intentions
express and coordinate their motivation to resolve the conflict

And also, depending upon the culture in question, confrontation may be an option to be deliberately deployed (Woodward, G., 1990; cf. e.g. Karp, 1985). As with other communication skills mentioned above, training in these areas typically makes use of role-play and discussion, is straightforward, and usually does not appear in ES/FL teacher education programs.

YOU TRY IT...

Role A: You are a bilingual EFL teacher; you have an excellent command of English and 40 years teaching experience. You are very skilled in giving grammatical explanations, working on translations as well as dealing with English literature. You are highly familiar with modern methods of teaching such as the audio-lingual method. Students in your classes respect you and are never bored. You understand their strengths and weaknesses because you are from their culture; you also know the textbooks that the school uses inside out and have an extensive collection of supplementary materials closely keyed to each chapter of these texts. Recently, one of the newly-hired foreign teachers has begun departing from the syllabus and students have complained. You mentioned this to the teacher, who responded by criticizing your teaching methods in front of the students. You have discussed whether or not to renew the teacher's contract with the principal.

Role B: You are a teacher of English, recently graduated from a prominent ESL teacher educational program. You have recently moved to a new country. Previously you picked up several foreign languages by living in the country where they were spoken. You are young, open, informal, and enthusiastic about the latest teaching techniques and materials. You believe that second language learning should be fun, and that it is essential that students have plenty of opportunities to communicate in class using stimulating materials that are keyed to their needs and interests. The textbooks of the school you have recently begun working for are antiquated and boring, and most of your students don't like them. You have discussed this with your students, and they agree. You have tried to persuade one of your senior colleagues to get rid of them, but he seems to have taken a personal dislike to you. Approach your colleague and try to resolve the matter.

Role C: Observer. Make notes of the participants' language. Do they use Johnson's strategies? Be ready to advise them when they have finished their discussion.

Rapport across cultures?

ES/FL teachers may face problems in establishing rapport as a result of being a member of a different culture to that of their students (cf. Prodromou, 1992).[13] Although we might guess that many of the strategies for developing interpersonal relationships, both with fellow teachers and students, may transfer across cultures, others may not.

While earlier research in this and the related area of classroom management generally reflected its times by assuming homogenous classes, more recent work in English-dominant countries reflects more pluralistic values[14] particularly salient in the field of multicultural and intercultural education. This work is oriented to fostering broader cultural understanding among mainstream or dominant-culture students, in all countries and is also intended to support the legitimate aspirations of minority groups for adequate and appropriate education in pluralistic societies (see e.g., Cushner, 1998; cf. Denoon, et al., 1996).

Probably the most long-developed area of this work concerns U.S. white–black relations in schools. Here, the area of "culturally relevant/responsive pedagogy" offers some suggestions or jumping-off places, when we are trying to decide how to foster rapport across cultural boundaries. Seeberg et al. (1998, pp. 283–84) summarize this area concisely:

Scholars advocate enhancing the cultural continuity between home/community and school (Shade, 1989; Sleeter, 1996; Swadener & Lubeck, 1995). Francesca Jackson's (1994) discussion of culturally responsive pedagogy is similar to the work of Gloria Ladson-Billings (1995) emphasizing "culturally relevant pedagogy." These researchers share the view that the responsibilities of educators include creating an environment that fosters positive intercultural interactions and reflects teachers' "cultural literacy," particularly in the cultures that their students bring to school. This could include sensitivity to oral literacy and different perceptual and learning styles, as well as many . . . intercultural communication issues.

Other voices in multicultural pedagogy have included Janice Hale-Benson's (1986) early work and Lisa Delpit's (. . . 1995) much-cited work on understanding the language and culture of power. Delpit argued that the implicit rules and expectations for success within dominant . . . cultures need to be made more explicit to children from marginalized subordinate class backgrounds . . . Ladson-Billing's work (1992) on successful teachers of Black children focused heavily on both culturally relevant pedagogy and relational work with students. In other words, successful multicultural education in the view of Ladson-Billings would require knowledge of and comfort with students' lived culture(s) as well as a relational approach to interacting with students and their families.

On the specific matter of rapport, Cazden (1988, pp. 168–70), looking at the teacher's classroom language, provides a number of examples showing how teachers from a range of cultures within the United States (Hispanic, Anglo, Amish) vary in the degree of social distance or closeness they establish with their students. She also points to cases where we can see the establishment of greater closeness, or "comembership" (Erickson & Schultz, 1982) across cultural differences, through mutual disclosure.

In search of answers to the matter of how to foster rapport in our classroom communities, those of us ES/FL teachers who teach across cultural boundaries may find ourselves becoming students of "comparative education." The area known as "comparative education" contrasts and compares the educational systems of different countries to understand and improve all such systems[15]; but sometimes it turns its attention to contrasting classroom practices, and interprofessional practices as well.

For example, Lewis's (1995) ethnography of Japanese elementary schools provides one answer to the question of whether some of the "tips" reviewed earlier in the chapter would transfer across cultures. It turns out that while U.S. teachers are told not to expect to be a buddy to the children, Japanese teachers are actively encouraged to be the children's friends. Similarly, Shimahara and Sakai (1995) in a comparative study of teacher education emphasize the comparatively greater responsibility of the teacher in Japan, versus the teacher in the United States, to foster teacher-student relationships, which contrasts with Jones and Jones' (1990) assertion that many U.S. teachers have been trained that this is not part of their responsibility. Finally, cross-cultural differences in one specific domain of interprofessional activity, the teacher meeting, are examined in a teacher research study by Caulk (1998). He found that German and expatriate EFL teachers at a university in Germany had such different expectations in the domain of meeting-related communication that rapport and innovation were seriously hindered until the expatriate side altered their practices. I look forward to a gradual increase in the number of reports our profession might have to draw on in this area, perhaps through the actions of teacher researchers.

11 *Working within the System: Institutional Structures and Reflective Teacher Development*

> • What is reflective teaching and do schools support it?
> • I want to continue reflecting with colleagues to develop my teaching, but my school isn't set up to facilitate this. What's going on?

Warm-up

How reflective has your teaching been lately? If you weren't in a practicum, would you be (so) reflective?

Throughout this book there has been an emphasis on reflective teaching as a means by which teachers can work, alone or with their students and colleagues, to develop their practice; some of these ideas and techniques appeared earlier, in Chapter 2. Without teachers who are able to engage in reflection, obviously a practicum could never foster teacher development. But as I have mentioned before, a practicum should not be the only period during a teacher's career in which a teacher develops.

The present book is intended to support a teaching practicum, but not just one that has only an immediate or short-term aspect. As I mentioned in the Introduction, it would be regrettable if there was only ever one time in a teacher's career when that teacher was helped to focus closely on their teaching. To forestall that, the present book is intended to improve teachers' command of skills and concepts that would foster long-term professional development, *as* they experience a practicum. In this light, as we come near to the end of any period of teaching practice, we should look forward to the next part of our teaching career, and ask, then, "Under what conditions apart from those of a formal practicum can teacher reflection and development best or most easily take place?"

Answers to this question may not necessarily be specific to ELT, EFL, or TESOL. ES/FL teaching has multiple contexts, of course – societal and cultural contexts, at least – and throughout this book I have emphasized the

180

language and cultural aspects of teaching practice that justify our reference to the literature of applied linguistics, educational linguistics, and second language studies, as well as the general literature of education. In this and the following chapter, which conclude the book, I move away from an immediate focus on what goes on inside the classroom, and lay out some ideas that contribute to, support, or in a sense, *surround* good (reflective) teaching practice; ideas which make the possibility of more than a short-term practicum conceivable in our future professional lives. The emphasis then, is less on practice, your own actual practice developed in a practicum, and more on how you might conceptualize the conditions for your future practice. These conditions, the contexts for reflective teaching and development, will be the institutional structures that surround us as teachers. To begin with, let's review the basic idea of reflective teacher development.

Concepts of reflective teaching

One of the earliest pieces of writing to appear in our literature that apprised the area of TESOL concerning the ideas of reflective teaching was Bartlett (1990). In his review of this material in one of the more substantial early collections dedicated to ES/FL teacher education, Bartlett sees the concept as becoming popular in the 1980s, and distinguishes a narrow form of reflection which views the classroom as not affected by social factors from a broader form of reflection, which he advocates.

The narrower version is associated with the work of Cruickshank (e.g., Cruickshank & Applegate, 1982) and even more so with the name of Schön (e.g., 1983). Bartlett (1990, p. 202) comments that "Cruickshank defines reflective teaching as the teacher's thinking about what happens in classroom lessons, and thinking about alternative means of achieving goals or aims." It involves "consider[ing] the teaching event thoughtfully, analytically and objectively (Cruickshank & Applegate, 1981, p. 4)." Similarly, Schön's version of the concept has been identified as individualistic. For example, Skrtic and Ware (1992, p. 208) remark,

he consistently characterizes reflection as a solitary act of volition, one in which the only discourse that takes place is between a practitioner and a problematic situation, a conversation in which "the situation talks back, the practitioner listens, and as he appreciates what he hears, he reframes the situation once again" (Schön, 1983, pp. 131–32).

Bartlett prefers a concept of reflecting on one's practice which involves both its social context, as well as matters of classroom technique. In this respect the intellectual lineage of this practice, associated with social critique and the role of teaching as improving society, goes back at least to educators such as John Dewey. Reflection, says Bartlett, "therefore has a double meaning. It involves the relationship between an individual's thought and action and the relationship between an individual teacher and his or her membership in a larger collective called society" (pp. 204–5).

I have asserted earlier the importance of one's colleagues in such a reflective process. This may be in the process of data gathering, or in coming up with solutions, or evaluating them – all areas in which some distancing or a second point of view, as well as some assistance with logistics, are likely to be highly desirable. Distance is necessary to reflect on aspects of our practice we may have become over-accustomed to. In addition, a critical, questioning, or skeptical friend can allow us to think over aspects of our practice that we have never thought to problematize. Bartlett provides a list of quite challenging questions, from which I here include a representative selection:

General questions
what counts as knowledge in second language teaching?
how is knowledge in language teaching organized?
whose interests are being served by the production and legitimation of this
    knowledge?

Specific questions
what does it mean to be a teacher? is the teacher I am the person I am?
where did the ideas I embody in second language teaching come from
    historically [and] how did I come to appropriate them?
whose interests do these ideas serve?
who has power in my classroom and how is it expressed?
what is the nature of knowledge that guides my teaching of content, who
    creates this knowledge [and] how did this knowledge emerge during the
    evolution of teaching?
what connections do I make with organizations outside the school … to
    demonstrate my active role in society?
do I wish to uncover the "hidden curriculum" – the inconsistencies – in my
    teaching?

Within the reflective process, following the collection of data pertinent to a particular aspect of practice upon which one is going to reflect, Bartlett identifies several key steps. The first is to interpret one's teaching by asking "what am I trying to do here?" – and Bartlett again stresses the importance of teachers seeing their practice as related to their participation as a citizen in society, asking themselves questions like "Are my purposes in selecting content intended to help develop a working citizen or an educated citizen or a person actively participating in a changing society?" (p. 211). The next step is "contesting," in which, says Bartlett, "we confront and perhaps begin to dislodge the complex system of reasons (theory) for our teaching actions" (p. 211). After these steps, it is necessary to think of changes to make and make them, as part of an ongoing cycle of development.[1]

Bartlett has aligned himself with those who see several levels of reflection, and is emphasizing the critical level. But I wonder whether institutions wish to see this degree of reflection among their teachers?[2] However, on the other hand, even to get educational institutions to support teacher reflection merely at the level of technique would be a major breakthrough in many if not most cases. The thrust of the present book has been to help you include in your reflective techniques a collaborative dimension and an awareness of the concept of the teacher development group as an informal support network operating independent of the institution(s) of its members. However, the responsibility for reflective, developmental practice should not be solely on the teachers' side. Possibilities have always existed, and sometimes manifest themselves, for educational institutions and systems to recognize their role in fostering teacher reflection and development. It is to that which I (shortly) turn.

FOR DISCUSSION

1. Do Bartlett's questions conform to your idea of reflection in teaching? Why, or why not?
2. Take two of Bartlett's questions and try to answer them in detail. (As ever, share your answers if possible.) This may assist with developing a broad conception of reflection; it may also assist if you are in the process of developing a philosophy of teaching.

School structure(s) supporting reflection and development

It has often been remarked that the typical teaching situation is one of isolation. The teacher development group is one attempt to respond to this, and, in breaking down isolation and opening up opportunities for peer discussion of practice, and thereby be a structure that supports reflection. Good interpersonal relations among teachers, i.e., "collegiality," are also needed for this. The social structures and systems of schools then, are potentially important to facilitate or inhibit reflection. Drawing conclusions from the general education literature on this topic for our own field, Freeman (1994, p. 188) comments,

> Schools and classrooms function as frameworks for interpretation in which certain actions and ways of being are valued and encouraged, while others are down played, ignored, and even silenced ... Learning how to negotiate these powerful environments is critical to becoming an effective teachers ... Often, because they are not adequately prepared for this environment, novice teachers can be defeated by it ... [T]he knowledge base of language teaching has [given] little or no attention ... to how schools function as systems, how power and meaning are sustained within them, and how teachers can act on those dynamics.

This recalls the concept of micropolitics touched on at the beginning of Chapter 5 and the skills of influencing one's colleagues referenced in Chapter 10. Freeman's point about the importance of seeing schools as systems which do or do not foster reflection should lead us to investigate in more detail what options face us, in schools and language programs. In the long run, if we have a choice about where to work, we may wish to choose a school whose administrative structure supports reflection and professional growth. If we do not have a choice, we may still try to work with administrations to make them more supportive of this sort of thing. There has been comparatively little direct study of the administrations of S/FL programs. Here I will draw on the remarks of theorists of educational administration Skrtic and Ware (1990) on schools as systems, supplemented with one of the few ELT-oriented discussions in this area, Davidson and Tesh (1997).

Around the world, schools in most countries are part of a hierarchical structure with power concentrated in the upper levels. Established patterns of school organization and management, perhaps in conjunction with larger social practices, result in the majority of these schools having formal arrangements which allow relatively little teacher input into school-wide policy. The words of one U.S. teacher engaged on a piece of reading research exemplify this:

> [In] the very act of doing the research, reflecting on my own practice ... I was often perplexed by a growing understanding of my personal inability to affect change and of the enormity of problems and circumstances over which I had no control. I did not set the staff development agenda; I was not a participant in curriculum decision making; I had no voice in determining policy; and I had no vehicle for influencing the messages about learning and literacy that students bring to school from home (Johnston, 1992, p. 35).

Major decision-making is in the hands of a principal, head, or (a more recent term) CEO – Chief Education Officer. Other bodies above the level of the principal, such as a board of governors, and so on, usually have additional authority.

Now this relatively hierarchical, nondemocratic system does not in itself necessarily mean that a school could not engage in professional development activities that go beyond the one-shot workshop, or foster collaborative reflection (see, for example, the case of state schools in Japan; Shimahara, 1995, 1998a). But it does suggest a system more likely to function as a bureaucracy, and thus one in which independent or professional action, and the reflection which supports it, are less likely to be valued or nurtured.

School organizational structures can be looked at in terms of the extent to which they provide for independent professional action, allow flexibility, foster reflection, and thereby development. Skrtic and Ware put this in terms of a three-part analysis, under the following headings: machine bureaucracy, professional bureaucracy, and adhocracy. The first of these is the classic bureaucracy of Weber,[3] a system in which the tasks to be done are repetitive and can be analyzed by the technocrats who set up the system; thereafter, workers following rules can almost without thinking accomplish what needs to be done. Because of its mechanical qualities, Skrtic & Ware refer to it as a "machine" bureaucracy, and Davidson and Tesh (1997, p. 178) call it the "mechanistic model." Moving one step away from this, a *professional* bureaucracy emerges when a bureaucratic organization does work that is "too complex to be rationalized, and thus too ambiguous to be standardized and formalized" (Skrtic & Ware, 1990, p. 210). Workers are trained intensively, becoming professionals, but specialize in different areas of work; clients are distributed across workers, and each professional works closely with clients but only loosely with fellow professionals.

I think the idea of a professional bureaucracy captures some of the key elements of the teacher's job and the systems within which many of us work. We do often have quite a lot of professional discretion, but at the same time we are not independent agents. We are not like the classic medical or legal professional – we do not "hang up our shingle" or put up our "brass plate"; we do not set up an office and deal with individuals each with their own idiosyncratic problems. On the contrary – we work in constraining hierarchical systems, and while it is true that we individualize our teaching somewhat, nevertheless there is a certain general category of client (student) that comes to us, whom we are competent or accustomed to dealing with. And though we do collaborate with colleagues within the same bureaucratic institution, we tend to do so somewhat distantly.

Skrtic and Ware assert that the overall system for managing even a *professional* bureaucracy tends to reflect "machine bureaucratic" ideas. Perhaps this is because educational administrators, though often once teachers them-selves, generally cease working with students in a primarily educative role, and instead may come to see both students and teachers in terms of the administrative system. In addition, when teachers become administrators, they naturally begin to reflect the pressures and practices of their superiors higher up in the educational-administrative hierarchy. Certainly in a number of countries and times, we find efforts to control and standardize teaching, a practice for which the term "de-professionalization" has been coined. At the same time, in some areas, we have seen the setting up of special programs for students with special needs (including ESL students), as the system (or its administrators) become less willing or capable of handling the diverse and unpredictable.

Srktic and Ware argue, and I find this plausible, that the bureaucratic el-ements in school are an important part of what militates against reflection. If standardization is the means by which efficiency is to be achieved, it is not necessary for workers to exercise discretion, creativity, analytic skills, and the ability to theorize in understanding new phenomena and problems in order to solve them. Therefore no space, time, or resources will be allo-cated to developing in workers (teachers) such abilities, which are seen as relatively uncalled for.

How could we describe a system in which workers really did need and develop these skills? Skrtic and Ware use the term "adhocracy": "a problem-solving organization configured to invent new programs" (p. 215). In it, workers (professionals) work together on teams with broad objectives, and as necessary they collaborate and adjust, with a need to talk things through and work together in which reflective thinking and a connection between theorizing and practicing are essential.

To some extent both the professional bureaucracy and the adhocracy are ways of dividing up what we get when we think of the mirror image of the machine bureaucracy. This conception – the likely opposite of the machine organization – was of interest to organization theorists of the 1960s, such as Likert (1967). A label for this kind of system is the "organic model" (Davidson & Tesh, 1997). Referring to what is obviously an ideal type (in the sense of not often fully realized in this world!), Davidson and Tesh describe it as

the one that maximizes flexibility and adaptability, encourages complete confidence and trust between superiors and subordinates. . . . Communication flows in all directions, both vertically and laterally. Teamwork is substantial, and decision making and control functions are shared widely throughout the organization. Training resources provided by the organization are outstanding as they seek to build upon the value and worth of each employee. The organic organization seeks to provide a supportive environment in which human resources are valued and personal growth and responsibility are stressed (p. 180).

Davidson and Tesh feel that at least to some extent, however, aspects of the organic model can be found in language teaching programs.[4] Certainly, in smaller, free-standing S/FL teaching programs, there has to be teacher flexibility, simply because a small staff must adapt to cope with changing market demands. For this reason, in such programs, Davidson and Tesh believe we are likely to find "a range of professional development activities [encouraged] for each faculty member" (p. 180). By their very nature, those programs in the private sector may well be autonomous – they do not have to grapple with several layers of control and multiple stakeholders. Also, the emphasis on lateral communication results in "cooperative teaching, peer coaching and observation, and joint writing and piloting of new materials" (ibid.). Obviously, these things are very much consistent with the sort of processes I have emphasized as fostering professional development and reflective practice, earlier in this book. Finally, Davidson and Tesh say that the organic model leads to programs valuing teamwork and establishing systems, typically committees, so that "decision making and control functions are shared widely throughout the program" (ibid.).

However, looking at the actual instructional resources of programs, no one model is best under all circumstances. The kind of programs Davidson and Tesh are oriented to sometimes have a large contingent of part-time or not fully-trained and qualified teachers in them. In that case, the demands on the teacher implied by the organic model, or the more adhocratic model, cannot be satisfied. The more that a program is staffed by full-time, graduate degree-holding specialists, the more a highly flexible, devolved, adhocratic model ought to be possible, on the other hand.

While the specialized world of Intensive English Programs may throw up some examples where there is such an array of well-qualified specialists mainly dealing with volunteer adult students, we may ask ourselves whether other parts of the ES/FL teaching world, with different resources and challenges, can equally well support organic models or adhocracies, however. Where might we find such schools? And if we can't find them, can we at least figure out what conditions would facilitate their emergence?

Shifts in school organization, or coexistence?

It is tempting, when considering alternatives in education, to assume that the present is better than the past and that because of progress the future will be better still. Or, in some more conservative traditions,[5] the past was a golden age, and we should look backward for inspiration. However, historical research in educational systems suggests that schools (in some cultures) have demonstrated remarkable stability over time (e.g., Cuban, 1993). In that case, we should be wary of simply looking to a particular era, whether past or present, for examples of what we would like to argue for. Our different models may coexist, or they may be found in this culture at this time, and in that culture at another time.

With that caveat, then, let me mention that in the present era, there *are* schools which show favorable organizational characteristics. These have sometimes been termed "collegial schools" (Little, 1987; cf. e.g. Sharan, Shachar, & Levine, 1999). In recent developments of research on this, Sykes (1999) draws on the work of the Center on Organization and Restructuring of Schools (CORS) to focus on schools which exhibit "school-wide professional community." This concept is defined as having five components: "shared norms and values," "reflective dialog," "deprivatization of practice," "school-wide focus on student learning," and "collaboration." In their multisite study of (U.S.) schools, CORS researchers observed that these characteristics of professional reflective practice are supported by the following structural factors: small school size, few programs requiring specialized staffing, and in particular, school autonomy. This is salient in the areas of creating programs, selecting staff, organizing staff development around local needs, and having schedules and workplaces that themselves encourage dialogue. While similar examples can be found outside of the country studied in this work, most state schools, it is widely agreed, do not manifest this sort of autonomy.

Apart from identifying actual examples, and again recognizing the dangers of looking for trends, are there any current patterns of change that might be of interest in this discussion? My answer is a tentative "yes," as follows. Because many state educational systems in pluralistic societies are, like the state itself, contested sites of political struggle, they encounter a continual series of reform efforts, which are often disguised efforts at control by one or another of the power players: political parties, teachers, unions, administrators, business representatives, and ethnic groups. From the 1980s on, in a number of developed countries[6] there were signs of a reform movement concerning public sector education. Though it seems to be a mixed bag of trends, some of them might be favorable to the topic of this chapter.

These reforms are associated with the term "school-based management" (SBM) (see, inter alia, Ogawa, 1994). Other terms used include "site-based management," "school-community based management (SCBM)," "charter schools," "local management of schools," "self-governing schools," "decentralized management," and "school-site autonomy." The common characteristic of such schools is that there is "some sort of representative decision-making council at the school, which may share authority with the principal or be merely advisory" (David, 1995, p. 6). Reasons advanced for schools to move to SBM have been that it will (a) increase student achievement, (b) increase local control of education, (c) trade increased school autonomy for increased accountability to the state, (d) provide a political reform (democratization), and (e) increase efficiency by decentralizing and deregulating so that teachers can do the job they have been professionally trained to do.

The core of SBM is participatory decision-making concerning a broad range of educational policy matters affecting each individual school, taking place at the school site itself. To be effective, this requires a well thought out committee structure, but in addition, enabling leadership. (This can include shared leadership, which can continue even in the absence of "official" leaders.) Furthermore, those involved in SBM suggest that long-term commitment from higher levels of administration, at district or even national level, is necessary.

A major problem in introducing SBM in established state schools is that the various groups or individuals involved may have no history of working together collaboratively. Equally, they are extremely unlikely to have had any training in working together in a democratic way. In practice, where SBM has been introduced, changes associated with it have often been rushed into place with little opportunities for learning and assistance. Educational personnel in SBM sites may have greater needs for skills of interprofessional facilitation and mediation; but explicit training in these matters is usually not part of teacher education, and years of largely individual professional practice within a hierarchical structure may have frozen into place working habits that are less useful under the new system. In addition, because of the effect of hierarchical administrative structures above the school level, schools themselves may have inadequate access to information such as budget and performance data which are needed for good site-based decision-making.

My primary reason for being hopeful about SBM in the present discussion is that providing schools with increased autonomy, particularly in terms of being separate from the administrative levels that previously supplied or organized in-service training, logically implies greater school-based responsibility for professional development, probably to be provided at the school site level itself. If this organizational change goes together with dissatisfaction with established models of in-service training, it could manifest itself in greater demand for the sort of professional development alternatives discussed earlier.

Unfortunately, there are also reasons for not being too optimistic about the utility to ES/FL teachers of SBM as implemented in reality, rather than as an ideal. First, the extent to which this is a global trend is questionable (cf. Green, 1997). For the time being it is probably only happening in the richer countries of Europe, North America, Australia, and New Zealand. Second, there are the low-level implementation problems I have mentioned. Third, it may be hard to strike a good balance between accountability and autonomy (cf. Whitty, Power, & Halpin, 1998).

That last point deserves a little explanation. In introducing a new "management by objectives" approach, an administrator might say to an employee, "I don't care what you do in detail; I simply want you to achieve these objectives, and I will monitor your achievement of them, not the methods you use to attain them. But of course, don't spend too much." Thus government authorities in some countries (cf. New Zealand Ministry of Education, 1988; UK govt., 1988) devolved control of the hiring or firing of teachers, and detailed control of budget, to local authorities and schools, while stepping up inspection and specification of curriculum at the national level. SBM-oriented changes, which have these sorts of characteristics, have been viewed with suspicion (e.g., Smyth, 1993). This sort of tension comes out in the remarks of Seeberg et al. (1998, p. 277), who first say that "Decentralized school districts, as enforced by the United States Supreme Court, particularly since 1974 give the technoeconomic bifurcation of American society its racial, income, and locational character." Critics thus blame some extremely unpleasant societal characteristics on decentralization of financial support for schools. These authors go on, however, to recognize that SBM, particularly that which is locally initiated, at the level of city or province, can lead to reforms that favor equity and pluralism. They provide as their example of "multicultural and equitable" reform "the city of Chicago [which] has been undergoing system reorganization through site-based management of schools" (p. 278).

A recent prominent survey of organizational matters in schools accounts for the remarkably small amount of change in this area, alluded to earlier, by depicting the area as characterized by a large number of forces in almost balanced tension. In particular, Ogawa, Crowson, and Goldring (1999) propose that so long as any set of professionals, like teachers, are to work in an organization that shares resources, responsibilities, and (supposedly) goals, there will be an unresolvable dilemma between centralizing and decentralizing forces. If this is largely correct, there is no reason to believe that we are moving altogether to a period of greater professional autonomy. However, I wonder if in a time of pushing and pulling we may not find opportunities for greater flexibility at the lower levels favoring teacher development groups, or other arrangements that would support a reflective perspective, and an orientation to long-term professional development.

FOR DISCUSSION

1. In your work experience so far, whether in teaching or elsewhere, have you ever been part of any of the three kinds of bureaucracy that are described above? On what basis do you assign the organization you worked in to one of those categories? Do you think those various categories could co-exist within the same school?
2. The discussion of school structures has concerned state schools exclusively (because of a lack of empirically-based studies on this topic of proprietary S/FL schools). From your experience or observation, what special characteristics might be found in the organizational structure of private, "proprietary," S/FL schools? How would this foster (or not) reflective teaching?
3. Why might democratic school structures support reflective teaching?
4. If you are familiar with countries or areas other than those mentioned above as involved in SBM-type developments, can you comment on the extent to which school structures in these areas are or are not exclusively hierarchical or nonparticipatory? Are you aware of specific sites with an orientation to professional development and reflective teaching?

12 Putting It Together and Starting Again – Another Model

- What sort of model would help me integrate my views of professional ES/FL practice thus far?
- In what form can I, as a teacher, present my current stage of development and accumulated experience to others?

Warm-up

Before reading further, sketch a diagram that shows the factors and conditions that foster your development as a teacher – both those that you have, and those you need but don't have. They could be social as well as psychological, at least.

In my experience, facilitating teacher development isn't easy. Among other difficulties is the reflexive nature of the job: the teacher educator has to present an excellent model of teaching practice in order to be credible when talking about teaching practice (while being closely observed by more than usually sensitive and well-informed "student" teachers)! Insofar as the present book should itself demonstrate good pedagogical practice, there needs to be a well-structured, clear, and *not rushed* concluding section to the "lesson." And it should support the overall goals of the lesson, and enable those participating in it to go away clear in their minds concerning what has been accomplished, and clear, too, on what "homework" or preparation for the next "lesson" needs to be done. A tall order, maybe; or rather old-fashioned sounding. More innovative or participatory approaches might involve the students more directly, asking *them* to summarize, perhaps. And of course, from a teacher development group perspective, there is no need for a "teacher educator" – teachers working together can serve as well. Nevertheless, as current group discussion leader, I will take responsibility, first, for a summary review, by way of another model that attempts to pull together some key concepts I have reviewed. I will then ask you to review what you have learned or gained from the experience.

Finally, one clear product that can arise out of a period of extended reflection is a teacher portfolio. This will be the subject of the final section.

Summary model-based review

Some years ago, Colton and Sparks-Langer (1993) presented a conceptual framework related to teacher development, based on their own extended practice as teacher educators (see Fig. 12-1) . It brings together many of the ideas and positions I have outlined in this book, and I discuss it here as a form of review, with the hope that it can serve as a mnemonic device for much of what we have covered. At the same time, it has its limitations,[1] and it will be up to the reader to extend and supplement it, replacing and adding elements as necessary. I think, as with some of the simpler models presented earlier in the book, it is something we can effectively react or respond to.

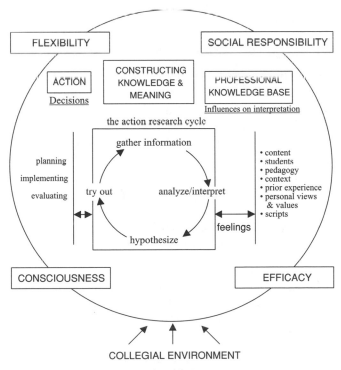

Fig. 12-1

For brevity, I will refer to it as the CSL model. (I have adapted it slightly for ease of presentation.)

Elements of the model

At the core of the model lies a sophisticated version of the action research cycle.[2] Here the model exemplifies a position that I articulated early in this material: that it is important to see teachers as actively involved in constructing knowledge and making meaning, through their own actions (that is, not being mere receivers of knowledge, whether pedagogical or concerning content/subject matter). And similarly, it is important to see teachers as constructing knowledge, that is, theorizing, about their practice, as opposed to engaged in an unconsidered, pretheoretical, and "intuitive" or "unconscious" set of procedures.

The authors describe the processes involved as follows:

First, the teachers are personally involved in a specific experience and choose to attend to some aspect of the experience. The teachers collect information about the experience from many possible areas including curriculum, students, school policies, and community interests.

Next the teachers begin to analyze the information gathered to develop mental representations – or theories – that help them interpret the situation at hand.

At this point, they suggest that teachers consult the professional knowledge base. This is done in two ways: "collaborative dialogue and professional readings" (p. 49). On the first, they comment, "New internal patterns of thinking are initiated externally through dialogue with a more skilled or knowledgeable individual." This is certainly common for the less experienced teacher. The more experienced teacher may simply need a peer teacher to bounce ideas off of or to use as a sounding board. It is quite probably the case that this, rather than directly accessing the professional literature, is how many if not most S/FL teachers proceed (Crookes & Arakaki, 1999). Nevertheless, as Colton and Sparks-Langer say, "Interaction with professional readings can lead to new patterns of thought" (p. 49). They comment,

Teachers' metacognitive scripts guide the reflections, questions, and considerations made when acquiring new information. As a result of this "exploratory experimentation" (Schön, 1983, 1987) – examination of the situation from multiple perspectives before making a decision – teachers may develop and use new and creative solutions.

Again it is important to notice that Colton and Sparks-Langer depict the teacher as using the professional literature as one of *several* sources of ideas, one viewed, perhaps skeptically, or at least not slavishly. And again, this is the position I exemplified when drawing on the remarks of Donna Johnson earlier. Naturally, I hope teachers will continue to consult the professional literature of the field as they go on in their careers. A position toward it that is neither dismissive nor slavish is what is needed.

Moving on, such teachers "develop possible hypotheses to explain the events and guide further action. They mentally test each hypothesis for its short-term effects and for its long-term social, moral and intellectual consequences." The inclusion of social and moral considerations is in line with the discussions presented earlier in this book. Teachers' recognition of their actions in these terms is crucial, else their work will be nothing more than wage labor, or a purely commercial transaction. Then action is taken and the cycle repeats itself. The cycle is set within broader action categories (to the left of the diagram): planning, implementation, and evaluation, which relate to the delivery of classroom instruction (as we have discussed earlier) in terms of curriculum and program.

The cycle is also supported by various categories of the professional knowledge base, which influence how a teacher interprets a particular teaching situation. In these areas, the model specifies content, students, pedagogy, and context; a division attributable to the influential work of Shulman (1987). The first concerns teachers' knowledge of the material being taught — in our case, primarily language and culture. This we have taken for granted in the present course of study. However, the second relates to a teacher's knowledge of the students themselves, as learners of a particular age, deriving beliefs and values from a culture, and having preferred ways of acting and learning. Here I have emphasized the importance of us, as teachers, being also investigators of our students' learning culture. I have referred to familiarity with students as crucial to teaching expertise. The third category, pedagogy, as in the present book is divided into "generic methods and theories applicable to any subject area" (p. 47), and that which is subject-specific (with which we have not been concerned in this work). Fourth in this group, context, "includes time of day, the cultural backgrounds ... of the community, and school, district and regional politics. What works in one situation," the authors comment, "may not work in another." Indeed — and hence the importance of finding out about "ethnopedagogies" and not ignoring the sociopolitical dimension particularly if we are teacher-guests in another culture.

Our model-builders have added to Shulman's original four components of the knowledge base for teaching three others. One's own prior experiences as a human being and teacher provide a storehouse of knowledge about past successful and unsuccessful actions, as well as a source for attempting to understand the situation from the students' point of view; and so Colton and Sparks-Langer wish to privilege rather than ignore this valuable personal element in teachers' knowledge. I have taken the position in the present work that it is important for us, as developing teachers, to review our "apprenticeship of observation" and to think over the teaching we were exposed to, and the institutions we were in, during our most impressionable years. Are we still acting out the scripts we were socialized into? As teachers, our personal histories are important, even if much of the professional literature of SL studies or applied linguistics does not operate from that perspective.

Relatedly, a teacher's social and personal values cannot be dismissed as irrelevant to teaching practice; a position I've advocated all through. Finally, an unusual but important emphasis is put on metacognitive scripts. The authors mention first that it is because we as teachers have well worked out scripts for classroom practice that we can concentrate sometimes on higher level, more demanding aspects of classroom practice (such as handling a classroom management problem simultaneous with delivering on-going content instruction). I have earlier referred to this with the term "automatization" – it is an essential aid to teaching, though it is also a danger if overly relied upon. The second aspect of this area of "scripts" also relates to automatization. Given the pace of most teaching days, we will be unable to reflect on our practice unless we routinize reflection, building it into our work and perhaps, as Colton and Sparks-Langer imply, develop a regular checklist of "the questions reflective teachers ask themselves to analyze a situation and plan the next course of action" (p. 47). One might compare this with the questions Bartlett has posed us (in Chapter 11), at a higher level of critical reflection, too. I hope that this period of study has heightened your reflective abilities.

The input of all these matters into the ongoing reflection and action research process is mediated by an element in the diagram labeled "feelings." Colton and Sparks-Langer observe, correctly I think, that "feelings have a huge influence on our ability to reflect – to interpret and respond to a situation" (p. 48). This is not intended to imply that feelings should be screened out, as somehow incompatible with rational reflection. Such a view is antihuman, and responsible for impoverished self-understanding, not to mention impoverished theories of human cognition. The integration of emotion and thought in more recent work on how we understand our worlds is one of the more productive trends in recent psychology and philosophy (see e.g., Damasio, 1994; Tallon, 1997; Turski, 1994).

The reflective and exploratory processes at the heart of the model require personal and social support. The former is subsumed under four headings, personal attributes, that Colton and Sparks-Langer take from the work of Costa and Garmston (1988; theorists encountered earlier in the section on lesson planning): efficacy, flexibility, social responsibility, and consciousness. The first is equivalent to believing one can make a difference. The second is broadly applicable – the teacher's improvisational skills, lack of dogmatism, and ability to see the other's perspective. Third is social responsibility. In the context of the United States that Colton and Sparks-Langer operate in, this is interpreted by them with reference to valuing democracy and encouraging "socially responsible actions in their students" (p. 50). Whether or not a teacher has any allegiance to democracy, however that broad term is understood, and whether or not such an allegiance could have a meaningful manifestation in all countries, I still think this attribute is important, because it implies or requires that teachers see their action not only within a given social context but having a moral and sociopolitical dimension. Fourth, consciousness: "the awareness of one's own thinking and decision making. Reflective teachers can explain to other professionals their reasoning behind given actions." Colton and Sparks-Langer decry what they call "intuitive teaching."[3] Teachers can teach, and teach well, without always being able to articulate what they are doing or the basis for their decisions, *but* an exclusive adherence to this form of practice can be of limited service to the rest of the profession. Other teachers will find it hard to learn from, and the individual who operates in this way will find it hard to reflect, and thereby develop, as a teacher. A counter-measure, here, is the teacher development group. Articulating one's practice with others supports these aspects of the teacher, providing a greater sense of efficacy, potentially defusing dogmatism (through engagement with other positions), and heightening consciousness.

Yet these personal attributes alone would leave all the burden on the individual teacher, and the lack of development in teachers and teaching systems around the world is, to my mind, directly attributable to the individualist culture that has grown up around school teaching in many areas (even in otherwise more collective cultures). My own personal history does not allow me to believe that change in social systems, whether schools, cultures, or countries, takes place primarily through the acts of isolated individuals (nor as a result of impersonal economic forces). Rather, it is networks, movements, collectives, and the force of men and women who undertake to work together for change, that turns the tides of ignorance and inequity against which many struggle and in which many drown each day. What this means for us as teachers is, among other things, the importance of a "collegial environment." Those rather comfortable words refer to conditions in which colleagues work together to "nurture thoughtful practice";

this we reviewed in Chapter 10. It also refers to the conditions for long-term reflective practice, covered in Chapter 11; "the system" in which teachers work has a lot to answer for.

This model, and your own

So this is a fairly comprehensive model, at least with reference to the present work. However, models or frameworks like the one I have presented here are obviously the selective construction of individuals who themselves have histories, values, and possibly even prejudices. They are not intended as empirically testable theory, but rather, to serve heuristic functions: in this case, to highlight aspects of teaching which the authors, like me, think are important, as well as present a structure by means of which they can be interrelated. They can also be used as "ammunition." The mere fact that one has a model of apparently adequate sophistication can aid in the search for funding of a program or project to which it relates. Colton and Sparks-Langer built a useful program of teacher education around theirs. And if you, the reader, are a "teacher-under-construction," you may wish to consider whether you too could make good ammunition, for an employment interview or portfolio, from your own framework, model, or philosophy of ES/FL teaching. It is important, I think, not to get too complex, but a framework of some kind surely can help us figure out what we think is important, and even what it is we still have to work on, as we continue the process of self-construction or reconstruction, as teachers.

FOR DISCUSSION

1. How does the Colton and Sparks-Langer framework relate to those presented earlier in this book?
2. What's missing, in your view, from the Colton and Sparks-Langer framework or what would you like to add to it? How would you modify it? What alterations are necessary if it is to be applied in an EFL context?
3. Looking back on what you have learned through the practicum, identify some of the key ways in which you think you have changed. What brought about those changes? In what ways do you think your development will continue after the practicum?

The teacher portfolio

Throughout this book, I have been emphasizing the bringing to consciousness of matters tacit, and the conscious development of models and conceptions of one's practice. As we conclude, temporarily, a period of heightened attention to practice, what should be done with what was conscious (besides returning it to unconsciousness)? One constructive response is to integrate it within a "teacher portfolio."

In the course of a couple of decades at most, the idea that professional teachers should have a portfolio, which in some ways represents their work as a teacher, has moved from being a fairly fringe idea to being very popular in some parts of the teaching world. Now, in education, as in some parts of the professions (such as architecture, or elsewhere, as in photography or modeling), practitioners will often gather together samples of their work, as well as credentials, statements of support, and the like.

One reason why a teacher might wish to develop a portfolio is because, as is widely recognized, a Certificate or qualification often doesn't do an adequate job of representing one's professional capabilities. Many an administrator has been known to utter some variation of "s/he has the degree, but can s/he teach?" One other general thrust for teacher portfolios may have been the combination of pressure for teacher certification via national- or state-mandated assessment practices in the United States, coupled with the move toward alternative, more realistic forms of assessment (besides discrete-point testing) in the classroom. Portfolios in student assessment became a popular initiative slightly before being advanced in the teacher education sphere, but a similar logic surrounds teacher portfolios as does student portfolios – we need methods of and bases for assessment that represent in a more realistic way the actual domains of practice that are being assessed.

In the United States, during the late 1980s, a government-funded project set up the National Board for Professional Teaching Standards, which further advanced teacher portfolios (Lyons, 1998). A definition proposed by one of those involved, Stanford University academic Lee Shulman, is widely quoted:

A teaching portfolio is the structured documentary history of a (carefully selected) set of coached or mentored accomplishments substantiated by samples of student work and fully realized only through reflective writing, deliberation, and serious conversation (1988, p. 36).

Writing with the TESOL professional in mind, Wolfe-Quintero and Brown (1998, p. 24) define the portfolio as

a purposeful collection of any aspects of a teacher's work that tells the story of the teacher's efforts, skills, abilities, achievements, and contributions to his/her students, colleagues, institution, academic discipline, or community.

Shulman's definition seems to reflect the teacher educator's view more, with its emphasis on mentoring and coaching; perhaps that of Wolfe-Quintero and Brown is more free-standing.

Why might you need a teacher portfolio?

One reason you might need a portfolio is purely pragmatic: you may need to submit one as part of a job application or as part of a periodic teacher evaluation exercise. Even from the brief discussion presented thus far, it should be obvious that a teacher portfolio allows a potentially vivid presentation of the results of teachers' experience; in that respect a portfolio allows a defense against the increasing availability of high academic qualifications in TESOL professionals – the less experienced job candidate may have higher academic qualifications than the more experienced candidate, and in the absence of a portfolio, perhaps some administrators will take, or be forced to take, the candidate whose formal qualifications are higher.

The second general reason I would advance has a less Machiavellian tinge: it may be professionally satisfying, and might contribute to the further development of various aspects of professional knowledge discussed earlier in this book, for a teacher to develop a record that documents improvements in performance and professional knowledge, and which by its nature asks them to provide documentary justification for their practice.

What's in a teacher portfolio?

The following list is from Wolfe-Quintero and Brown (p. 27):

1. A cover letter . . .
2. An updated résumé . . .
3. A statement of your teaching philosophy, including discussions of:
   a. the theoretical underpinnings of your belief system and how your belief system affects materials selection, teaching strategies, and classroom management.
   b. a description of what you actually do in the classroom, why doing things that way benefits your students, and how you know when teaching strategies are working well.
4. Samples of your work, including: a videotaped class . . . syllabi . . . tests . . . students' work . . . your feedback . . . original materials . . .
5. Selected comments from evaluations or observations of your teaching . . .

6. Other items: letters of recommendation, thank-you letters from students or colleagues, awards or certificates, pictures of classroom activities, [and] whatever best represents your professional abilities and accomplishments.

Most items in a portfolio will need interpretation for the reader, as Brown and Wolfe-Quintero make clear. Thus the cover letter itself should explain the purpose and organization of the portfolio. The examples of your work will need supporting documents, which might include a lesson plan but also some indication of the extent to which the lesson is typical, and your comments on it. Not all teachers make test-writing an integral part of their practice, but if you include a test as a portfolio item, the reader would benefit from an indication about how this specific test reflects your views about assessment and grading. Similarly, students' work is not necessarily informative on its own, and commentary that relates it to your teaching would be appropriate. Similarly, comments from evaluations or observations should be placed in context and remarks from the teacher concerning how s/he interprets or responds to the comments would be helpful. The overall thrust of commentary may depend on how a teacher intends or believes the portfolio will be used on a given occasion.[4]

YOU TRY IT...

If you have already developed a portfolio, share it with your peers. If you have not yet done so, begin the process. Using Wolfe-Quintero and Brown's list of headings – which do you already have, or have material for? Which are going to be difficult or take time to acquire or develop?

Envoi

With the idea of a complex model of your views on teaching to be (re)constructed, and a teaching portfolio under way or under revision, this is by no means the end for your period of heightened reflection and teacher development. However, we are here coming to the physical conclusion of this book (more or less). The Colton and Sparks-Langer model should be "grist to the mill" of your own reflective model-making minds. I hope that it together with what has gone before will be of use to you as you continue the never-ending process of teacher development. Your philosophy of teaching statement can be a powerful centerpiece in the portfolio that will serve as a continuing and growing record of your work and your professional orientation.

Going forward, the path for ES/FL teachers and their schools is not particularly clear at the time of writing. Pundits have been alluding to an increased pace of change in the world for a long time. Is it really the case, or does it just seem that way? Will it be the case that S/FL teachers will have to continuously retool, and if so, will the skills they have honed through a practicum continue to be of service, even if transferred from the classroom to a virtual medium through information technology? Will schools finally begin to change under these and other pressures, or will they continue to resist? My view is that they badly do need to change. I hope that readers of this book will be active in trying to shift these dinosaurs in a direction that would facilitate teacher development at least; shifting it from being a solitary burden to something shared and supported. Perhaps for that to happen, teachers with a change orientation need to take steps to secure positions of influence. But that is a matter for a different stage in the careers of most readers of this book, perhaps. And perhaps it is a story for a different book. . . . S/FL teaching, and schools, still do not get the respect they deserve given the importance of what they do. We cannot afford to be complacent and we must not shut our eyes to the difficulties. It seems to me that professionals cannot really develop unless *the profession* develops. Let us commit ourselves to a form of teaching that will move toward that end.

FOR DISCUSSION

What lies in your future? How can you make S/FL teaching a rewarding profession that has fewer frustrations, in your lifetime?

Appendix A
Teacher Development Groups: Growth Through Cooperation

Katrina Oliphant

Throughout the body of this text, I have continually stressed the importance of teachers helping teachers, and I have in a number of places discussed the concept of the teacher development group. Throughout I take for granted that this sort of thing is needed if teachers are to move forwards efficiently and with speed in their professional development. Accordingly, in this appendix further detail on this vital topic is provided. This appendix was originally written as a term paper on the topic by one of my students, and I am most grateful to the author, Katrina Oliphant, for allowing me to include it here.

Graham Crookes

Introduction

As an experienced EFL teacher working toward a Master's degree in my area, I often pondered the career choices that would be available to me upon completion of my program. Having made the commitment to professional development implicit in my decision to return to university, I hoped to find a position in an EFL setting that would nurture my desire for continued growth as a teacher. But how realistic was that prospect? My experience had shown me that many schools are indifferent to teacher development; in fact, they often hire teachers with no qualifications. Profit, rather than the quality of teaching, guides their decision-making. As long as their students continue to accept unqualified (and thus low-paid) teachers, such schools have no motivation to hire professionals who will demand higher salaries.

I believe that the majority of ES/FL teachers have no choice but to look outside the school environment for opportunities to further their development. While there are many activities that can be done on one's own, such as attending conferences, keeping abreast of ESOL literature, and researching one's own class, the typical harried teacher, who may hold down a variety of part-time jobs, may just not make the time for them. What then is the answer? I believe joining forces with other like-minded teachers is the solution. The motivation, stimulation, and pleasure that can be lacking in a solitary quest for professional growth can be found in the formation of a teacher development group.

In the field of education, the concept of teachers coming together to foster personal and professional growth is well-documented, though discussions of this are rare in the ESOL literature.[1] Such groups go by many different names, which often reflect the focus of the group, e.g. "collegial support groups," "personal effectiveness groups," "teacher development groups," "teacher study groups," "teacher support groups" or "teams," "teacher groups," "teachers' learning cooperatives," "teachers' networks" and "teachers' support networks." I will use the terms "teachers' groups," "teacher networks," and "teacher development groups" interchangeably to encompass all groups working toward teachers' growth.

Purposes

The reasons given for organizing teacher networks generally fall into two main categories: (a) emotional support and (b) professional support and growth. As personal and professional issues are very often interrelated, the intent may be to focus on both areas.

For many of the groups, which have formed in order to give personal support to their members, an important issue is burnout, which can be defined as "some degree of physical, emotional, and attitudinal exhaustion related to occupational stress" (Kirk & Walter, 1981). Factors often influencing burnout are "feelings of isolation, loneliness, and lack of support" (Kirk & Walter, 1981). Isolation is a problem inherent in most teaching situations as "(t)he combination of the self-contained classroom and a heavy teaching schedule gives teachers few opportunities to share common problems or sustain an intellectual life" (Boyer, 1983 , cited in Armour, 1985). The term "alienation" can be used to describe the situation in which many teachers find themselves. The lack of control over curriculum design, the obligation to perform administrative (as opposed to teaching) duties, the lack of interaction with other teachers, as well as time and economic pressures all contribute to this state of alienation, a relationship of undesirable separation between people and their working environment.

The feeling of being isolated from other teachers is compounded by the gulf that often exists between teaching staff and school administration. Some teachers hope to diminish the sense of separateness between the two by encouraging administrators to join their groups. In one case (Joyce et al., 1989), a school district formed teacher study groups in which administrators were active, with the belief "that the development of shared understandings would develop vertical and horizontal social cohesiveness, thereby reducing administrator-teacher divisions while increasing cooperation between classrooms and teams of teachers."

The interconnectedness of personal and professional concerns are clear in the feelings of isolation and/or alienation experienced by many teachers. The difficulties encountered in their jobs negatively affect their state of mind. For the expatriate EFL teacher, faced with the additional problems related to functioning within a different culture, the feeling of isolation may be even more acute.

Many teachers define their purpose for creating a network as enhancing professional growth or support, which can be manifested in a variety of ways depending on the needs of the group. For example, a very specific type of professional support was sought by the teachers both in the "writing support program for junior faculty women," which Gainen (1993) describes, and in the high school English teachers writing group, which Flythe (1989) organized: to aid the teachers in producing writing for publication. (Once again the line between personal and professional support is hazy. Gainen states that the support the group offers "may serve to quell self-doubts and strengthen hard-won, but sometimes fragile professional identities.") The purpose of some other groups is related to the study and practice of a certain approach – "whole language" in the case of Watson and Bixby's support group (1994). To others it involves the teaching of a specific skill, which for Armour's network was writing (1985). Recent years have seen the growth of the teacher research movement, in which groups of teachers seek professional growth through their own research (Schecter & Ramirez, 1992).

Logistics

Once an ES/FL teacher has decided to start a group, there is the question of logistics. Who should join? How can potential members be found? How many members is optimal? Where can meetings be held? How long should they last and how often should they take place? Exploring the answers others have given to these questions can be helpful when faced with the challenge of organizing one's own network.

Member selection

The goals one has in mind when forming the group will help determine the types of members to seek out. Kirk and Walter (1981) distinguish between "topical" groups, which are primarily concerned with a specific topic, and groups formed according to membership criteria, such as teachers of the same grade:

Membership should be considered a key ingredient in the potential success of the group. The ability to identify with each other enhances the group's productivity potential. If the group is too divergent, the members may need to spend valuable time educating each other in the idiosyncrasies of their divergent tasks and the various organizational structures. On the other hand, an overly homogenous group may serve to inhibit the breadth and general scope of discussion. For these reasons, it is better to consider both criteria to attempt to include teachers in the organization who have somewhat similar tasks yet to include a broad interpersonal base that will enable topical variety. This will then tend to stimulate a more interesting and thus more functional group experience.

The advantages and disadvantages of homogeneity should be carefully weighed. Should teachers of other age groups be asked to join? How is the balance between local teachers and expatriates? Would it be beneficial, for example, for teachers in an international elementary school to join a group with teachers from private adult language schools? Should school administrators be encouraged to join?

Finding members

Several methods of finding members have been offered in the literature:

- Give a "well-advertised short course with practical sessions offering concrete solutions for classroom problems." At the end, give the teachers who attend a questionnaire regarding interest in further meetings (Wolff & Vera, 1989).
- Call two other teachers who share similar values about teaching and have them call others (Watson & Bixby, 1994).
- "Start with a few people and attract new members by word of mouth so that the group grows slowly" (Wolff & Vera, 1989).
- Obtain a list of teachers who have attended local workshops or conferences and send them letters soliciting their participation (Armour, 1985).
- Put up notices in staff rooms in local schools.

Group size

How many members should the ideal group have? Kirk and Walter (1981) maintain that the ideal number is between five and eight, because "(t)oo many members make it easy for some shy or inhibited members to blend into the background and possibly evolve into dissatisfied and/or angry group members." They believe that smaller groups allow "flexibility of time schedules, greater potential participation for group members, and generally, a higher level of group cohesion." Large groups, on the other hand, draw from "a wealthier fund of information and sharing," but, because of their size, "limit the amount of time for individual sharing and the generally more personal quality of discussion."

Before forming a group, one should consider the benefits of a small one versus a large one. When the initial group has been formed the members may want to consider limiting membership. Wolff and Vera (1989) suggest the possibility of a compromise: Teachers can form a large group, which breaks up into subgroups, with the meetings taking place more frequently within the smaller group context.

Meeting place and time

Watson and Bixby (1994) suggest meeting in "a home, a school, a restaurant, [or] a church." The important point is that it be a safe, comfortable, neutral place, which is relatively convenient for all of the group members. Will there be interruptions from children, phones, and so forth, if a member's home is chosen? Is rotating homes a possibility? If meeting at a school is an option, will the teachers feel in any way inhibited? Kirk and Walter (1981) discourage "marathon" meetings, while Armour's group prefers their meetings to last for three or four hours (including dinner). Once again the amount of time to dedicate to a session depends on the time constraints of the individuals in the group. Teachers with small children may not be able to meet for extended periods of time, or they may prefer to have long meetings once a month.

Goals

Once the group has been formed and the meeting time and place have been established, the issue of the group's goals must be addressed. General aims will have been set by the organizers, but these can be renegotiated by the whole group at the first meetings. If the group members do not know each other, they may want to work toward short-term goals that can be achieved within a limited time frame (Wolff & Vera, 1989). At the end of an initial period, the teachers can evaluate the group's progress and set new and perhaps longer-term objectives. Will there be a specific focus, for example, becoming classroom researchers, or learning about a specific teaching approach? Or will the goals be broader, such as "encouraging student autonomy and cooperation" or "breaking away from traditional teacher roles" (Plumb, 1988)?

Organization

Groups can be structured in a variety of ways. In many of the school-based groups, facilitators lead the meetings. The first important question to think of when organizing a teachers' group is whether or not there will be facilitators or leaders. Kirk and Walter (1981) advocate a democratic approach, and suggest avoiding groups "if there is a self-appointed leader who attempts to dominate and manipulate the group." Plumb ascribes the success of her group to the fact that it was "organized by teachers, for teachers," all with equal responsibility. How can a group without leaders actually function? Must the organizer be prepared to do more than his or her share of the work during the first year, as Wolff and Vera (1989) warn? The Philadelphia Teachers' Learning Cooperative (1984) found an interesting solution for their group, which they describe as "cooperative with all responsibilities shared." They have an annual chairperson for the planning meetings who is responsible for maintaining notes, while each week there is a different chairperson, presenter, and note-taker. Even if a group prefers a looser organizational structure, certain tasks must be performed. The group should decide what these tasks will be and who will perform them. Will notes be taken? If so, by whom? How will voting take place? How will activities be chosen? What kind of roles will the members play in the group and in the meetings themselves? Many of the first meetings will have to be dedicated to working out these complex issues of group organization.

Activities

After establishing the goals and group structure, the next step is to decide how meeting time will be spent. Will the sessions be focused on one topic or will they be divided into time segments devoted to different activities? Will activity types change from meeting to meeting, or will there be standard types? Will activities be performed outside of meeting time? Organizing time well, so that there is a feeling of being productive is important. Wolff and Vera (1989) cite a "lack of methodical approach to work" as one of the principal complaints voiced by teachers involved in development groups in Spain.

When choosing the activities that the group will perform, one might want to think in terms of some general types of activities. Some of these are sharing, feedback, personal/professional goal-setting, brainstorming, problem-solving, presentation of new information, discussion, planning, experimentation, research, reading, writing, evaluation, community organizing, and socializing. Most activities will incorporate two or more of these features. For example, an activity in which one shares experiences in the classroom may be followed by feedback from the group, or presentation of materials could be followed by experimentation with them in the classroom, with experiences shared later in the meeting.

The number of activities a teacher development group can perform is endless. Here are some sets of possible activities I have grouped together from the literature on teacher networks.

- Record observations of learning and teaching in one's classroom in a "learning log."
- Take part in peer observation.
- Videotape your class, and bring the tape to the meeting to be discussed by the group.

- Staff review: Teacher gives detailed description of one student and brings examples of student's work. Group discusses problems and gives recommendations.
- Reflection: One word, which relates to an issue important to the group, is chosen. The group then brainstorms on paper for five minutes. Each person then shares the feelings and thoughts that were generated.

- Bring in speakers to discuss a chosen topic.
- Make plans to attend language conferences as a group.
- Write letters to administrators and policymakers.
- Organize local workshops or conferences about topics relevant to teaching EFL in the area in which you live.

- Have all members bring in materials they like and discuss them.
- Develop materials as a collaborative effort.
- Give articles to be read at home, with discussion taking place later at a meeting.
- One person presents a teaching technique, which he or she must have already used in class. Others then try it in their classes. Later the group members discuss their experiences with the technique.
- Individual teachers investigate topics related to their field and lead group discussions.

- Create a handbook, divided into different sections, for notes, reflections, articles, etc.
- Create a mini-library for group members' use.
- Publish a newsletter discussing the activities of the group.
- Write collaborative articles.

- Teachers develop the design of research that is to be carried out in the classroom.
- Research particular learning difficulties related to your EFL students.

Possible guidelines

It may be a good idea to establish a set of guidelines that the group agrees to follow. I have drawn up a list of suggestions, based on the authors cited. They are offered here only as the starting point for discussion, rather than as rules to be observed.

- Don't spend too much time on complaints, particularly those of one person. Focus on "achievements and accomplishments," as well.
- Offer feedback that is supportive.
- Remember the importance of listening.
- Be punctual and if you cannot attend a meeting let others know.
- Make a serious commitment to the group.
- Come to an agreement with other group members about how you will deal with confidentiality.
- Remember that "the purpose of the group is not to provide therapy for personal problems for which professional assistance might be advisable."
- Talk in meeting should be formal discussion, "not informal, teachers' lounge chat."
- Remember that you shouldn't "expect everything to work every time . . . there are good weeks and bad weeks."
- Focus on the practical: "Try new ideas instead of just talking about them."
- Focus on "offer(ing) support and encouragement to each other in solving problems," rather than on complaining.
- Give all members specific tasks.
- Put all suggestions in writing.
- Don't forget to have fun!

Problems and issues that may come up

The act of coming together as individuals, each one with his or her own values, beliefs, and personality, in a group setting is bound to bring up a certain number of issues and/or problems. A teachers' group is certainly no exception. Upon creation of a network, members may want to discuss potential problems and decide on strategies for dealing with them. The following is a list of issues to keep in mind:

Irregular attendance: How will this be dealt with? Should members notify the group if they cannot attend a meeting?

Personal problems: How will the group limit discussion of personal problems, if at all?

Untrained teachers: Many may be reluctant to join because of a lack of interest. If untrained teachers do join, they may feel intimidated by the others. How can the group best encourage and support them?

Lack of time: How can the best use be made of the precious time devoted to group activities?

Sponsorship of the group: Should a group seek school sponsorship? Deming (1984) says that "sponsorship is a crucial issue and should be considered carefully." She believes that school sponsorship should be avoided if possible, so as to "minimize faculty resistance." On the other hand, some teachers might welcome the opportunity to take part in group activities during paid school time.[2]

Creating trust: Many of the authors mentioned agree with Deming (1984) about the primacy of creating "a safe, supportive environment." Activities where teachers share their personal experiences or socialize informally may help to foster closeness. Knowing that they will be supported and not criticized when expressing their ideas and feelings will encourage the group members to trust one another. The difficulty of establishing trust is augmented when administrators from the same school are part of the group. The benefits of allowing administration personnel to join must be weighed against the possibility of teachers feeling intimidated by their presence.

Sharing responsibility: How can the group avoid a situation where a few members are doing most of the work? If some members are contributing more to the discussions, it may be that the others are shy or intimidated. What can be done to change this situation?

Learning to work together: Different people have different personality styles and ways of working. What can be done to accommodate these different styles?

Dealing with controversy: Armour (1985) discusses the friction caused by a discussion of standardized testing and the use of basal readers. Although she is "still not sure how to handle controversy at a network meeting," she states that "surviving controversy strengthened our sense of unity." What kind of strategies can be used to deal with controversy?

Positive outcomes

According to the teachers who have written about their experiences with teacher development groups, the rewards to be gained are substantial. Here are a few of the benefits of working together with other teachers for personal and professional growth:

Greater awareness: Teachers may attain an increased understanding of the issues involved in the teaching profession and of the problems they share with their colleagues.

Increased motivation: Armour (1985) speaks of one member of the group who found the motivation to request a grant, which she was awarded, through her contact with other group members. Matlin and Short (1991) state that some of the teachers who participated in their study groups "have attended courses at the university. Others have presented at national conferences, and all have renewed their focus on teaching and learning."

Better teaching: Teachers studying, exchanging ideas, experimenting with techniques and materials, researching their own classrooms, can only serve to improve their abilities as teachers. Matlin and Short (1991) discuss the "innovative changes" in teaching that took place because of involvement in a teaching group.

Benefits to students: Improvement in teaching, of course, will directly affect the students. Teachers, according to Matlin and Short (1991), "after seeing how powerful it is to be in charge of their own learning ... are making the same experience possible for their students." Joyce et al. (1989) discuss the "positive effects on students when teachers in their school districts took part in study groups. Both the students' involvement in their own learning and their achievement showed significant increases."

Joy of sharing: According to Armour (1985), teachers are "hungry" to discuss their teaching with others, but "talking about teaching [is] almost illegal in some classrooms." She speaks of the initial "exhilaration" and "euphoria" the teachers felt as they shared their feelings and experiences with the group.

Connection to others: The experience of working together intimately as a group can help teachers overcome their sense of isolation. Personal gratification can come not only from sharing one's experiences, but also from the feeling of having helped others with one's support (Kirk & Walter, 1981). Raiser (1987) says that teachers in her network have become "active advocates," not only of their students, but also of one another.

New ways of thinking: Matlin and Short (1991) believe that the changes teachers can make go beyond the simple addition of new techniques to their repertoire; they can actually change their way of thinking.

Empowerment: Membership in a teachers' group can be an empowering experience as teachers begin to question the pronouncements of the "experts" and to have more faith in their own abilities, according to Matlin and Short (1991). They state that teachers in their group no longer passively accept certain conflicts (for example, the discrepancy between the new literacy curriculum and the method for evaluating students), and now seek alternative ways of dealing with them. The Philadelphia Teachers' Learning Cooperative (1984) state that they occasionally invite speakers to give talks, but believe that they can learn more from one another.

Conclusion

In this account I have attempted to elaborate on the issues that are involved in the creation of a teacher development group. I present many questions, because I believe that prescriptions are inappropriate, while awareness is fundamental if one is to make the most of the potential offered by the group. Much can be learned from those who have already experienced the benefits, and difficulties, of working together in a network, but each group must choose the form, content, and goals best suited to its unique situation.

Involvement in a teacher development group requires much in terms of time, patience, and commitment. This is repaid by the benefits we receive as teachers, i.e. the "opportunity to think through (our) own beliefs, share ideas, challenge current instructional practices, blend theory and practice, (and) identify professional and personal needs" (Matlin & Short, 1991). I agree that "the alternative to action is isolation, cynicism, stagnation, a failure to fulfill one's potential as a creative human being, and in very practical terms, poorer quality programs and less successful students" (Crookes, 1995). On a personal level, I feel empowered by the knowledge that, no matter where I end up teaching, I can continue to grow both professionally and personally through cooperation with other teachers who share my desire for development.

FOR DISCUSSION

1. If you are using this book in conjunction with a formal period of professional development, to what extent would it be possible for the class to have some of the characteristics of a teacher development group?

Do the institutional characteristics of the class interfere with its teacher development group aspects? For example, who sets the agenda for the class, and what responsibilities are there for facilitating?

2. Have you ever participated in a teacher development group or in any similar activity? If so, what were some of its strengths and weaknesses?

3. If you are currently teaching, and were to set up or participate in a teacher development group at your present school, what would be some of the problems you might face?

Appendix B
NEA Code of Ethics

Code of Ethics of the Education Profession

Preamble

The educator, believing in the worth and dignity of each human being, recognizes the supreme importance of the pursuit of truth, devotion to excellence, and the nurture of the democratic principles. Essential to these goals is the protection of freedom to learn and to teach and the guarantee of equal educational opportunity for all. The educator accepts the responsibility to adhere to the highest ethical standards. The educator recognizes the magnitude of the responsibility inherent in the teaching process. The desire for the respect and confidence of one's colleagues, of students, of parents, and of the members of the community provides the incentive to attain and maintain the highest possible degree of ethical conduct. The Code of Ethics of the Education Profession indicates the aspiration of all educators and provides standards by which to judge conduct. The remedies specified by the NEA and/or its affiliates for the violation of any provision of this Code shall be exclusive and no such provision shall be enforceable in any form other than the one specifically designated by the NEA or its affiliates.

PRINCIPLE I Commitment to the Student. The educator strives to help each student realize his or her potential as a worthy and effective member of society. The educator therefore works to stimulate the spirit of inquiry, the acquisition of knowledge and understanding, and the thoughtful formulation of worthy goals. In fulfillment of the obligation to the student, the educator – 1. Shall not unreasonably restrain the student from independent action in the pursuit of learning. 2. Shall not unreasonably deny the student's access to varying points of view. 3. Shall not deliberately suppress or distort subject matter relevant to the student's progress. 4. Shall make reasonable effort to protect the student from conditions harmful to learning or to health and safety. 5. Shall not intentionally expose the student to embarrassment or disparagement. 6. Shall not on the basis of race, color, creed, sex, national origin, marital status, political or religious beliefs, family, social or cultural background, or sexual orientation, unfairly – a. Exclude any student from participation in any program b. Deny benefits to any student c. Grant any advantage to any student. 7. Shall not use professional relationships with students for private advantage. 8. Shall not disclose information about students obtained in the course of professional service unless disclosure serves a compelling professional purpose or is required by law.

PRINCIPLE II Commitment to the Profession.   The education profession is vested by the public with a trust and responsibility requiring the highest ideals of professional service. In the belief that the quality of the services of the education profession directly influences the nation and its citizens, the educator shall exert every effort to raise professional standards, to promote a climate that encourages the exercise of professional judgment, to achieve conditions that attract persons worthy of the trust to careers in education, and to assist in preventing the practice of the profession by unqualified persons. In fulfillment of the obligation to the profession, the educator – 1. Shall not in an application for a professional position deliberately make a false statement or fail to disclose a material fact related to competency and qualifications. 2. Shall not misrepresent his/her professional qualifications. 3. Shall not assist any entry into the profession of a person known to be unqualified in respect to character, education, or other relevant attribute. 4. Shall not knowingly make a false statement concerning the qualifications of a candidate for a professional position. 5. Shall not assist a noneducator in the unauthorized practice of teaching. 6. Shall not disclose information about colleagues obtained in the course of professional service unless disclosure serves a compelling professional purpose or is required by law. 7. Shall not knowingly make false or malicious statements about a colleague. 8. Shall not accept any gratuity, gift, or favor that might impair or appear to influence professional decisions or action.

– Adopted by the NEA 1975 Representative Assembly

Appendix C
Use of This Book by the
Teacher Educator

The arrangement of this book is fairly conventional, and I hope fosters its use in a variety of circumstances, both formal and informal. Besides use by the individual reader, and by groups of student teachers with a teacher educator in colleges and universities, I would be disappointed if the book were not also occasionally used by small groups of teachers working outside of an institution formally supporting teacher education. However, I was also asked to provide some guidance for teacher educators using it, concerning how the material might be situated within the practicum/professional development process.

As I mention in the Introduction, there is (in my mind, at least) a rationale to the sequence of topics. However, obviously other sequences are possible. Teacher educators might disagree about the extent to which a group they are working with might need to prioritize attention to classroom techniques over, or in advance of, attention to developing a philosophy of teaching. Some might find an urgent need to focus immediately on, say, lesson planning, simply in order to begin practical activity with relatively inexperienced teachers, in which case Chapters 4 and 6 would be the place to start. Others may feel that the actual importance of a teacher's views and values is so great in determining practice that Chapters 3 and 5, though challenging, should at least be reviewed swiftly before moving on.

Time considerations are probably going to be what really determines the extent of use of the discussion questions, some of which might also well lend themselves to teacher research investigations.

If the implications of my support of the concept of the teacher development group are carried through, this would imply the teacher educator handing over responsibility for discussion of some topics and sections to individual student teachers, of course. Similarly, if a group of individuals using the book really does think through and develop its goals for professional development, it would then follow that there should be some discussion of which (as opposed to all) of the chapters in the book would be drawn upon.

Some teacher preparation programs I am familiar with require a piece of teacher research as a graduation requirement to be done in connection with a student teacher's practice teaching. Where there is such a requirement or something similar, a number of the chapters here might lend themselves to this. For example, if teachers (whatever their status) wish truly to reflect on and develop their teaching in a particular area, they might select one of the chapters and either choose one of the *You try it* sections to be worked through in detail, or possibly even one of the discussion questions might provide a stimulus for such work. I would not have made such extensive use of mainstream educational research in this book if there had been sufficient (E)S/FL-focused studies to draw upon; in their absence there is certainly need and justification for any amount of teacher research in most if not all of the topics covered here, in my opinion.

Given the obvious importance I attach to the idea of a (personal, practical) philosophy of teaching throughout this book, a teacher educator using it may wish to require a statement of philosophy of teaching as some culminating activity when working with this text. As I have mentioned, from my own experience this is not easy even for teachers in midcareer to develop, unless they have been encouraged to think in such terms from early in their experience. Indeed, if time is short, perhaps classroom or group meeting time could be spent on discussion that works directly towards such statements rather than that working through all the discussion questions.

Finally, given the increasing popularity of teacher portfolios, it is also possible early to turn to the section on teaching portfolios (end of Chapter 12) and use that as a guiding project to orient to while using other sections of this book.

Appendix D
Working with a Cooperating Teacher

This book can be used by groups of like-minded teachers working together in a variety of contexts, and of course, one of those contexts is the formal, institutionally-supported short-term teaching practicum. Within this context, beginner or near-beginner teachers may be provided with the opportunity to develop their teaching under the guidance of a "cooperating teacher." Because of my interest in the idea of long-term professional development of one's teaching practices, I have emphasized the possibilities of groups of teachers with various amounts of experience working together as a basis for teacher development. However, it is clearly the case that an important and common basis for the development of a teacher is a one-to-one relationship with a senior teacher with assigned responsibilities as a mentor[1] and model. The following discussion is intended to assist such an arrangement.

A cooperating teacher or master teacher (and other terms are possible) usually provides a model to be observed, if not imitated, and also provides a classroom context (their own classroom, usually) in which the junior teacher will assist and teach. Close supervision and immediate feedback is the dominant expectation (though not always the rule) under these circumstances. Cooperating teachers are obviously extremely important in practicum contexts, and in at least one study (Funk, et al., 1982) they were identified as the most important significant other by student teachers – more important, that is, than their peers or the practicum supervisor. Other past research is summarized by Zahorik (1988, p. 9) to the effect that "supervision is dominated by the cooperating teacher," influencing both student teachers' attitudes and classroom actions. And indeed, one well-known past review (Bowman, 1979) suggested that the "university supervisor's effectiveness is so insignificant that this type of supervision ought to be discontinued" (Zahorik, ibid.)!

The inexperienced student teacher who has a helpful and wise cooperating teacher is in a favored position indeed. As noted, in the traditional format, these individuals are senior teachers, and the student teachers work (unpaid) alongside them and under their direct supervision. With more experienced student teachers, modifications of the traditional arrangement may some-times be possible and used. In some cases, a teacher who has an established teaching position may also be enrolled in a degree program, and may be able to do their practice teaching in their own class, with some semi-formal con-sultative relationship with a "teaching colleague" (instead of a "cooperating teacher"). This individual would be another teacher with plenty of experi-ence with whom the student teacher establishes a professional dialogue, most likely through the intervention or arrangement of a practicum super-visor. In this case there will not be minute-to-minute supervision, and the relationship is typically less hierarchical and more egalitarian.[2]

Unfortunately, since few regular schools are set up with administrative structures that are truly designed to foster teacher learning, connections be-tween and among student teacher, cooperating teacher, and practicum super-visor are often less than satisfactory. At a time of increasing "intensification" of teachers' work in many parts of the world, being a cooperating teacher is still something extra, and it is certainly, therefore, something that deserves to be planned for by institutions and for which teachers should be rewarded. It is not something that can or should be taken for granted; indeed, all of us would be a lot better off if there was greater recognition that this is an institutional responsibility, not something to be done out of a teacher's individual sense of professional responsibility (cf. Ganser, 1996).

For a student teacher to get the most from the relationship under con-sideration may require a willingness to ask questions (diplomatically) and to try to understand the situation from the point of view of the cooperat-ing teacher. The questions will be the better for being informed by what has been written and investigated about this aspect of supervised teaching practice, thus it may be helpful to offer some background and perspective on working with a cooperating teacher, for those readers of this book who find themselves in such a relationship.

As usual, within the field of TESOL, since teacher education in our area has been an area comparatively neglected by researchers until recently, our literature provides relatively little discussion (however based) of the mat-ter of being a cooperating teacher or working with one. The mainstream education field provides a body of work in its journal literature which has been growing in recent years; and for a particularly clear statement of prac-tice by one cooperating teacher, see Wood (1991). Even so, we continue to find comments like "we still know little about how the relationship be-tween a cooperating and preservice teacher develops" (Agee, 1996, p. 280), or, "limited information has appeared about student teaching from the co-operating teacher's point of view" (Koerner, 1992, p. 46; cf. Goodfellow, 1994; Kremer-Hayon, 1991; Dunn & Taylor, 1993). Besides the journal literature, there are only a handful of book-length treatments (e.g. Balch & Balch, 1987, on which I have drawn fairly extensively in the following section; see also Hunter, 1962; Pelletier, 1995).

Institutional background; history and the present

The beginnings of student teaching and the concept of a cooperating teacher may have been presaged by developments in Jesuit-run schools in Europe in the sixteenth century. However, a clear institutional context is more obvious in the development by the seventeenth century French educator, de la Salle, of "an elementary laboratory school for the sole purpose of providing practice teaching" (Johnson, 1968, p. 10) in 1685. This has been referred to as the first "normal school" or "training college" for teachers. The idea was swiftly taken up in Germany by Francke, where it became incorporated into the practices of the rapidly evolving German university system.[3] Educational reformers like Pestalozzi, Herbart, and Froebel made use of the concept in the institutions they worked in, and it naturally also functioned as a means of spreading their ideas through the training of teachers. By the eighteenth century, other developments such as the monitorial and pupil-teacher systems had assisted the idea that student teachers were somewhat like apprentices to skilled craft workers, at a time when apprenticeships were one of the most widespread forms of practical education and far more common than teacher education in universities or colleges. Out of these ideas came the normal school movement which, alongside increasing state support for education in the more economically developed nations, placed practice teaching with its master, cooperating, or supervising teacher on a firm and widespread institutional footing throughout many countries by the middle of the nineteenth century.

One subsequent shift in dominant arrangements since then was the move to implement practice teaching in regular schools, as opposed to "model" or "normal" schools. The original institutional setup often implied a practice teaching school as the heart of the teacher training institution, or at least an "experimental school" adjacent to and administratively part of the teachers college. Johnson (1968, p. 197) comments that in the United States,

during the 1920s there was a marked increase in the use of off-campus practice teaching.... [This] was partially due to the fact that the normal schools grew to the point at which their model schools could no longer handle all of the practice teachers. Also, there was a feeling that the public school could provide a more typical teaching situation for the practice teacher.

Turning now to the present – since ES/FL is taught in such a wide range of institutional contexts, the formats in which practica can involve a cooperating teacher are also very diverse. There are still situations which closely approximate the "in-house" experimental school, where senior teachers, as a regular part of their professional responsibilities every term or semester take on junior student teachers in a cooperating teacher role. The cooperating teacher would receive compensation, possible release time, and may have taken a formal course on being a cooperating teacher.[4] They may have support materials and corresponding bureaucratic, grading or report-writing responsibilities. At the other end of the scale, those with responsibilities for finding cooperating teachers may contact senior teachers in their area very occasionally, asking them to volunteer for a responsibility which they may take on only a few times in their professional career; and if they have been asked to volunteer for unpaid extra work, they may not expect to have to provide more than a minimal accounting of the student teacher's efforts, nor may they receive or want formal training for their role. Finding placements for student teachers is not necessarily easy, and Potthoff and Alley (1996, p. 95) comment

All too often, the realities of placement decisions, such as availability of quality sites, convenient locales, cooperation of local districts, etc., override any ideological goals or systematic programs established by program faculty [i.e., practicum supervisors].

What will student and cooperating teachers do?

Some indications concerning typical cooperating teacher practices are provided by Grimmett and Ratzlaff (1986). These authors compared several previous empirical investigations in this area done in Canada and the United States across several decades. The most general, shared practices or responsibilities were that

the cooperating teacher provide[s] the student teacher with the information and resource materials basic to teaching in a practice situation. They would also involve student teachers in planning and evaluating learning experiences and regularly give them focused feedback through lesson observation and conferencing (p. 48).

Some sort of progression from observation, through assistance, to possibly a full responsibility for the discharge of actual lessons, has been identified in the earliest discussions (e.g., Bagley, 1922) and would appear to be standard (cf. Caruso, 1998). It would also be common for some degree of coplanning of lessons to occur, which (if the student teacher is very inexperienced) could be highly directive at first, moving through a collaborative phase, and ending, perhaps, with lesson plans simply being approved or even taken for granted toward the end of this period. Many student teachers working with a cooperating teacher will be obliged to use preexisting materials specified either by the cooperating teacher or the school as a whole, though some will have the chance to choose their own materials or even make their own.

Grimmett and Ratzlaff's review identified some additional functions, which appeared only in studies of cooperating teachers done closer to the present, e.g.,

teach ... student teachers the skills of presentation and classroom management. At the same time, cooperating teachers ... encourage the development of professional responsibility in student teachers through careful induction, positive support of [student teachers'] experimental behavior, and the provision of [extensive and varied] opportunities to study the learning process (p. 48).

The precise details of what student teachers will do with a cooperating teacher naturally vary greatly depending on site, local practices, cultures, time duration of the practicum placement, and so forth. Besides national culture, Grimmett and Ratzlaff were able to identify other key factors that could cause variation, such as

the 'ethos' of the preparation program ... the timing (i.e., early or late field experience) and the length of the practicum ... and the developmental maturity level of student teaching supervision participants (Grimmett & Ratzlaff, 1986, p. 48).

Such variation may also be the result of a general lack of administrative explicitness in this area, as Griffin (1986) reported that groups of cooperating teachers indicated that they had not received much formal guidance concerning their responsibilities toward their student teachers.

In many cases, the cooperating teacher will tell the student teacher explicitly what is expected; ideally these requirements will also have been gone over by the supervisor as well. It is possible, of course, that there can be a lack of congruence between those two authority figures. The student teacher's need to negotiate between the two positions under these circumstances is an unfortunate consequence of a triadic relationship that has sometimes (e.g. Yee, 1969) been called "unstable." It will, therefore, be necessary for student teachers to clarify, diplomatically and courteously, the various aspects of the situation that will affect them, including notably the matter of any formal grading of the student teacher.

YOU TRY IT...

1. Ask for some statement of your role and responsibilities as a student teacher with a cooperating teacher, if you have not already received one. If possible, and if necessary, obtain this separately from cooperating teacher and supervisor. Compare, and seek clarification from them on any discrepancies. Check your findings with other student teachers.
2. A range of possibilities exist concerning what the supervisor may have requested your cooperating teacher to do by way of making a report on your teaching, submitting a grade, and so on. Take the necessary steps, if possible, to be clear on this aspect of your placement. Compare the answers you receive from your cooperating teacher to your questions on this point to those you receive from your supervisor. Check and clarify with any fellow student teachers, if possible, as well.
3. Are you getting as much direction as you want from your cooperating teacher? Or is it too much or too little? Your needs and preferences may be different from those of your peers, but compare them if possible. Can you identify specific areas (e.g., lesson plans, feedback on your teaching, the actual content of lessons, and language items) where you are getting either too much or too little direction? If necessary, in collaboration with your peers or your supervisor, plan how to take up such matters with your cooperating teacher the next time you meet.

Pros and cons for both sides

The cooperating teacher

In my experience, most cooperating teachers would freely admit that they benefit from most, if not all, student teachers.[5] The student teacher provides additional person-power in the classroom, to start with (Caruso, 1998). In addition, one obvious positive aspect for the teacher newly taking on the responsibility of aiding a student teacher is that it provides an opportunity to get away from the isolating aspects of teaching. While it is widely agreed that the absence of a chance to work with others is a problematic aspect of the teaching profession, changes addressing this are slow to manifest themselves in reality, despite the many efforts at school restructuring in recent years (cf., e.g., DiPardo, 1996). Being a cooperating teacher allows at least one regular in-classroom collaboration to occur naturally.

Besides providing actual support for the cooperating teacher in the classroom, a key benefit to the cooperating teacher is the possibility for professional development. For example, in a study (Koerner, 1992) of "eight experienced cooperating teachers" working at the elementary level (on the U.S. mainland), the researcher identified two prominent themes in trying to answer the question, "How does this role [of cooperating teacher] affect the professional development of the cooperating Teacher?" These were "reflection about self as a practitioner and reflections about the teaching profession" (p. 52). She comments,

To instruct student teachers about how to become teachers, cooperating teachers had to think about the essential elements of teaching and decide what knowledge the student teachers needed. . . . [I]t seems that it is a necessary, if not always explicitly stated, part of the cooperating teacher experience. . . .

Some reported that they had re-examined their classroom organization, materials, and instruction. Others thought about their short- and long-term goals. All reported having thought about themselves as teachers. Having student teachers in their classrooms gave these veteran teachers opportunities to think about the knowledge they had acquired through the years. [One teacher said]:

"It's funny how this situation can provide a mirror for me. I never even considered that possibility when I first agreed to have a student teacher. I'm seeing through her that I AM an experienced teacher. The years have taught me things I didn't learn in college" (pp. 52–53).

Reflection about the profession also occurred, because the cooperating teachers had to evaluate their student teachers and say if they were competent (cf. Tollefson & Kleinsasser, 1992). Cooperating teachers are gatekeep ers to the profession, with considerable responsibilities to their colleagues, since one of the defining qualities of a profession is that its members police themselves. Koerner (1992) comments that "the student teaching experience offers cooperating teachers opportunities to plan their future as career professionals" (p. 53). Here she provides no further detail, but remarks that "All the teachers liked being partners with the university . . . as classroom teachers they seldom received any positive feedback from colleagues or administrators" (ibid.).

We should not pretend that there are not some downsides to being a cooperating teacher sometimes. Not all teachers want to begin a working relationship with another influential and possibly challenging, even if junior, professional while running a classroom. Not all student teacher placements go off without a hitch. Some of the problems and difficulties that the cooperating teacher experiences are documented by Koerner (1992) – intrusions in routines, demands on time, and feelings that one's own work is likely to be discussed and critiqued out of earshot in university seminars. Applegate and Lasley's (1982) extensive study of almost 200 cooperating teachers analyzed the problems they encountered and placed them in the following categories: (1) student teachers' orientation to teaching; (2) understanding the role of the university; (3) lack of student teacher and university interest in school norms; (4) student teachers' attitudes and skills; (5) low student teacher enthusiasm; and (6) student teachers' lack of planning and organization skills.

The student teacher

Despite suggesting in the subsection immediately above that the cooperating teacher does benefit from his/her assignment, the primary beneficiary must, conceptually, be the student teacher, the one who has surely more to learn. However, even here there can be some negatives. We've discussed the constraints that might be experienced that would be particularly felt by those doing student teaching who nevertheless have already accumulated some or perhaps considerable classroom experience, a feature particularly of some parts of the ES/FL world. Other problems can occur more for administrative reasons. Lemma (1993) in a review of problems identified cases where "declining contact and insufficient feedback and encouragement" caused difficulties, a vivid first-person account of this sort of situation being provided by Hawkey (1996). One general problem can occur if a cooperating teacher takes the not uncommon view that since it is hard to articulate one's principles for teaching, student teachers will learn more from experiencing and doing teaching than being told about it. For some student teachers, their cooperating teacher may come across as insufficiently explicit (as was the case for some practice teaching cases studied by Borko & Mayfield, 1995). Also problematic are cases where the cooperating teacher has a substantially different approach to the subject matter or to the nature of teaching, than does the student teacher. Agee (1996) suggests that gender may play a role here.

Cooperating teacher relationships

As soon as one has a colleague of any kind visiting and assisting, and eventually teaching in one's classroom on a regular basis, some sort of relationship has to be worked out. Having a sense of the range of possibilities in the cooperating teacher-student teacher relationship can assist the student teacher. Cooperating teachers can be more or less directive, may or may not be willing to listen to the student teacher or accept their way of doing things; and with time being always a concern in teaching, may or may not have adequate time to engage with a student teacher. It would be unusually favorable circumstances if a student teacher finds s/he is the cooperating teacher's top priority. Most cooperating teachers are still going to be concerned with the learning of their regular students as the primary concern, and a student teacher may have to recognize and go along with that.

How a student teacher and a cooperating teacher relate may be more or less left to them, or it may be guided by outside forces. In the area of TESOL, individuals may enter teaching without a qualification and proceed and be successful before gaining a substantive degree in the area. And in mainstream education a somewhat similar situation occurs, when student teachers come to education after some years of work elsewhere, as opposed to entering straight from a B. Ed. course. Under these circumstances, such student teachers and their cooperating teachers may be able to work in a team relationship right from the start.

A recent qualitative study of five pairs of student and cooperating FL teachers of high school Spanish in the United States (Hall & Davis, 1995) sheds useful light on some of the aspects of the relationships that can develop. Hall and Davis identify six: "clearing-house, expert/mentor/master teacher, facilitator, mediator, motivator, and friend" (p. 35). One might expect that for most of these, it would be the senior teacher who is the "giving" member of the relationship, but that is not always the case. The authors comment with respect to the "facilitator" role that

to facilitate the experiences of another, one did not necessarily have to be an expert in the experience nor possess much information about it. Instead, what was perceived to be more important to the enactment of this role was being open to the possibility of having different experiences, making the other aware of them, and making it easy for the other to pursue [them] (p. 36).

Similarly, for the "clearing-house" role, while it may be the case that the experienced teacher has access to materials, the junior may be more in touch with the more academic sources of information. However, these two aspects of the relationship, along with that of "mediator," were found by the authors to be what they call "complementary" in most of the cases they studied, by which they mean unequal, and it was indeed the cooperating teacher who was in the expert or dominant role. On the other hand, the master teacher aspect, the motivator aspect, and the friend aspect were found to be reciprocal in three of the five cases. This was in part because some of the teacher-student pairs opted for team teaching; or in another case, they taught each other's lesson plans, allowing feedback to be not just from senior to junior.

FOR DISCUSSION

What is your relationship with your cooperating teacher? How hierarchical is it, or, how teamlike? Which of Hall and Davis's aspects is primary?

Communication between student and cooperating teacher – important and difficult questions

In one program familiar to me[6] which favors a teaming relationship between cooperating and student teacher, an initial task (required by the program administrators) of the cooperating teacher-student teacher pair is to jointly write down and negotiate their philosophy of teaching, that is, what their fundamental beliefs as teachers are. This can be productive for both parties, and student and cooperating teacher are supported and encouraged to establish a relationship in which mutual challenge is possible (rather than the traditional apprenticeship). When it works, it can work well. One cooperating teacher said of her classroom experience.

While one person taught, the other was always observing, writing down anecdotes, gathering data and providing feedback. We always held continuous discussions. We didn't name it as such and just did it naturally. . . . That really helped us to help each other, get to know one another, and get to know the students intimately. It gave us a basis for dialoguing and planning to implement new ideas/ strategies (Phelan, McEwan, & Pateman, 1996, p. 341).

In fact, both aspects of these areas of reflection tie in with a point increasingly made about teachers' knowledge: that the traditional conceptions of academic knowledge have made no place for, and have denied the validity of other forms of knowledge, notably the knowledge of practice (e.g., Day, 1992; Freeman & Johnson, 1998). One reason for this, besides immediate effects of power, is that such knowledge is often tacit. Only when skilled practice is viewed and compared with unskilled practice can we discover what a teacher really "knows"; yet the conditions of teaching provide almost no opportunity or encouragement for a teacher to articulate that knowledge – until, that is, the student teacher comes along. Not articulating this knowledge, on the one hand, and having only one conception of official knowledge, that provided by the university during initial socialization into the profession, the teacher may not realize how much she really knows until forced to articulate this for the benefit of her student teacher. Alternatively, it may be the case that a cooperating teacher believes that what works for them may not work for the student teacher, or again, believes that knowledge about teaching is acquired through trial and error, and experience, rather than through direct instruction or telling. The instructions and comments cooperating teachers may provide can, as a result, be abbreviated or restrained (cf. Gonzalez & Carter, 1996, inter alia).

Besides the fact that much of the expert teacher's knowledge may be tacit, a related problematic concern is that the expert and the novice teacher are likely to see the same classroom event differently. This is documented in Gonzalez and Carter's (1996) U.S. study of 13 cooperating-student teacher dyads, in which they review a range of classroom events salient to pairs of cooperating and student teachers, but which were reflected on or interpreted differently by them. Gonzalez and Carter point to the importance of "personal narratives and life histories in learning to teach." The "broader and more fully elaborated narrative frame" that experienced teachers have certainly helps them, professionally. At the same time,

novices enter teacher education programs with richly formulated, deeply personal, and quite persistent understandings of what it means to teach. These understandings, derived from being pupils in classrooms, serve as theoretical frameworks within which novices interpret and judge suggestions by educational faculty or classroom teachers and invent a personal meaning for the experiences they have in the field (p. 45).

Fundamentally, these investigators feel that communication between student and cooperating teacher runs the risk of being "demanding and perplexing for both parties" (p. 45) though obviously potentially very useful. They advocate that the two sides work toward a common understanding of events, by way of more extended conversations informed by sharing of personal experience and background than may commonly occur (or be possible).

Finally, a slightly more pessimistic position on the differences that student and cooperating teacher may take, and their effects, has long been articulated in this literature. This is that student teachers may acquire a somewhat progressive approach to teaching as a result of their university coursework, but it is swiftly washed out during their student teaching. Some have said this is due to the influence of their likely more conservative cooperating teacher (Yee, 1969; Edgar & Warren, 1969). Others suggest that this is simply the result of the bureaucratic nature of school as an institution (Hoy & Rees, 1977). In Bunting's study of 17 cooperating-student teacher pairs, significant though not radical change occurred in 10 of the student teachers. Bunting (1988, p. 46) also found that

[cooperating] teachers who possessed more flexible, adaptable views more often witnessed movement in this direction by [student teachers] under their supervision. [Cooperating] teachers with more extreme views more often witnessed no change in the views of candidates assigned to them.

I am not aware of any similar study in the world of TESOL, but student teachers working with cooperating teachers may wish to track changes in their views during this time, and consider how their interactions with their cooperating teachers affect such changes.

YOU TRY IT...

1. When you have established a suitable degree of rapport, that is, after some time within your placement as a student teacher, ask your cooperating teacher to articulate her/his principles for some aspect of teaching. Depending on the response, you may also try asking him or her the broad question, "What is your philosophy of teaching?" On the basis of the responses you get, do you think s/he is accessing tacit knowledge or more active knowledge?

2. How would you describe the feedback or input you get from your cooperating teacher?

3. Do you think there are substantial differences between your own personal history as a pupil in a classroom and that of your cooperating teacher? Similarly, are there differences between your cooperating teacher and yourself in terms of your experiences as classroom second language learners? If so, how do these differences affect the communication between you and your cooperating teacher?

4. The fact that the field of TESOL sees itself as trying to improve ES/FL teaching around the world suggests that in many places, dominant aspects of curriculum and instruction are inadequate. Potthoff and Alley (1996) suggest that one criterion for selecting a cooperating teacher should be "challenging beliefs," and it is desirable to place a student teacher with a cooperating teacher who is trying to improve TESOL, who is "teaching against the grain" (in the famous phrase of Cochran-Smith, 1991). To what extent are you and your cooperating teacher "teaching against the grain" of TESOL? Is such a thing possible, in student teaching in general, or in your particular placement? (As a *student* teacher, would you prefer to go "with the flow" instead of "against the grain"?)

Notes

Introduction

1. I am not putting this forward as a model, but simply as background. Many alternatives exist, and a more extended and integrated practicum is certainly possible (cf. Stoynoff, 1999).
2. I'll use these three terms interchangeably. TESOL is a mainly U.S.-oriented usage, ELT appears particularly in UK sources; ES/FL is a common, though still loaded, general term (cf. Nayar, 1997).
3. Cf. Maher and Tetreault (1994); "Positionality involves the notion that since our understanding of the world and ourselves is socially constructed, we must devote special attention to the differing ways individuals from diverse social backgrounds construct knowledge and make meaning" (Kincheloe & Steinberg, 1998, p. 3).
4. That's probably one reason why I think the field of TESOL tends to be a bit inward-looking, though it's getting better.
5. Different traditions in ES/FL teacher preparation handle practice teaching differently, though I believe the present work will be of interest to all. University-based EFL teacher preparation in EFL countries usually includes a practice teaching or practicum experience at the level of the first degree. Many teachers beginning in these traditions go on to do (post)graduate work in ESL countries, which themselves differ in regard to practica in what are typically courses in applied linguistics. Readers may wish to register the point that in the UK-influenced tradition, an MA usually does not contain any practice teaching; the MA student is assumed to be technically proficient in the classroom on the basis of previous certificate-level instruction. In the United States or North American tradition, on the other hand, an MA may be the first qualification of a teacher, and consequently often contains a practicum.
6. Cf. Cumming (1989); Brinton & Holten (1989); Guillaume & Rudney (1993).
7. E.g., Tom (1984); see Chapter 5.
8. This has been relatively nonformal, with little attempt either to present putative internal, cognitive, mechanisms by which such development might

take place, nor to make use of existing adult learning theory in which to situate such understandings (cf. Feldman, 1997; Smylie, 1995).

9. I am thus suggesting an alternative viewpoint on teacher development to that identified by Nunan and Lamb (1996, drawing on Pak, 1986), who say "Ultimately, teaching will probably only improve through self-analysis and self-evaluation" (p. 234).

10. Hawai'i itself is sometimes claimed to be a place where "east" meets "west"; but this ignores the matter of the indigenous inhabitants, whose bodies form the meeting ground of imperial powers of both hemispheres.

11. Cf. Lvovich (1997); Baumeister (1986).

12. Self-actualization as a goal a teacher might have is beginning to be discussed: see hooks (1995); Srivastava (1997); it is not confined to western cultures (Tu, 1993).

13. My ideas about role as socially constructed, and self as under transformation, echo ideas that are "in the air" in the last decade or two. In the literature of ELT, some, rather compressed use of them is to be found in e.g. Pierce (1995, 1996). A useful brief survey is Hekman's (1995) discussion of Foucault's concept of the (human) subject, or self, from which the following is taken: "The Cartesian [understanding of the] subject . . . is [something] predetermined, in the sense that it is 'given'; it is . . . incapable of moving beyond the rigid boundaries that define it. Once we abandon the Cartesian subject, however, subjects become not social dupes but acts of self-creation: 'From the idea that the self is not given to us I think there is only one possible consequence: we have to create ourselves as a work of art.' . . . On Foucault's account, this self-creation is accomplished through a kind of discursive mix. At any given time we find ourselves confronted with an array of discourses of subjectivity, scripts that we are expected to follow. We can accept the script that is written for us or, alternatively, piece together a different script from other discourses that are extant in our particular circumstances. It is important to note that this concept of subjectivity does not involve an appeal to a core, or essential, self. It is not a matter of 'finding' our true, authentic self. Rather, we employ the tools (scripts) available to us in our situation. Furthermore, our application of these tools is a creative act; it can even be an act of resistance. What emerges from Foucault's theory, then, is that subjectivity is a potential to be realized, not a truth to be deciphered." (Hekman, 1995, p. 82).

14. Laursen, 1992; Popkin & Vanderjagt, 1993.

Chapter 1

1. For one historical instance, see National Education Association (1939).
2. Newble & Cannon, 1991; Kellough, 1990.

3. Historical sources include Bobbitt (1918), Mager, (e.g., 1962) and Tyler (1950). Bobbitt's concern with societal and work-related needs in curriculum design makes him a precursor to the development of the field of ESP, which picked up on the goals and instructional objectives movement of Mager and Tyler and introduced them to ELT. See e.g. Kliebard (1970) for a critique of Tyler.
4. Feldman's is a useful definition of an increasingly hard to manage conceptual area; see Philips for a good recent survey.

Chapter 2

1. Assuming, of course, that ES/FL teachers do have careers; but see Johnston (1997).
2. Attributed to both poet W. H. Auden and novelist E. M. Forster.
3. For further discussion of the role of diary-keeping in personal development, see Wiener and Rosenwald (1993). Those with a research orientation may also learn some useful lessons from Numrich's (1996) recent analysis of what she, as a practicum supervisor, learned from her students' "teaching diaries."
4. An increasingly wide and useful range is available, including specifically in the ELT field – see, for example, Waynryb (1992), or some of the appendices in Richards and Lockhart (1994); also Willerman, McNeely, and Koffman (1991).
5. See Richards and Lockhart (1995, pp. 22–27) for more extended guidelines of this kind.
6. Besides the common meaning of this term ("helping to run a meeting") a more technical sense has become widespread: an extended consultation by an outside specialist to aid the development of an organization, such as a company. This is not the sense implied here.
7. A very preliminary introduction to this area with a TESOL setting is given in Reznich (1985), and with the IEP/service English sector in mind, Davidson and Tesh (1997) provide a useful review drawing on Jay (1976). Further guidance for the educational field is provided by Miller & Kantrow (1998); a more extended treatment of group facilitation to serve professional development and institutional problem-solving is Webne-Behrman (1998).
8. At the same time, experiencing discussions in which leadership functions are extensively distributed like this may also allow teachers to run such discussions collaboratively with their own students. That is, the students would be enabled, indeed required to take an active functional role in the discussion, which in a second language classroom would presumably facilitate participation.

9. I recognize that that pair of terms is increasingly, and rightly, under attack. I hope the reader will excuse the use of a dichotomy that does only minimal justice to a highly complex matter (discussed by e.g., Braine, 1998; Liu, 1999; Medgyes, 1992, 1994; Phillipson, 1992; Rampton, 1990; and Tang, 1997; see also Kamhi-Stein, Lee, & Lee, 1999).

10. Simply telling individuals in such a group that it is ok to "pass" if they are called upon directly may address this.

11. The third was acquiring instructional routines. However, this point was vigorously disputed by Grossman (1992; who also questions the basis for the selection of the 40 studies of teacher learning Kagan reviewed). See Chapter 9.

12. A simple cybernetic system is a thermostat. It has a goal state to be maintained or achieved, and it does so through getting feedback from the environment and acting on it.

13. In the quote that follows Johnson espouses, though does not name, a constructivist psychology of teacher learning.

Chapter 3

1. According to Griffin (1993, p. 167), this topic is neglected in U.S. teacher education programs.

2. I note again the inadequacy of this dichotomy.

3. Teaching members of this sector of the ES/FL community are in some sense the elite; whether native speaker or non-native speaker, they typically hold graduate qualifications and are to some extent internationally mobile, and are probably better paid and have better working conditions than the average indigenous EFL teacher in a state elementary or high school. As a natural (economic) consequence, this sector has the strongest links to the academic sectors of the field, to publishing houses and to the university-based discipline of applied linguistics.

4. In addition, of course, an approach which is widely used is for teachers-in-development to reflect and try to bring their views about teaching to consciousness, as a starting point. (For some examples of exercises of this type, see Zinn, 1990, and for our field, see Pennington, 1990.) I still think it is worthwhile to engage with historical and philosophical traditions pertinent to education as well.

5. These two senses of the term are identified by Brezinka (1971/1992), in an extended treatment, as the most common and most justifiable meanings.

6. As soon as I refer to empirical theories of SLA, I must be careful, terminologically. Older empirical theories of SLA/T, not to mention "Methods," sometimes get the word "philosophy" attached to them, and that is not what I have in mind in the present discussion.

7. I recognize that there are also non-Western sciences – see especially the work of Joseph Needham (Needham et al., 1954–2000; cf. Habib & Raina, 1999) but these have been overwhelmed, and their validity is only recently being re-recognized (cf. Selin, 1992).

8. In addition, some specialists in this area prefer not to present an exposition solely by way of a review of concepts, issues, theories or positions, but to consider the kind of real cases where teachers must exercise judgment which would be informed by their personal philosophies of teaching (e.g., Heslep, 1997).

9. At the risk of complicating an already complex matter, I should mention that neither Western philosophy nor Eastern philosophy are free of mutual influences. Confucius was widely read in France during the Enlightenment, Goethe was familiar with Chinese literature, Leibnitz the I Ching, Hegel with Lao Tze, Schopenhauer the Bhagavad-Gita, Heidegger and Zen were mutually engaged, and so on. For details see e.g., Clarke (1997).

10. I will take up some aspects of the other options in Chapter 5.

11. Cited in Battistoni (1985, p. 70); presumably this would not have applied to women and slaves.

12. First in Prussia, France, and the northern United States, with the UK and southern Europe lagging well behind, according to Green (1990; cf. Green, 1997).

13. The intersection of the literatures of the history of education and comparative education are important here (e.g., Lincicome, 1995; Röhrs & Lenhart, 1995, inter alia).

14. Reagan, for example, in discussing Islamic education, explicitly separates "the traditional Islamic educational system" from "the Western-inspired, formal educational systems that are found today in most Islamic countries" (1996, p. 132).

15. Whether of the West or not, because the nation-state is a political entity largely constructed on models that first emerged in Europe.

16. Noddings (1995) points out that Rousseau embodied the antifemale views of his time and treated the genders in a very unequal fashion in his discussion of education (as in Book Five of *Emile*).

17. For example, Dewey's "New Education" model "had been advocated by Japanese liberal educators in the 1920s" (Kobayashi, 1985, p. 96).

18. Though this was primarily a result of the U.S. Occupation, "some commentators . . . interpreted [this] as a revival of the pre-war Japanese liberal education movement" (Kobayashi, 1986, p. 96). For further general discussion, see Horio, (1988), and Spring, (1998).

19. Perhaps we are about to see a re-awakening of interest in the histories of our fields (cf. Thomas, 1998).

20. These authors were addressing S/FLT generally, not just the teaching of English. In this area see also Howatt (1984), Pugh (1996) and Newmark (1948).
21. That approach, which in the United States was subsequently revamped as the popular "Natural Approach" (Krashen & Terrell, 1983).
22. Compare Clark's (1987) analysis of major curricular trends in ES/FL interpreted in terms of philosophies of education and schooling.

Chapter 4

1. Other reasons for being particularly tentative here come from the SLA and classroom research literature. Consider (1) there are still some theorists (e.g., Krashen) for whom conscious attention to language is immaterial in SL learning; (2) structural syllabi assume an entire class is psycholinguistically ready to learn the official teaching point of a specific class, which is implausible given SLA research on developmental sequences; (3) one salient study suggests that students are learning or at least paying attention to a wide variety of aspects of the target language in a SL class, but very often not the points the teacher is working on (Slimani, 1992).
2. Richards' (1998) study of planning, cited earlier, also addresses some matters of timing.
3. Though it is occasionally tackled by S/FL teachers; e.g. Antes (1996).
4. An alternative source within the teaching literature on this topic is the work of Neill (1991; Neill & Caswell, 1993). However, the approach seems highly culture specific, indeed parochial, and could be used merely as a source of possible hypotheses by teachers working outside a very traditional sector of the UK education system. Miller (1988) is a rather brief survey.
5. In the S/FLT literature, detail here is mainly at the level of anecdote. Some more substantial non-SL related references are Shilling (1992) and Shapiro (1999).
6. The study by Book et al. (1985) supports the hypotheses that (1) students of teachers trained to use explicit explanation are more aware of what they had been taught than students of teachers who are not similarly trained and (2) there is a significant positive relationship between teacher explanation and student metacognitive awareness.
7. For more than you ever wanted to know on this topic, see also Keefe and Smith (1997).

Chapter 5

1. The technocratic orientation of much of the academic field associated with the profession is the reason for this; influenced, perhaps, by the expatriate

status or experiences of an influential section of its practitioners. Most of these individuals by their status are prevented from playing a full role in the civic and moral life of their host country.

2. Politics concerns the distribution of resources under conditions of power inequity. Hawkesworth (1992, p. 27): "The central question for political research then is 'who gets what, when, how' (Lasswell [1936])." Similarly, Dove (1986, p. 32): Politics "concerns the procedures by which scarce resources are allocated and distributed.... between groups who uphold and those who challenge the status quo."

3. I include myself here. However, this seems also to be a more general problem, existing even in mainstream education. See Rich (1984).

4. To argue that women, or men, have some inherent attributes in the moral domain is "essentialist," and many question the viability of such a position. Most of the authors cited in this paragraph draw their conclusions from within their own cultures, which again tend to be white middle or upper class. Obviously there is room for debate and for a better empirical grounding of this important line of research and theory.

5. See Vandrick (1997) and Nelson (1999) for TESOL-related work oriented to this population.

6. The United States' National Education Association (NEA, 1977), the American Association of School Administrators (AASA, 1976); the American Association of University Professors (1987); cf. e.g., Chadwick, 1994; Rich, 1984. That of the AASA is ten times the length of the NEA. The other major professional organization for teachers in the United States, the AFT, does not have an ethics code [according to Rich, 1984]. For further discussion, see e.g. Sockett (1990).

7. A less-commonly recognized source of growth for the early applied linguistics field (cf. Richards, 1970).

8. See Gorlin (1994) for an extensive listing of professional codes, including many which have an international orientation or claim. An explicitly international charter seems to be more common among professional organizations in the natural sciences or engineering than among professions such as law or medicine.

9. Ex-TESOL President Dick Allwright (1991, p. 2) states "my own special interest as a member of the Executive Board of TESOL has been in the concept of internationalism, which I interpret as being centrally concerned with cooperation among people and associations in different countries." A more recent TESOL President, David Nunan, continued TESOL's concern in this area (e.g., Nunan, 2000).

10. Though it is not necessarily in line with those of the other kind of international NGO, the transnational corporation (TC)!

11. Woods (1996, p. 27) says "A belief articulated in the context of a 'story' about concrete events, behaviors, and plans, is more likely to be

grounded in actual behavior" than reflect what one might wish to do, or like to believe.

Chapter 6

1. More detailed work identifies fourteen potential components of lesson plans, but confirms that experienced teachers do not plan in such detail (Maroney & Searcy, 1996).
2. Knezevic and Scholl (1996, p. 83), as preservice S/FL teachers, reported "on average we spent four hours per week together preparing for four hours of classes ... at one of our homes, a local cafe, or a favorite restaurant." This is praiseworthy, but what are the implications for those carrying a heavier teaching load? White (1989, p. 185) remarked, "Initially student teachers' ratio of input to output time is fairly low. They often look like 'bag ladies' lugging home a shopping bag of texts and resource books nightly. After several weeks of intense exhaustion, they find that constant heroic effort ... cannot be sustained: they cannot prepare for several hours for each lesson plan if they are teaching for six hours a day."
3. For recent references see So (1997).
4. Donmoyer (1983, p. 39) comments: "Improvisation is not often discussed by educators."
5. The term has two meanings. This one derives from the psychological planning literature, and means a single person planning while also acting. Later in the chapter we will encounter a second meaning, when two individuals plan together.
6. For a little more on this topic, see Cazden (1988); and also on the matter of lesson structure.
7. Or alternatively, a move of educational social psychology from disciplinary margin to center stage; cf. Williams and Burden (1997).

Chapter 7

1. Even the concept of a discipline is increasingly questioned or seen as having feet of clay: Becher (1989), Gibbons, et al. (1994), Lemaine, et al. (1976), inter alia.
2. And not even that of Stern tells us how ES/FL teachers themselves learn. For a diagram on that point, see Freeman & Johnson (1998).
3. Some good references that could be used to follow up this important matter of the personalization of professional knowledge in our area, all cited by Golombek, are: Ulichny (1996), Burns (1996), and Moran (1996).

Chapter 8

1. Compare, for example, Brown's (1994) popular introductory handbook. The author proposes a concern for intrinsic motivation as a principle in TES/FL which should appear in teaching each of the four skills and in testing as well.
2. The section that follows draws on Crookes & Schmidt (1991). For a more detailed treatment of the topic from a S/FL viewpoint, see Williams and Burden (1997); for recent book-length treatments see Brophy (1998) for elementary and secondary education, and Brown, Armstrong, and Thompson (1998) for post-secondary education.
3. "It is believed and stated by many educators that when individuals in the class are motivated they work energetically and purposefully" (Bany & Johnson, 1975, p. 192).
4. There have been published materials that made a selling point of this, such as Maley et al. (1980). Jones and von Baeyer (1983) was an ES/FL text which contained exercises which encouraged students to express their curiosity about how the language they are learning works. I feel that these are exceptions, however, and the utilitarian character of most government-supported EFL materials lie far below most commercial materials in their appeal to curiosity.
5. See also Green's (1993) work on activities – their enjoyment and effectiveness.
6. See Wyman (1998) for a brief note of how his program did in fact modify the perspectives of some unsuccessful or resistant ESL immigrant students, with positive results.

Chapter 9

1. Although a dominant viewpoint, the topic can of course be addressed from any number of theoretical perspectives, not just that one. Historical & cultural perspectives are also illuminating – see, e.g., Shimahara (1998b).
2. Chaudron and Valcarcel (1988, summarized in Crookes & Chaudron, 1991) formed a comprehensive list from work on EFL classrooms in Spain which contained 37 activities in total.
3. To put it another way: as an outside observer, if you do not recognize some behavior as orderly, in fact if you do not recognize it as a phenomenon at all, it may be because you are ignorant of the rules that govern, indeed, constitute it.

Chapter 10

1. "L'enfer, c'est les Autres."
2. The same has been true elsewhere in education, and in other professional fields (Cohen, 1982; Cahn, 1987); Cummings et al. (1989)

suggests little is known about how teachers solve interpersonal social problems.

3. The most recent development in applied linguistics literature in this area is a return to the old research field of "group dynamics," popular in the 1960s and 70s, to investigate its implications for the language classroom. Senior (1997) does this briefly, and Dörnyei and colleagues (Dörnyei & Malderez, 1997; Ehrman & Dörnyei, 1998) have taken a more extended approach to this literature.

4. Admittedly, these surveys draw mainly on U.S. or European studies.

5. The first phase of the "knowledge base for teachers" literature, e.g. Reynolds (1989), is "notably silent on the issue of student-teacher rapport," comments Kagan (1993, p. 145).

6. And thus overlaps with another potentially interesting area for us, that of "professional education."

7. The following lists group headings taken with slight modification from Brookfield (1990, pp. 147–176). They derive from a conceptual analysis of the topic, rather than research. Brookfield works mainly in the field of adult education, but here is writing for the college teacher. He observes that "the rich literature on adult learning and adult education is rarely acknowledged, let alone drawn upon, in most works on college teaching" (1990, p. xv).

8. This refers to the cases where successful school learning is inconsistent with a learner's self-image or given identity. Thus, if you are working class, and working class kids hate school (or at least, you believe this), how can you succeed in school and still be working class?

9. In presenting these summaries, extracts, and suggestions, I have to some extent been drawing on the field of communication studies, within the subsection of communication studies related to education, or to teacher-student communication. The area is too vast to summarize further, though it seems to be one with some potentially rich insights for the ES/FL teacher, and an area not yet much taken up by researchers into S/FL classrooms. Past empirical studies in this area have identified aspects of teacher communication linked to positive student evaluations, including "teacher communication style" (TCS-Kearney and McCroskey 1980, p. 533, broken down into "assertiveness, versatility and responsiveness"), "self-disclosure" (Sorensen 1989) and "perceived understanding" (Cahn 1987); see also Nussbaum and Scott (1980).

10. Unfortunately, this study did not have a process component – we are unable to tell which of the sixty humanistic exercises (described in Moscowitz, 1978) the teachers experienced in their training course, besides those they developed themselves, were implemented in their classes, nor how they were implemented.

11. Johnson and Johnson (1982), in a review of 37 studies of cooperative learning for which there was "interpersonal attraction data" find that in 35 of them "cooperative learning promoted greater interpersonal attraction" (pp. 112–113). The efficacy of cooperative learning in building positive interpersonal relations among second language students has also been demonstrated in at least one small investigation (of high school French as a SL classes – Gunderson and Johnson, 1980).
12. For further details see e.g., Kagan (1992), Hultman (1998).
13. The most obvious cases concern expatriate native-speaker teachers, but as English is increasingly a world possession these are not the only cases. Amin (1997) discusses the cases of minority ESL teachers in Canada whose students did not accept them fully on the basis of their ethnicities.
14. "The concepts and strategies ... have been field-tested ... with students who are African American, Hispanic, Native American, Asian, Anglo, poor, rich, learning disabled, emotionally disturbed, and talented and gifted," claims one confident classroom management text (Jones with Jones, 1998, p. xiii).
15. For a recent overview, see Shriewer (2000). Those wishing to explore other source areas for developing cross-cultural rapport might wish to consider the literature on cross-cultural communication, for example, cross-cultural interpersonal communication (e.g. Ting-Toomey & Korzenny, 1991), and cross-cultural counseling (e.g. Pedersen, 1982).

Chapter 11

1. For much more extensive discussion including practical tips on reflective practice, see Ghaye and Ghaye (1998); and to move beyond the teacher, see e.g. Sparks-Langer (1992).
2. Or, for that matter, the mainstream of ELT? In one of the major outgrowths of this concept for TESOL, Richards and Lockhart's *Reflective teaching in second language classrooms*, the authors acknowledge (1994, pp. 16–17) Bartlett's work and use the term "critical" in their introductory sections, but do not take up the critical dimension in detail or define the term as Bartlett does.
3. Weber is one of the founding figures of sociology, noted among other things for his definitional exploration of the concept of "bureaucracy" (e.g. Andreski, 1983).
4. Their focus is specifically on the service English or Intensive English Program sector of the United States.

5. Those of classical antiquity in Europe, and of Confucius, in the East.
6. The global breadth of this movement, or lack of it, is addressed by Lawton (1990) and Lauglo (1996), among others.

Chapter 12

1. I should mention that the model was developed from experience with *pre-service* teachers. This doesn't show up particularly strongly.
2. Colton and Sparks-Langer do not actually use this term in the original paper.
3. Though see Noddings and Shore (1984) for a wide-ranging survey of the senses of this word in teaching; including some of its more positive attributes.
4. For more on this topic, see, in our field Johnson (1996); elsewhere McLaughlin and Vogt (1996) and the volume 25 special issue of *Teacher Education Quarterly.*

Appendix A

1. The only substantive discussion, appearing since this work was originally drafted, is Clair (1998).
2. This point appears in Clair (1998). The two teacher study groups she investigated were organized by an outside specialist (Clair herself), who attended all meetings, and they carried university credit. Considerable tension was experienced as members expected the specialist to provide direct instruction and supply materials, whereas the specialist hoped the teachers would collaborate with her on a more equal basis.

Appendix D

1. Being a cooperating teacher is a special case of being a mentor. I do not discuss the overarching concept, but note that mentoring is a responsibility of many senior teachers that is gaining increased attention in recent years. See e.g., Maynard (1997), Pascarelli (1998), and Reiman and Thies-Sprinthall (1998).
2. Hall and Davis (below) use the term "teaching pair," which does not refer to the junior teacher as a student teacher. This seems particularly appropriate to some parts of the field of TESOL, where, because of unorthodox or uncontrolled entry to the "profession," teachers may gain considerable experience before taking a standard qualification, such as the MA.
3. The modern research university is widely regarded as having started in Germany.

4. For a description of one such course, see Caruso (1998).
5. Gibbs and Montoya (1994, p. 1) report their survey in which "97 percent of [149 cooperating teacher] respondents perceived benefits in working with student teachers for both the classroom students and their own personal professional development."
6. The University of Hawai'i College of Education M.E.T. program – a Masters of Education in Teaching for non-traditional entrants to teaching.

References

[UK Govt.], 1988. Educational Reform Act. London: Her Majesty's Stationery Office.

Abbott, G. 1992. The proper study of ELT. In A. van Essen & E. I. Burkart (eds.), *Homage to W. R. Lee: Essays in English as a Foreign or Second Language* (pp. 21–27). Berlin: Foris.

Agee, J. M. 1996. "I was kind of hoping for a woman": issues of lived experience in the preservice-cooperating teacher relationship. *English Education, 28*(4), 280–302.

Alatis, J., & Straehle, C. A. 1997. The universe of English: imperialism, chauvinism, and paranoia. In L. E. Smith & M. L. Forman (eds.), *World Englishes 2000* (pp. 1–20). Honolulu, HI: University of Hawai'i Press.

Allwright, D. 1991. *Exploratory teaching, professional development, and the role of a teachers' association* (CRILE Working Paper #7). Lancaster, UK: Centre for Research in Language Education, University of Lancaster.

American Association of School Administrators [AASA]. 1976. *AASA statement of ethics for school administrators and procedural guidelines.* Arlington, VA: AASA.

American Association of University Professors. 1987. Statement on professional ethics. *Academe, 73*(4), 49.

Ames, C. 1984. Competitive, cooperative, and individualistic goal structures: a cognitive-instructional analysis. In R. E. Ames & C. Ames (eds.), *Research on motivation in education* (vol. 1, pp. 177–207). New York: Academic Press.

Ames, C. 1986. Effective motivation: the contribution of the learning environment. In R. S. Feldman (ed.), *The social psychology of education* (pp. 235–256). Cambridge: Cambridge University Press.

Amin, N. 1997. Race and the identity of the nonnative ESL teacher. *TESOL Quarterly, 31*(3), 580–583.

Andreski, S. (ed., trans.). 1983. *Max Weber on capitalism, bureaucracy, and religion: a selection of texts.* Boston: Allen & Unwin.

Antes, T. A. 1996. Kinesics: the value of gesture in language and in the language classroom. *Foreign Language Annals, 29*(3), 439–448.

Applegate, J. H., & Lasley, T. J. 1982. Cooperating teachers' problems with preservice field experience students. *Journal of Teacher Education, 33*(2), 15–18.

Armour, M. 1985. Energy RX for writing teachers: plug into a network. *Language Arts, 62*, 759–764.

Ashton-Warner, S. 1958. *Spinster.* New York: Touchstone.

Ashton-Warner, S. 1963. *Teacher.* New York: Simon and Schuster.

Ashworth, M. 1991. Internationalism and our 'strenuous family.' *TESOL Quarterly 25*(2), 231–243.

Auerbach, E. 1991. Politics, pedagogy, and professionalism: challenging marginalization in ESL. *College English, 1*(1), 1–9.

Bagley, W. D. 1922. Preparing teachers for the urban service. *Educational Administration and Supervision, 7*, 400.

Bailey, F. 1996. The role of collaborative dialogue in teacher education. In D. Freeman & J. C. Richards (eds.), *Teacher learning in language teaching* (pp. 260–280). Cambridge: Cambridge University Press.

Bailey, K. 1992. The process of innovation in language teacher development: what, why, and how teachers change. In J. Flowerdew, M. Brock, & S. Hsia (eds.), *Perspectives on language teacher education* (pp. 253–282). Hong Kong: City Polytechnic of Hong Kong.

Bailey, K. M. & Celce-Murcia, M. 1979. Classroom skills for ESL teachers. In M. Celce-Murcia and L. McIntosh (eds.), *Teaching English as a second or foreign language* (pp. 315–330). Rowley, MA: Newbury House.

Baker, S. B., Swisher, J. D., Nadenichek, P. E., & Popowicz, C. L. 1984. Measured effects of primary prevention strategies. *The Personnel and Guidance Journal, 63*, 459–463.

Balch, P. M., & Balch, P. E. 1987. *The cooperating teacher.* Lanham, MD: University Press of America.

Ball, D. L., & Feiman-Nemser, S. 1988. Using textbooks and teachers' guides: a dilemma for beginning teachers and teacher educators. *Curriculum Inquiry, 18*(4), 401–423.

Bandura, A. 1982. Self-efficacy mechanism in human agency. *American Psychologist, 37*, 747–755.

Bandura, A., & Schunk, D. H. 1981. Cultivating competence, self-efficacy, and intrinsic interest through proximal self-motivation. *Journal of Personality and Social Psychology, 41*, 586–598.

Bany, M. A., & Johnson, L. V. 1975. *Educational social psychology.* New York: Macmillan.

Barnes, D. (ed.) 1971. *Language, the learner and the school.* Harmondsworth, UK: Penguin.

Bar-Tal, Y., & Bar-Tal, D. 1986. Social psychological analysis of classroom interaction. In R. S. Feldman (ed.), *The social psychology of education:*

current research and theory (pp. 132–149). Cambridge: Cambridge University Press.

Bartlett, L. 1990. Teacher development through reflective teaching. In J. C. Richards & D. Nunan (eds.), *Second language teacher education* (pp. 202–214). Cambridge: Cambridge University Press.

Bartu, H. 1991. The social relations in a language classroom: a neglected issue. *System, 19*(3), 225–233.

Bashiruddin, A., Edge, J., & Hughes-Pelegrin, E. 1990. Who speaks in seminars? Status, culture and gender at Durham University. In R. Clark, N. Fairclough, R. Ivanic, N. McLeod, J. Thomas, & P. Meara, *Language and power* (pp. 74–84). London: CILT/BAAL.

Bassano, S. 1986. Helping learners adapt to unfamiliar methods. *ELT Journal, 40*(1), 13–19.

Bateson, G. 1972. *Steps to an ecology of mind.* New York: Ballantine.

Battistoni, R. M. 1985. *Public schooling and the education of democratic citizens.* Jackson, MI: University Press of Missouri.

Baumeister, R. F. 1986. *Identity: Cultural change and the struggle for self.* New York: Oxford University Press.

Baumeister, R. F. 1991. *Meanings of life.* New York: Guilford Press.

Baumeister, R. F., Heatherton, T. F., & Tice, D. M. 1994. *Losing control.* New York: Academic Press. (ch. 4: Self-management)

Becher, T. 1989. *Academic tribes and territories: intellectual enquiry and the cultures of disciplines.* Milton Keynes: Open University Press.

Bechtold, J. 1983. Planning the lesson. *TESL Talk, 14*(1&2), 142–149.

Bell, J. 1988. *Teaching multilevel classes in ESL.* San Diego, CA: Dormac.

Benson, M. 1991. Attitudes and motivation towards English: A survey of Japanese freshmen. *RELC Journal, 22*(1), 34–48.

Benson, P., & Voller, P. (eds.) 1997. *Autonomy and Independence in Language Learning.* London: Longman.

Berger, P. L., & Luckmann, T. 1966. *The social construction of reality.* Harmondsworth, UK: Penguin.

Bey, T., & Holmes, C. T. (eds.). 1992. *Mentoring: Contemporary Principles and Issues.* Reston, VA: Association of Teacher Educators

Birch, B. M. 1993. Prosocial communicative competence in the ESOL classroom. *TESOL Journal, 3*(2), 13–16.

Black, P. J. 1998. *Testing: friend or foe?* London: Falmer Press.

Blase, J., & Anderson, G. L. 1995. *The micropolitics of educational leadership: from control to empowerment.* New York: Cassell.

Blum, L. 1980. *Friendship, altruism and morality.* Boston, MA: Routledge.

Boak, G. 1998. *A complete guide to learning contracts.* Aldershot, UK: Gower.

Bobbitt, F. 1918. *The curriculum.* Boston, MA: Houghton, Mifflin.

Boli, J., & Thomas, G. M. (eds.). 1999. *Constructing world culture: international nongovernmental organizations since 1875.* Stanford, CA: Stanford University Press.

Book, C. L., et al. 1985. A study of the relationship between teacher explanation and student metacognitive awareness during reading instruction. *Communication Education, 34*(1), 29–36.

Boostrom, R. 1991. The nature and functions of classroom rules. *Curriculum Inquiry, 21*(2), 193–216.

Borg, S. 1998. Teachers' pedagogical systems and grammar teaching: a qualitative study. *TESOL Quarterly, 32*(1), 9–38.

Borko, H., & Livingston, C. 1989. Cognition and improvisation: differences in mathematics instruction by expert and novice teachers. *American Educational Research Journal, 26*(4), 473–498.

Borko, H., & Mayfield, V. 1995. The roles of the cooperating teacher and university supervisor in learning to teach. *Teaching and Teacher Education, 11*(5), 501–18.

Boulding, E. 1988. *Building a global civic culture.* New York: Teachers College Press.

Bourdieu, P. (trans. R. Nice). 1977. *Outline of a theory of practice.* Cambridge: Cambridge University Press.

Bowers, C. A., & Flinders, D. J. 1990. *Responsive teaching: an ecological approach to classroom patterns of language, culture, and thought.* New York: Teachers College Press.

Bowman, N. 1979. College supervision of student teaching. *Journal of Teacher Education, 30*(3), 29–30.

Bowyer, C. H. 1970. *Philosophical perspectives for education.* Glenview, IL: Scott, Foresman.

Braine, G. 1998. *Non-native educators in English language teaching.* Hillsdale, NJ: Erlbaum.

Brammer, L. M. 1985. *The helping relationship: process and skills* (3rd. edn.). Englewood Cliffs, NJ: Prentice-Hall.

Brezinka, W. 1992. *Philosophy of educational knowledge* (trans. J. S. Brice & R. Eshelman; originally published 1971). Dordrecht: Kluwer.

Brindley, G. 1989. The role of needs analysis in adult ESL programme design. In R. K. Johnson (ed.), *The second language curriculum* (pp. 63–78). Cambridge: Cambridge University Press.

Brinton, D., & Holten, C. 1989. What novice teachers focus on: the practicum in TESL. *TESOL Quarterly, 23*(2), 343–350.

Brislin, R. W., Chushner, K., Cherrie, C., & Yong, M. 1986. *Intercultural interactions.* Beverly Hills, CA: Sage.

Britzman, D. P. 1991. *Practice makes practice: a critical study in learning to teach.* New York: SUNY Press

Brookfield, S. 1985. (ed.). *Self-directed learning from theory to practice*. San Francisco, CA: Jossey-Bass.

Brookfield, S. 1986. *Understanding and facilitating adult learning*. San Francisco, CA: Jossey-Bass.

Brookfield, S. D. 1990. *The skillful teacher*. San Francisco, CA: Jossey-Bass.

Brophy, J. & Kher, N. 1986. Teacher socialization as a mechanism for developing student motivation to learn. In R. S. Feldman (ed.), *The social psychology of education* (pp. 257–288). Cambridge: Cambridge University Press.

Brophy, J. 1998. *Motivating students to learn*. New York: McGraw Hill.

Brown, G., & Atkins, M. 1997. Explaining. In Hargie, O. D. W. (ed.), *The handbook of communication skills* (2nd. edn.; pp. 183–212). London: Routledge.

Brown, H. D. 1994. *Teaching by principles: an interactive approach to language pedagogy*. Englewood Cliffs, NJ: Prentice Hall Regents.

Brown, K., & Peterson, J. 1997. Exploring conceptual frameworks: framing a world Englishes paradigm. In L. E. Smith & M. L. Forman (eds.), *World Englishes 2000* (pp. 32–47). Honolulu: University of Hawai'i Press.

Brown, R. 1992. Max Van Manen and pedagogical human science research. In W. Pinar & W. Reynolds (eds.), *Understanding curriculum as phenomenological and deconstructed text* (pp. 41–63). New York: Teachers College Press.

Brown, S., Armstrong, S., & Thompson, G. 1998. *Motivating students*. London: Kogan Page.

Brubacher, J. W., Case, C. W., & Reagan, T. G. 1994. Values, ethics, and reflective teaching (Ch. 6 of *Becoming a reflective educator*). Thousand Oaks, CA: Corwin Press.

Bruner, E. M. 1986. Ethnography as narrative. In E. M. Bruner & V. Turner (eds.), *The anthropology of experience* (pp. 139–155). Urbana, IL: University of Illinois Press.

Bruner, J. 1986. *Actual minds, possible worlds*. Cambridge, MA: Harvard University Press.

Bruner, J. 1987. Life as narrative. *Social Research, 54*, 11–32.

Bull, B. L., Fruehling, R. T., & Chattergy, V. 1992. *The ethics of multicultural and bilingual education*. New York: Teachers College Press.

Bunting, C. 1988. Cooperating teachers and the changing views of teacher candidates. *Journal of Teacher Education, 39*(2), 42–46.

Burnett, J. H. 1973. Event description and analysis in the microethnography of urban classrooms. In F. A. J. Ianni & E. Storey (eds.), *Cultural relevance and educational issues* (pp. 287–303). Boston, MA: Little, Broom.

Burns, A. 1996. Starting all over again. In D. Freeman & J. C. Richards (eds.), *Teacher learning in language teaching* (pp. 11–29). Cambridge: Cambridge University Press.

Burns, A. 2000. *Participatory action research and ESL.* New York: Cambridge University Press.

Burns, A., & Hood, S. (eds.). 1995. *Teachers' voices: exploring course design in a changing curriculum.* Macquarie University: National Centre for English Teaching and Research.

Burns, A., & Hood, S. (eds.). 1998. *Teachers' voices: Australian teachers' perspectives on teaching mixed-level immigrant groups.* Macquarie University: National Centre for English Teaching and Research.

Cahn, D. D., Jr. 1987. *Letting go* (Chapter 9, Teacher-student relationships). New York: SUNY Press.

Carr, W., & Kemmis, S. 1986. *Becoming critical: education, knowledge, and action research.* London: Falmer Press.

Carter, K. 1990. Teachers' knowledge and learning to teach. In W. R. Houston (ed.), *Handbook of research on teacher education* (pp. 291–310). New York: Macmillan.

Caruso, J. J. 1998. What cooperating teacher case studies reveal about their phases of development as supervisors of student teachers. *European Journal of Teacher Education, 21*(1), 119–132.

Caulk, N. 1998. Intercultural faculty meetings. In J. C. Richards (ed.), *Teaching in action: case studies from second language classrooms* (pp. 132–136). Washington DC: TESOL.

Cazden, C. 1981. Social contexts of learning to read. In J. T. Guthrie (ed.), *Comprehension and teaching: research reviews* (pp. 118–139). Newark, DE: International Reading Association.

Cazden, C. B. 1988. *Classroom discourse.* Portsmouth, NH: Heinemann.

Chadwick, R. F. (ed.). 1994. *Ethics and the professions.* Aldershot, UK: Avebury.

Chalfant, J. C., & Pysh, M. V. 1989. Teacher assistance teams: Five descriptive studies on 96 teams. *Remedial and Special Education, 10*, 49–58.

Charles, C. M. 1992. *Building classroom discipline* (4th edn.). New York: Longman.

Chatfield, C. 1997. Intergovernmental and nongovernmental associations to 1945. In J. Smith, C. Chatfield, & R. Pagnucco (eds.), *Transnational social movements and global politics* (pp. 19–41). Syracuse University Press.

Chaudron, C. 1988. *Second language classrooms.* Cambridge: Cambridge University Press.

Chaudron, C., & Valcarcel, M. 1988. *A process-product study of communicative language teaching.* Murcia, Spain: Universidad de Murcia.

Chiang, P. 1981. *Non-governmental organizations at the United Nations.* New York: Praeger.

Chick, J. K. 1996. Safe-talk: collusion in apartheid education. In H. Coleman (ed.), *Society and the language classroom* (pp. 21–39). Cambridge University Press.

Chiseri-Strater, E. 1991. *Academic literacies: the public and private discourse of university students*. Portsmouth, NH: BoyntonCook/Heinemann.

Clair, N. 1998. Teacher study groups: persistent questions in a promising approach. *TESOL Quarterly, 32*(3), 465–492.

Clark, C. M. & Peterson, P. L. 1986. Teachers' thought processes. In M. C. Wittrock (ed.), *Handbook of research on teaching* (3rd. edn.; pp. 255–296). New York: Macmillan.

Clark, John L. 1987. *Curriculum renewal in school foreign language learning*. Oxford: Oxford University Press.

Clarke, J. J. 1997. *Oriental enlightenment: the encounter between Asian and Western thought*. London: Routledge.

Clarke, M., & Silberstein, S. 1988. Problems, prescriptions, and paradoxes in second language teaching. *TESOL Quarterly, 22*(4), 685–700.

Clifford, J. 1986. On ethnographic allegory. In J. Clifford & G. Marcus (eds.), *Writing culture* (pp. 98–121). Berkeley, CA: University of California Press.

Cochran-Smith, M. 1991. Learning to teach against the grain. *Harvard Educational Review, 61*(3), 279–310.

Cody, M. J., & McLaughlin, M. L. (eds.). 1990. *The psychology of tactical communication*. Philadelphia: Multilingual Matters.

Cohen, D. 1982. Skills, professional education and the disabling university. *Studies in Higher Education, 10*, 175–186.

Cohen, L., Manion, L., & Morrison, K. 1996. *A guide to teaching practice* (4th. edn.). London: Routledge.

Coleman, H. (ed.). 1996a. *Society and the language classroom*. Cambridge University Press.

Coleman, H. 1996b. Shadow puppets and language lessons: interpreting classroom behavior in its cultural context. In H. Coleman (ed.), *Society and the language classroom* (pp. 64–85). Cambridge University Press.

Coles, R. 1989. *The call of stories: teaching and the moral imagination*. Boston, MA: Houghton Mifflin.

Colton, A. B., & Sparks-Langer, G. M. 1993. A conceptual framework to guide the development of teacher reflection and decision-making. *Journal of Teacher Education, 44*(1), 45–54.

Conoley, J. C. 1989. Professional communication and collaboration among educators. In M. C. Reynolds (ed.), *Knowledge base for the beginning teacher* (pp. 245–254). Oxford: Pergamon.

Cooper, H. & Tom, D. Y. H. 1984. SES and ethnic differences in achievement motivation. In R. E. Ames & C. Ames (eds.), *Motivation in education* (vol. 1, pp. 209–242). New York: Academic Press.

Cooper, J. E. 1991. Telling our own stories: the reading and writing of journals and diaries. In C. Witherell & N. Noddings (eds.), *Stories lives tell: narrative and dialogue in education* (pp. 96–112). New York: Teachers College Press.

Costa, A. L., & Garmston, R. 1985. Supervision for intelligent teaching. *Educational Leadership, 42*(5), 70–80.

Costa, A., & Garmston, R. 1988. *Cognitive coaching manual.* Stanford, CA: Institute for Instructional Behavior.

Cripwell, K. 1979. A question of pace. In S. Holden (ed.), *Teacher training* (pp. 47–50). London: Modern English Publications.

Crites, S. D. 1971. The narrative quality of experience. *Journal of the American Academy of Religion, 39*, 292–311.

Crookes, G. 1986. *Task classification: a cross-disciplinary review.* Technical Report no. 4, Center for Second Language Classroom Research, Social Science Research Institute, University of Hawai'i.

Crookes, G. 1989. Planning and interlanguage variation. *Studies in Second Language Acquisition, 11*(4), 367–383.

Crookes, G. 1993. Action research for SL teachers – going beyond teacher research. *Applied Linguistics, 14*(2), 130–144.

Crookes, G. 1995. Teacher action for the prerequisites for teacher development. In L. Y. Shem (ed.), *Proceedings of the 1994 ASOCOPI Congress.* Colombia: ASOCOPI.

Crookes, G., & Arakaki, L. 1999. Teaching idea sources and work conditions in an ESL program. *TESOL Journal, 8*(1), 15–19.

Crookes, G., & Chaudron, C. 1991. Principles of second language teaching. In M. Celce-Murcia (ed.), *Teaching English as a second or foreign language* (2nd. edn., pp. 46–67). New York: Newbury House.

Crookes, G., & Lehner, A. 1998. Aspects of process in a critical pedagogy teacher education course. *TESOL Quarterly, 32*(2), 319–328.

Crookes, G, & Schmidt, R. W. 1991. Motivation: reopening the research agenda. *Language Learning, 41*(4), 469–512.

Cruickshank, D. R., & Applegate, J. H. 1981. Reflective teaching as a strategy for teacher growth. *Educational Leadership, 38*, 553–554.

Cruickshank, D. R., & Metcalf, K. K. 1995. Explaining. In L. W. Anderson (ed.), *International encyclopedia of teaching and teacher education* (2nd. edn.; pp. 232–238). New York: Pergamon.

Csikszentmihalyi, M. & Nakamura, J. 1989. The dynamics of intrinsic motivation: a study of adults. In C. Ames & R. Ames (eds.), *Research on motivation in education* (vol. 3, pp. 45–71). San Diego, CA: Academic Press.

Cua, A. S. 1998. *Moral vision and tradition: essays in Chinese ethics.* Washington, DC: Catholic University of America Press.

Cuban, L. 1993. *How teachers taught: constancy and change in American classrooms, 1890–1990* (2nd. edn.). New York: Teachers College Press.

Cumming, A. 1989. Student teachers' conceptions of curriculum: toward an understanding of language-teacher development. *TESL Canada Journal, 7*(1), 33–51.

Cummings, A. L., Murray, H. G., and Martin, J. 1989. Protocol analysis of the social problem solving of teachers. *American Educational Research Journal, 26*, 25–43.

Cushner, K. (ed.). 1998. *International perspectives on international education.* Mahwah, NJ: Erlbaum.

Dahllöf, U. S. 1971. *Ability grouping, content validity and curriculum process analysis.* New York: Teachers College Press.

Damasio, A. R. 1994. *Descartes' error: emotion, reason, and the human brain.* New York: Putnam.

David, J. L. 1995. The who, what, and why of site-based management. *Educational Leadership, 53*(4), 4–9.

Davidson, J. O., & Tesh, J. S. 1997. Theory and practice in language program organizational design. In M. A. Christison & F. L. Stoller (eds.), *A handbook for language program administrators* (pp. 177–197). Burlingame, CA: Alta Book Center Publishers.

Day, R. R. 1992. Models and the knowledge base of second language teacher education. In E. Sadtono (ed.), *Issues in language teacher education* (pp. 38–48). Singapore: Regional Language Center.

deCharms, R. 1984. Motivation enhancement in educational settings. In R. E. Ames & C. Ames (eds.), *Motivation in education* (vol. 1, pp. 275–310). New York: Academic Press.

Della-Dora, D., & Blanchard, L. J. (eds.). 1979. *Moving toward self-directed learning.* Alexandria, VA: Association for Curriculum Supervision and Development.

Delpit, L. 1995. *Other people's children: cultural conflict in the classroom.* New York: The New Press.

Deming, A. L. 1984. Personal effectiveness groups: A new approach to faculty development. *Journal of College Student Personnel, 25*, 54–60.

Denoon, D., et al. (eds.). 1996. *Multicultural Japan: palaeolithic to postmodern.* New York: Cambridge University Press.

De Volder, M. L., & Lens, W. 1982. Academic achievement and future time perspective as a cognitive-motivational concept. *Journal of Personality and Social Psychology, 44*, 20–33.

Dewey, J. 1904/1965. The relation of theory to practice in education. In M. Borrowman (ed.), *Teacher education in America: a documentary history* (pp. 1401–1471). New York: Teachers College Press.

Dickinson, L. 1987. *Self-instruction in language learning.* Cambridge University Press.

DiPardo, A. 1996. Seeking alternatives: the wisdom of collaborative teaching. *English Education, 28*(2), 109–126.

Doenau, S. J. 1985. Classroom structuring. In T. Husen & T. N. Postlethwaite (eds.), *International encyclopedia of education* (pp. 755–765) New York: Pergamon.

Donaldson, E. L. (ed.). 1995. *Caring for your voice.* Calgary, Canada: Detselig Enterprises.

Donato, R., & Adair-Hauck, B. 1992. Discourse perspectives on formal instruction. *Language Awareness, 1*(2), 73–89.

Donmoyer, R. 1983. Pedagogical improvisation. *Educational Leadership, 40*(4), 39–43.

Dörnyei, Z., & Malderez, A. 1997. Group dynamics and foreign language teaching. *System, 25*(1), 65–81.

Dörnyei, Z., & Schmidt, R. (eds.). 2001. *Motivation and second language acquisition.* Honolulu: National Foreign Language Resource Center/ University of Hawai'i Press.

Dove, L. 1986. *Teachers and teacher education in developing countries.* London: Croom Helm.

Doyle, W. 1986. Classroom management. In M. C. Wittrock (ed.), *Handbook of research on teaching* (3rd. edn.; pp. 392–431). New York: Macmillan.

Duff, P. A. 1995. An ethnography of communication in immersion classrooms in Hungary. *TESOL Quarterly, 29*(3), 505–537.

Duke, B. C. 1973. *Japan's militant teachers; a history of the left-wing teachers' movement.* Honolulu: University Press of Hawai'i.

Duke, D. L. 1990. Setting goals for professional development. *Educational Leadership, 47*(8), 71–75.

Dunn, T. G., & Taylor, C. A. 1993. Cooperating teacher advice. *Teaching and Teacher Education, 9*(4), 411–423.

Dweck, C. S. 1986. Motivational processes affecting learning. *American Psychologist, 41*, 1040–1048.

Edelsky, C., Draper, K., & Smith, K. 1983. Hookin' 'em in at the start of school in a "whole language" classroom. *Anthropology and Education Quarterly, 14*, 257–281.

Edgar, D., & Warren, R. 1969. Power and autonomy in teacher socialization. *Sociology of Education, 42*, 386–399.

Edge, J. 1992. Co-operative development. *ELT Journal, 46*(1), 62–70.

Edge, J. 1993. *Cooperative development: professional self-development through cooperation with colleagues.* London: Longman.

Edge, J. 1996. Cross-cultural paradoxes in a profession of values. *TESOL Quarterly, 30*(1), 9–30.

Ehrman, M. E., & Dörnyei, Z. 1998. *Interpersonal dynamics in second language education: the visible and invisible classroom.* Thousand Oaks, CA: Sage.

Ellis, R. 1999. *SLA Research and Language Teaching.* Oxford University Press.

Emmer, E. T., Sanford, J. P., & Anderson, L. 1980. Effective classroom management at the beginning of the school year. *Elementary School Journal, 80*(5), 219–231.

Eraut, M. 1994. *Developing professional knowledge and competence.* Philadelphia, PA: Falmer Press.

Erickson, F. 1982. Classroom discourse as improvisation: relationships between academic task structure and social participation structure in lessons. In L. C. Wilkinson (ed.), *Communicating in the classroom* (pp. 153–181). New York: Academic Press.

Erickson, F., & Schultz, J. 1982. *The counselor as gatekeeper.* New York: Academic Press.

Evans, S. H. & Dansereau, D. F. 1991. Knowledge maps as tools for thinking and communication. In R. F. Mulcahy, R. H. Short, & J. Andrews (eds.), *Enhancing learning and thinking* (pp. 97–120). New York: Praeger.

Fanselow, J. 1987. *Breaking rules.* New York: Longman.

Fanselow, J. F. 1988. "Let's see": contrasting conversations about teaching. *TESOL Quarterly, 22*, 113–130.

Feiman-Nemser, S., & Beasley, K. 1997. Mentoring as assisted performance: a case of co-planning. In V. Richardson (ed.), *Constructivist teacher education* (pp. 108–126). Philadelphia, PA: Falmer Press.

Feldman, A. 1996. Coming to understand teaching as a way of being: Teachers as knowers, reasoners and understanders. Paper presented at the Second International Conference on Teacher Education, July 1–4, 1996, Netanya, Israel.

Feldman, A. 1997. Varieties of wisdom in the practice of teachers. *Teaching and Teacher Education, 13*(7), 757–773.

Floden, R. E., & Clark, C. M. 1988. Preparing teachers for uncertainty. *Teachers College Record, 89*(4), 505–520.

Flythe, V. L. 1989. Beginning a faculty writing group. *English Journal, 78*, 62–63.

Freeman, D. 1982. Observing teachers: Three approaches to in-service training and development. *TESOL Quarterly, 16*, 21–28.

Freeman, D. 1989. Teacher training, development, and decision making: a model of teaching and related strategies for language teacher education. *TESOL Quarterly, 23*(1), 27–45.

Freeman, D. 1991. "To make the tacit explicit": teacher education, emerging discourse, and conceptions of teaching. *Teaching & Teacher Education, 7*(5/6), 439–454.

Freeman, D. 1992. Language teacher education, emerging discourse, and change in classroom practice. In J. Flowerdew, M. Brock, & S. Hsia (eds.), *Perspectives on language teacher education* (pp. 1–21). Hong Kong: City Polytechnic of Hong Kong.

Freeman, D. 1993. Renaming experience/reconstructing practice: developing new understandings of teaching. *Teaching and Teacher Education, 9*, 485–498.

Freeman, D. 1994. Educational linguistics and the knowledge base for teaching. In J. E. Alatis (ed.), *Language, communication, and social meaning* (GURT '94; pp. 180–197). Washington, DC: Georgetown University Press.

Freeman, D. 1996. The "unstudied problem": research on teacher learning in language teaching. In D. Freeman & J. C. Richards (eds.), *Teacher learning in language teaching* (pp. 351–378). Cambridge: Cambridge University Press.

Freeman, D. 1998. *Doing teacher-research: from inquiry to understanding.* New York: Heinle & Heinle.

Freeman, D., & Johnson, K. E. 1998. Reconceptualizing the knowledge-based of language teacher education. *TESOL Quarterly, 32*(3), 397–418.

Freeman, D., & Richards, J. C. (eds.). 1996. *Teacher learning in language teaching.* New York: Cambridge University Press.

Freeman, Y. S., & Freeman, D. E. 1998. *ESL/EFL teaching: principles for success.* Portsmouth, NH: Heinemann.

Fuller, F. F., & Bown, O. H. 1975. Becoming a teacher. In K. Ryan (ed.), *Teacher education* (74th yearbook of the National Society of the Study of Education, part 2, pp. 25–52). Chicago: University of Chicago Press.

Funk, F. F. et al. 1982. The cooperating teacher as most significant other: a competent humanist. *Action in Teacher Education, 4*(2), 57–64.

Gainen, J. 1993. A writing support program for junior faculty women. *New Directions for Teaching and Learning, 53*, 91–100.

Ganser, T. 1996. The cooperating teacher role. *Teacher Educator, 31*(4), 283–291.

Gatenby, E. V. 1948/1967. Reasons for failure to learn a foreign language. Reprinted in W. R. Lee (ed.), *E.L.T. selections 1* (pp. 1–10). London: Oxford University Press.

Gebhard, J. G. 1984. Models of supervision: Choices. *TESOL Quarterly, 18*, 501–514.

Gegeo, D. 1998. Indigenous knowledge and empowerment: rural development examined from within. *The Contemporary Pacific, 10*(2), 289–315.

Ghaye, A., & Ghaye, K. 1998. *Teaching and learning through critical reflective practice.* London: David Fulton Publishers.

Gibbons, M., et al. 1994. *The new production of knowledge: the dynamics of science and research in contemporary societies*. Thousand Oaks, CA: Sage.

Gibbs, L. J, & Montoya, A. L. 1994. The student teaching experience: are student teachers the only ones to benefit? Paper presented at the Annual Meeting of the Association of Teacher Educators, Atlanta GA; Eric Document 373025.

Gilligan, C. 1982. *In a different voice: psychological theory and women's development*. Cambridge, MA: Harvard University Press.

Godwin, W. 1793a/1976. *Enquiry concerning political justice, and its influence on modern morals and happiness* (3rd. edn.). Harmondsworth, UK: Penguin.

Godwin, W. 1793b/1966. *Four early pamphlets*. Gainesville, FL: Scholars Reproduction Press.

Goldberg, M. 1982. *Theology and narrative: a critical introduction*. Nashville, TN: Abingdon.

Golombek, P. R. 1998. A study of language teachers' personal practical knowledge. *TESOL Quarterly, 32*(3), 447–464.

Gonzalez, L. E., & Carter, K. 1996. Correspondence in cooperating teachers' and student teachers' interpretations of classroom events. *Teaching and Teacher Education, 12*(1), 39–47.

Good, J., & Brophy, T. L. 1987. *Looking in classrooms*. (ch. 12 Improving Classroom Teaching). New York: Harper & Row.

Goodfellow, J. 1994. Cooperating teachers: images and the art of connoisseurship. *Australian Journal of Early Childhood, 19*(3), 28–33.

Goodman, J. 1988. Constructing a practical philosophy of teaching: a study of preservice teachers' professional perspectives. *Teaching & Teacher Education, 4*(2), 121–137.

Gordon, T. 1974. *Teacher effectiveness training*. New York: Wyden.

Gore, J., & Zeichner, K. 1991. Action research and reflective teaching in preservice teacher education: a case study from the United States. *Teaching and Teacher Education, 7*(2), 119–136.

Gorlin, R. A. (ed.). 1994. *Codes of professional responsibility* (3rd edn.) Washington, DC: Bureau of National Affairs.

Gouran, D. S. 1991. Rational approaches to decision-making and problem-solving discussion. *Quarterly Journal of Speech, 77*, 343–384.

Gower, R., & Walters, S. 1983. *Teaching practice handbook*. Oxford: Heinemann.

Green, A. 1990. *Education and state formation*. London: Macmillan.

Green, A. 1997. *Education, globalization, and the nation state*. New York: St. Martin's Press.

Green, J. M. 1993. Student attitudes toward communicative and non-communicative activities: do enjoyment and effectiveness go together? *Modern Language Journal, 77*(1), 1–10.

Griffin, G. A. 1986. Issues in student teaching: a review. *Advances in Teacher Education* (vol. 2, pp. 239–279). Norwood, NJ: Ablex.

Griffin, R. 1993. Teaching values: the later years. (Chapter 17 of *Teaching in a secondary school*). Hillsdale, NJ: Erlbaum.

Grimmett, P. P., & Erickson, G. L. (eds.). 1988. *Reflection in teacher education*. London: Pacific Educational Press.

Grimmett, P. P., & Ratzlaff, H. C. 1986. Expectations for the cooperating teacher role. *Journal of Teacher Education, 37*(6), 41–50.

Grossman, P. L. 1992. Why models matter: an alternative view on professional growth in teaching. *Review of Educational Research, 62*(2), 171–179.

Grotjahn, R. 1991. The research programme "subjective theories." *Studies in Second Language Acquisition, 13*, 187–214.

Guillaume, A. M., & Rudney, G. L. 1993. Student teachers' growth toward independence: an analysis of their changing concerns. *Teaching and Teacher Education, 9*(1), 65–80.

Gump, P. V. 1975. *Ecological psychology and children*. University of Chicago Press.

Gumperz, J. J. 1977. Sociocultural knowledge in conversational interference. In M. Saville-Troike (ed.), *Linguistics and anthropology* (pp. 191–214). Washington DC: Georgetown University Press.

Gunderson, B., & Johnson, D. 1980. Building positive attitudes by using cooperative learning groups. *Foreign Language Annals, 13*(1), 39–43.

Habib, I., & Raina, D. (eds.). 1999. *Situating the history of science: dialogues with Joseph Needham*. New York: Oxford University Press.

Hadfield, J. 1992. *Classroom dynamics*. Oxford: Oxford University Press.

Hale-Benson, J. 1986. *Black children: their roots, culture and learning styles* (rev. edn.). Baltimore, MD: Johns Hopkins Press.

Hall, E. T. 1959. *The silent language*. Greenwich, CT: Fawcett.

Hall, J. K., & Davis, J. 1995. What we know about relationships that develop between cooperating and student teachers. *Foreign Language Annals, 28*(1), 32–48.

Halliday, M. A. K. 1985 *An introduction to functional grammar*. London: Edward Arnold.

Hamm, C. M. 1989. *Philosophical issues in education: an introduction*. New York: Falmer Press.

Harmer, J. 1982/1991. *The practice of English language teaching*. Longman.

Harrington, H. 1994. Teaching and knowing. *Journal of Teacher Education, 45*, 190–198.

Hawkesworth, M. 1992. The science of politics and the politics of science. In M. Hawkesworth & M. Kogan (eds.), *Encyclopedia of government and politics* (pp. 5–39). London: Routledge.

Hawkey, W. S. 1996. A student teacher's journal. *Phi Delta Kappan, 77*(5), 352–359.

Hawkins, J. N. 1994. Issues of motivation in Asian education. In H. F. O'Neill & M. Drillings (eds.), *Motivation – theory and research* (pp. 101–115). Hillsdale, NJ: Erlbaum.

Hayhoe, R. (ed.). 1992. *Education and modernization: the Chinese experience.* Oxford: Pergamon Press.

Hekman, S. J. 1995. *Moral voices, moral selves: Carol Gilligan and feminist moral theory.* University Park, PA: Pennsylvania State University Press.

Heslep, R. D. 1997. *Philosophical thinking in educational practice.* Westport, CT: Praeger.

Heyman, R. D. 1986. Formulating topic in the classroom. *Discourse Processes, 9*, 37–55.

Hobbs, T. (ed.). 1992. *Experiential training: practical guidelines.* London: Tavistock/Routledge.

Hodge, B. 1993. *Teaching as communication.* London: Longman.

Hoffman, J. C. 1986. *Law, freedom, and story: the role of narrative in therapy, society and faith.* Waterloo, Canada: Wilfred Laurier University Press.

Holec, H. 1980. *Autonomy and foreign language learning.* Oxford: Pergamon.

Holliday, A. 1992. Tissue rejection and informal orders in ELT projects: Collecting the right information. *Applied Linguistics, 13*(4), 403–424.

Holliday, A. 1996. Large- and small-class cultures in Egyptian university classrooms: a cultural justification for curriculum change. In H. Coleman (ed.), *Society and the language classroom* (pp. 86–104). Cambridge University Press.

Holly, M. L. H. & Mcloughlin, C. S. 1989. Professional development and journal writing. In M. L. H. Holly & C. S. McLoughlin (eds.), *Perspectives on teacher professional development* (pp. 259–283). London: Falmer Press.

hooks, bell. 1995. *Teaching to transgress.* London: Routledge.

Horio, T. 1988. *Educational thought and ideology in modern Japan: state authority and intellectual freedom.* Tokyo: University of Tokyo Press.

Howatt, A. P. R. 1984. *A history of English language teaching.* London: Oxford University Press.

Hoy, W., & Rees, R. 1977. The bureaucratic socialization of student teachers. *Journal of Teacher Education, 28*(1), 23–26.

Hubbard, P., Jones, H., Thornton, B., & Wheeler, R. 1983. *A training course for TEFL.* Oxford: Oxford University Press.

Hudelson, S., & Faltis, C. 1993. Redefining basic teacher education: preparing teachers to transform teaching. In G. Guntermann (ed.), *Developing language teachers for a changing world* (pp. 23–40). Lincolnwood, IL: National Teachers Council.

Hudson, P. J. 1989. Instructional collaboration: creating the learning environment. In S. H. Fradd & M. J. Weismantel (eds.), *Meeting the needs of culturally and linguistically different students* (pp. 106–129). Boston, MA: College-Hill.

Huerta-Macias, A. 1995. Alternative assessment: responses to commonly asked questions. *TESOL Journal 5*(1), 8–11.

Hultman, K. 1998. *Making change irresistible: overcoming resistance to change in your organization.* Palo Alto, CA: Davies-Black Publishing.

Hunter, E. 1962. *The cooperating teacher at work: case studies of critical incidents.* New York: Bureau of Publications, Teachers College, Columbia University.

Ingram, D. E. 1982. Developing a language program. *RELC Journal, 13*(1), 64–86.

Iseno, K. 1998. Stimulating participation in a college classroom. In J. C. Richards (ed.), *Teaching in action: case studies in second language classrooms* (pp. 139–142). Washington DC: TESOL.

Jackson, F. 1994. Seven strategies to support a culturally responsive pedagogy. *Journal of Reading, 37*(4), 298–303.

Jackson, P. W. 1986. *The practice of teaching.* New York: Teachers College Press.

Jackson, P. W., Boostrom, R. E., & Hansen, D. T. 1993. *The moral life of schools.* San Francisco, CA: Jossey-Bass.

Jay, A. 1976. How to run a meeting. *Harvard Business Review, 54*(2), 43–57.

Ji, Y. 1997. Creating real communication via the game "Breaking the Ice." *Guidelines, 19*(1), 67–73.

Johnson, D. M. 1992. *Approaches to research in second language learning.* New York: Longman.

Johnson, D. W. 1987. *Human relations and your career* (2nd. edn., Ch. 10). Englewood Cliffs, NJ: Prentice-Hall.

Johnson, D. W., & Johnson, F. P. 1982. *Joining together: group theory and group skills* (2nd. edn.). Englewood Cliffs, NJ: Prentice-Hall.

Johnson, D. W., & Johnson, R. T. 1975. *Learning together and alone.* Englewood Cliffs, NJ: Prentice-Hall.

Johnson, J. 1968. *A brief history of student teaching.* DeKalb, IL: Creative Educational Materials.

Johnson, K. E. 1996. Portfolio assessment in second language teacher education. *TESOL Journal, 6*(2), 11–14.

Johnson, K. E. 1996. The vision versus the reality: the tensions of the TESOL practicum. In D. Freeman & J. C. Richards (eds.), *Teacher learning in language teaching* (pp. 30–49). Cambridge: Cambridge University Press.

Johnston, B. 1997. Do EFL teachers have careers? *TESOL Quarterly, 31*(4), 681–712.

Johnston, P. 1992. The ethics of our work in teacher research. In T. Newkirk (ed.), *Workshop 4 – the teacher as researcher* (pp. 31–40). Portsmouth, NH: Heinemann.

Jones, L. & von Baeyer, C. 1983. *Functions of American English*. Cambridge: Cambridge University Press.

Jones, T. S. 1981. Intercultural communication research. In S. Thomas (ed.), *Communication theory and interpersonal attraction* (pp. 121–128). New York: Ablex.

Jones, V. F. and Jones, L. S. 1990. *Comprehensive classroom management* (3rd. edn.). Boston, MA: Allyn & Bacon.

Jones, V. F. with Jones, L. S. 1998. *Comprehensive classroom management* (5th. edn.). Boston, MA: Allyn & Bacon.

Joyce, B., Murphy, C., Showers, B., & Murphy, J. 1989. School renewal as cultural change. *Educational Leadership, 47*, 70–77.

Kagan, D. M. 1992. Professional growth among preservice and beginning teachers. *Review of Educational Research, 62*, 129–169.

Kagan, D. M. 1993. *Laura and Jim and what they taught me about the gap between educational theory and practice*. Albany, New York: SUNY Press.

Kamhi-Stein, L., Lee, E., & Lee, C. 1999. How TESOL programs can enhance the preparation of nonnative English speakers. *TESOL Matters, 9*(4), 1–5.

Kaplan, R. B. 1995. Applied linguistics, AAAL, and the political scene. *AILA News, 10*(1), 2–3.

Karp. H. B. 1985. *Personal power*. New York: American Management Association.

Katz, M. S., Noddings, N., & Strike, K. A. (eds.). 1999. *Justice and caring: the search for common ground in education*. New York: Teachers College Press.

Kearney, P., & McCroskey, J. C. 1980. Relationships among teacher communication style, trait and state communication apprehension and teacher effectiveness. In D. Nimmo (ed.), *Communication yearbook 4* (pp. 533–551). New Brunswick, MN: Transaction Books.

Keefe, R., & Smith, P. (eds.). 1997. *Vagueness: a reader*. Cambridge, MA: Bradford/MIT Press.

Keller, J. M. 1983. Motivational design of instruction. In C. M. Reigeluth (ed.), *Instructional design theories and models* (pp. 386–433). Hillsdale, NJ: Erlbaum.

Kellough, R. D. 1990. *A resource guide for effective teaching in postsecondary education: planning for competence*. Lanham, MD: University Press of America.

Kelly, Louis G. 1969. *25 centuries of language teaching; an inquiry into the science, art, and development of language teaching methodology*. Rowley, MA; Newbury House.

Kemmis, S., & McTaggart, R. 1988. *The action research planner* (3rd. edn.). Geelong, Australia: Deakin University Press.

Kida, H., Ohno, R., Kanaya, T., Kato, K., & Watanabe, R. 1983. Japan. In R. M. Thomas & T. N. Postlethwaite (eds.), *Schooling in East Asia* (pp. 52–89). Oxford: Pergamon.

Kidd, J. R. 1973. *How adults learn.* New York: Association Press.

Kincheloe, J. L., & Steinberg, S. R. 1998. Addressing the crisis of whiteness. In J. L. Kincheloe, S. R. Steinberg, N. M. Rodriguez, & R. E. Chennault (eds.), *White reign* (pp. 3–30). New York: St. Martin's Press.

Kirk, W., & Walter, G. 1981. Teacher support groups serve to minimize teacher burnout: Principles for organizing. *Education, 102*, 147–150.

Kliebard, H. 1970. The Tyler rationale. *School Review, 78*, 259–272.

Klopf, D. W., & Cambra, R. E. 1983. *Speaking skills for prospective teachers.* Englewood, CO: Morton Publishing.

Knapp, M. S. et al. 1991. *Teaching for meaning in schools that serve the children of poverty.* Washington, DC: United States Department of Education.

Knezevic, A., & Scholl, M. 1996. Learning to teach together: teaching to learn together. In D. Freeman & J. C. Richards (eds.), *Teacher learning in language teaching* (pp. 79–96). Cambridge: Cambridge University Press.

Knowles, M. C. 1982. *The modern practice of adult education.* Chicago: Follett.

Kobayashi, T. 1986. From educational borrowing to educational sharing: the Japanese experience. In C. Brock & W. Tulasiewicz (eds.), *Cultural identity and educational policy* (pp. 92–113). New York: St. Martin's Press.

Koerner, M. E. 1992. The cooperating teacher: an ambivalent participant in student teaching. *Journal of Teacher Education, 43*(1), 46–56.

Kohn, A. 1991. Caring kids: the role of the schools. *Phi Delta Kappan, 72*, 496–506.

Kowalski, T. J. 1988. *The organization and planning of adult education.* New York: SUNY Press.

Kozol, J. 1982. *Alternative schools: a guide for educators and parents.* New York: Continuum (Revised edition of: *Free schools*, 1972).

Krashen, S. D. 1977. Some issues relating to the Monitor Model. In H. D. Brown, C. Yorio, & R. Crymes (eds.), *On TESOL '77* (pp. 144–158). Washington DC: TESOL.

Krashen, S. D., & Terrell, T. 1983. *The Natural Approach.* San Francisco, CA: Alemany Press.

Kremer-Hayon, L. 1991. The stories of expert and novice student teachers' supervisors: perspectives on professional development. *Teaching & Teacher Education, 7*(5/6), 427–438.

Kuty, M. 1992. Fur mehr Freude am Fremdsprachenunterricht. Teil 1: Get-to-Know Activities (For more fun in second-language instruction. Part 1: Get-to-Know Activities). *Fremdsprachenunterricht, 36*(2), 77–78.

Kwo, O. 1996. Learning to teach English in Hong Kong classrooms. In D. Freeman & J. C. Richards (eds.), *Teacher learning in language teaching* (pp. 295–319). Cambridge: Cambridge University Press.

La Fontaine, F. 1998. The effects of a continual enrollment policy on classroom dynamics. In J. C. Richards (ed.), *Teaching in action: case studies from second language classrooms* (pp. 195–198). Washington, DC: TESOL.

Ladson-Billings, G. 1992. Liberatory consequences of literacy: a case of culturally relevant instruction for African American students. *Journal of Negro Education, 61*(3), 378–391.

Ladson-Billings, G. 1995. *Dream keepers: successful teaching with African-American children*. San Francisco, CA: Jossey-Bass.

Land, M. L. 1987. Vagueness and clarity. In M. J. Dunkin (ed.), *The international encyclopedia of teaching and teacher education* (pp. 392–397). Oxford: Pergamon.

Lasswell, H. 1936. *Politics: who gets what, when, how.* New York: McGraw-Hill.

Lauglo, J. 1996. Forms of decentralization and the implications for education. In J. Chapman, W. L. Boyd, R. Lander, & D. Reynolds (eds.), *The reconstruction of education: quality, equality and control.* London: Cassell.

Laursen, J. C. 1992. *The politics of skepticism in the ancients, Montaigne, Hume, and Kant.* New York: E. J. Brill.

Lawton, S. 1990. Why restructure? An international survey of the roots of reform. *Journal of Education Policy, 8*(2), 139–154.

Lemaine, G., et al. 1976. *Perspectives on the emergence of scientific disciplines.* The Hague: Mouton.

Lemma, P. 1993. The cooperating teacher as supervisor: a case study. *Journal of Curriculum and Supervision, 8*(4), 329–42.

Lepper, M. R. 1983. Extrinsic reward and intrinsic motivation: implications for the classroom. In J. M. Levine & M. C. Wang (eds.), *Teacher and student perceptions: implications for learning* (pp. 281–317). Hillsdale, NJ: Erlbaum.

Lepper, M. R., Greene, D., & Nisbett, R. E. 1973. Undermining children's intrinsic interest with extrinsic rewards: a test of the "overjustification" hypothesis. *Journal of Personality and Social Psychology, 28*, 129–137.

Lewis, C. C. 1995. *Educating hearts and minds: reflections on Japanese preschool and elementary education.* New York: Cambridge University Press.

Lewis, M. 1998. Diverse levels and diverse goals in a community class. In J. C. Richards (ed.), *Teaching in action: case studies from second language classrooms* (pp. 278–282). Washington, DC: TESOL.

Lewis, M., & Hill, J. 1985. *Practical techniques for language teaching.* Hove, UK: Language Teaching Publications.

Likert, R. 1967. *The human organization: its management and value.* New York: McGraw-Hill.

Lincicome, M. E. 1995. *Principle, praxis, and the politics of educational reform in Meiji Japan.* Honolulu: University of Hawai'i Press.

Little, J. W. 1987. Teachers as colleagues. In V. Richardson-Koehler (ed.), *Educators' handbook: a research perspective* (pp. 491–518). New York: Longman.

Littlejohn, A. P. 1983. Increasing learner involvement in course management. *TESOL Quarterly, 17*(4), 595–608.

Liu, J. 1999. Nonnative-English-speaking professionals in TESOL. *TESOL Quarterly, 33*(1), 85–102.

LoCastro, V. 1996. English language education in Japan. In H. Coleman (ed.), *Society and the language classroom* (pp. 40–58). Cambridge University Press.

Locke, E. A., & Latham, G. P. 1990. *A theory of goal setting and task performance.* Englewood Cliffs, NJ: Prentice-Hall.

Lockhart, C. 1990. Co-operative teacher development: new observations on observation. *Perspectives* [Working Papers of the Department of English, City Polytechnic of Hong Kong], *2*, 43–57.

Long, M. H., & Crookes, G. 1992. Three approaches to task-based syllabus design. *TESOL Quarterly, 26*(1), 27–56.

Long, M. H., & Porter, P. A. 1985. Group work, interlanguage talk, and second language acquisition. *TESOL Quarterly, 19*(2), 207–228.

Lopes, L. P. Da M. 1995. What is this class about? Topic formulation in an L1 reading comprehension classroom. In G. Cook & B. Seidlhofer (eds.), *Principle and practice in applied linguistics* (pp. 349–362). Oxford: Oxford University Press.

Lortie, D. C. 1975. *Schoolteacher: a sociological study.* Chicago, IL: University of Chicago Press.

Loughran, J., & Russell, T. 1997. Meeting student teachers on their own terms: experience precedes understanding. In V. Richardson (ed.), *Constructivist teacher education* (pp. 164–181). London: Falmer Press.

Lvovich, N. 1997. *The multilingual self.* Mahwah, NJ: Erlbaum.

Lyons, N. 1983. Two perspectives: on self, relationships, and morality. *Harvard Educational Review, 53*(2), 125–145.

Lyons, N. 1990. Dilemmas of knowing: ethical and epistemological dimensions of teachers' work and development. *Harvard Educational Review, 60,* 159–180.

Lyons, N. (ed.). 1998. *With portfolio in hand: validating the new teacher professionalism.* New York: Teachers College Press.

MacIntyre, A. 1981. *After virtue.* Notre Dame, IN: University of Notre Dame Press.

Maehr, M. L. & Archer, J. 1987. Motivation and school achievement. In L. G. Katz (ed.), *Current topics in early childhood education* (pp. 85–107). Norwood, NJ: Ablex.

Mager, R. F. 1962. *Preparing instructional objectives.* Palo Alto, CA: Fearon.

Maher, F. A. & Tetreault, M. K. T. 1994. *The feminist classroom.* New York: Basic Books.

Maley, A., Duff, A., & Grellet, F. 1980. *The mind's eye: using pictures creatively in language learning.* Cambridge: Cambridge University Press.

Manderlink, G., & Harackiewicz, J. M. 1984. Proximal versus distal goal setting and intrinsic motivation. *Journal of Personality and Social Psychology, 47,* 918–928.

Manicas, P. 1982. The human sciences: a radical separation of psychology and the social sciences. In P. F. Secord (ed.), *Explaining human behavior* (pp. 155–173). Beverly Hills, CA: Sage.

Manicas, P. 1987. *A history and philosophy of the social sciences.* New York: Basil Blackwell.

Markus, H. R., & Kitayama, S. 1991. Culture and self: Implications for cognition, emotion, and motivation. *Psychological Review, 98*(2), 224–253.

Marland, P. W. 1995. Implicit theories of teaching. In L. W. Anderson (ed.), *International encyclopedia of teaching* (2nd. edn. pp. 131–136). Oxford: Pergamon.

Maroney, S. A., & Searcy, S. 1996. Real teachers don't plan that way. *Exceptionality, 6*(3), 171–189.

Marshall, K. A. 1998. Improving time management. In J. C. Richards (ed.), *Teaching in action: case studies from language classrooms* (pp. 3–9). Washington DC: TESOL.

Master, P. 1983. The etiquette of observation. *TESOL Quarterly, 17*(3), 497–501.

Matlin, M., & Short, K. G. 1991. How our teacher study group sparks change. *Educational Leadership, 49,* 68.

Maynard, T. (ed.). 1997. *An introduction to primary mentoring.* London: Cassell.

McCall, A., & Andringa, A. 1997. Learning to teach for justice and equality in a multicultural social reconstructionist teacher education course. *Action in Teacher Education, 18*(4), 57–67.

McCombs, B. L. 1994. Strategies for assessing and enhancing motivation: keys to promoting self-regulated learning and performance. In H. F. O'Neill & M. Drillings (eds.), *Motivation: theory and research* (pp. 49–69). Hillsdale, NJ: Erlbaum.

McCombs, B. L. 1984. Processes and skills underlying continued motivation to learn. *Educational Psychologist, 19*(4), 199–218.

McCombs, B. L. 1988. Motivational skills training: combining metacognitive, cognitive, and affective learning strategies. In C. E. Weinstein, E. T. Goetz & P. A. Alexander (eds.), *Learning and study strategies* (pp. 141–169). New York: Academic Press.

McCombs, B. L., & Whisler, J. S. 1997. *The learner-centered classroom and school: strategies for increasing student motivation and achievement.* San Francisco, CA: Jossey-Bass.

McGrath, I., Davies, S., & Mulphin, H. 1992. Lesson beginnings. *Edinburgh Working Papers in Applied Linguistics, 3*, 92–108.

McLaughlin, H. J. 1991. Reconciling care and control: authority in classroom relationships. *Journal of Teacher Education, 42*, 82–195.

McLaughlin, M., & Vogt, M. 1996. *Portfolios in teacher education.* Newark, DE: International Reading Association.

McMurray, D. L. 1998. Teaching large university classes in Japan: classroom management. In J. C. Richards (ed.), *Teaching in action: case studies in second language classrooms* (pp. 213–218). Washington, DC: TESOL.

Medgyes, P. 1992. Native or non-native: who's worth more? *ELT Journal, 46*(4), 340–349.

Medgyes, P. 1994. *The non-native teacher.* New York: Macmillan.

Mehan, H. 1979. *Learning lessons: social organization in a classroom.* Cambridge, MA: Harvard University Press.

Mezirow, J. 1991. *Transformative dimensions of adult learning.* San Francisco, CA: Jossey-Bass.

Middlehurst, R., & Kennie, T. 1997. Leading professionals: towards new concepts of professionalism. In J. Broadbent, M. Dietrich, & J. Roberts (eds.), *The end of the professions?* (pp. 50–68). London: Routledge.

Miles, M. B., Saxl, E. R., & Lieberman, A. 1988. What skills do educational "change agents" need? An empirical view. *Curriculum Inquiry, 18*, 157–193.

Miller Retwaiut, H. L. 1994. *Cross-cultural communication difficulties of some Micronesians in entry-level employment interviews in Hawaii.* Unpublished MA thesis (University of Hawai'i at Manoa, English as a Second Language; no. 2367).

Miller, B., & Kantrow, I. 1998. *A guide to facilitating cases in education.* Portsmouth, NH: Heinemann.

Miller, P. W. 1988. *Nonverbal communication* (3rd. edn.). Washington, DC: National Education Association.

Mink, L. 1978. Narrative form as a cognitive instrument. In R. Canary & H. Kozicki (eds.), *The writing of history* (pp. 129–142). Madison, WI: University of Madison Press.

Moran, P. M. 1996. "I'm not typical." In D. Freeman & J. C. Richards (eds.), *Teacher learning in language teaching* (pp. 125–153). Cambridge: Cambridge University Press.

Moscowitz, G. 1978. *Caring and sharing in the foreign language class: A sourcebook on humanistic techniques.* Rowley, MA: Newbury House.

Moscowitz, G. 1981. Effects of humanistic techniques on attitude, cohesiveness, and self-concept of foreign language students. *Modern Language Journal, 65*, 149–157.

Moscowitz, G., & Hayman, J. 1974. Interaction patterns of first year, typical and "best" teachers in inner city schools. *Journal of Educational Research 67*(5), 224–30.

Moscowitz, G., Benevento, J., & Furst, N. 1973. Sensitivity in the foreign language classroom. In J. W. Dodge (ed.), *Reports of the working committees* (pp. 13–57). Northeast conference on the teaching of foreign languages.

Moustakas, C. 1966. *The authentic teacher: sensitivity and awareness in the classroom.* Cambridge, MA: H. A. Doyle.

Moyer, B., & Tuttle, A. 1983. Overcoming masculine oppression in mixed groups. In [various authors, no editor] *Off their backs* (pp. 25–29). Philadelphia: New Society Press.

Mulholland, J. 1994. *Handbook of persuasive tactics: a practical language guide.* London: Routledge.

Murdoch, I. 1970. *The sovereignty of good.* London: Routledge & Kegan Paul.

Murphey, T. 1994. Tests: Learning through negotiated interaction. *TESOL Journal, 4*(2), 12–16.

Musumeci, D. 1997. *Breaking tradition: an exploration of the historical relationship between theory and practice in second language teaching.* New York: McGrawHill.

Mutoh, N. 1998. Management of large classes. In J. C. Richards (ed.), *Teaching in action: case studies of language classrooms* (pp. 35–37). Washington, DC: TESOL.

Narayan, K. 1991. "According to their feelings": teaching and healing with stories. In C. Witherell & N. Noddings (eds.), *Stories lives tell: narrative and dialogue in education* (pp. 113–135). New York: Teachers College Press.

National Education Association. 1939. *Personal growth of the teacher.* Washington, DC: Dept. of supervisors and directors of instruction, NEA.

National Education Association [NEA]. 1977. Code of ethics of the education profession. In National Education Association, *NEA Handbook 1977–78.* Washington DC: National Education Association.

Nayar, P. B. 1997. ESL/EFL dichotomy today: language politics or pragmatics? *TESOL Quarterly, 31*(1), 9–37.

Needham, J., et al. 1954–2000. *Science and civilisation in China* (vols. 1–7). Cambridge: Cambridge University Press.

Neill, S. 1991. *Classroom nonverbal communication.* London: Routledge.

Neill, S., & Caswell. 1993. *Body language for competent teachers.* London: Routledge.

Nelson, C. 1999. Sexual identities in ESL: Queer Theory and classroom inquiry. *TESOL Quarterly, 33*(3), 371–391.

New Zealand Ministry of Education. 1988. *Tomorrow's schools: the reform of educational administration in New Zealand.* Wellington: Government Printer.

Newble, D., & Cannon, R. 1991. *A handbook for teachers in universities and colleges* (rev. edn.). London: Kogan Page.

Newmark, M. 1948. *Twentieth century modern language teaching; sources and readings.* New York: Philosophical Library.

Newton, D. A., & Burgoon, J. K. 1990. The use and consequences of verbal influence strategies during interpersonal disagreements. *Human Communication Research, 16,* 477–518.

Nicholls, J. G., & Thorkildsen, T. A. (eds.). 1995. *"Reasons for learning": expanding the conversation on student-teacher collaboration.* New York: Teachers College Press.

Noddings, N. 1984. *Caring, a feminine approach to ethics and moral education.* Berkeley: University of California Press.

Noddings, N. 1995. *Philosophy of education.* Boulder, CO: Westview Press.

Noddings, N., & Shore, P. J. 1984. *Awakening the inner eye: intuition in education.* New York: Teachers College Press.

Nolasco, R., & Arthur, L. 1994. *Large classes.* Hemel Hempstead, UK: Phoenix ELT/Modern English Publications/International Book Distributors.

Numrich, Cl. 1996. On becoming a language teacher: insights from diary studies. *TESOL Quarterly, 30*(1), 131–154.

Nunan, D. 1993. Action research in language education. In J. Edge & K. Richards (eds.), *Teachers develop teachers research* (pp. 39–50). Oxford: Heinemann.

Nunan, D. 2000. Auditing our international initiative. *TESOL Matters, 10*(1), 3.

Nunan, D., & Lamb, C. 1996. *The self-directed teacher.* Cambridge University Press.

Nussbaum, J. F., & Scott, M. D. 1980. Student learning as a relational outcome of teacher-student interaction. In D. Nimmo (ed.), *Communication Yearbook, 4* (pp. 553–564). New Brunswick, MN: Transaction Books.

Ogawa, R. T. 1994. The institutional sources of educational reform: the case of School-Based Management. *American Educational Research Journal, 31*(3), 519–548.

Ogawa, R. T., Crowson, R. L., & Goldring, E. B. 1999. Enduring dilemmas of school organization. In J. Murphey & K. S. Louis (eds.), *Handbook of educational administration* (2nd. edn.; pp. 277–296). San Francisco: Jossey-Bass.

Oxford, R. L. (ed.). 1996. *Language learning motivation: pathways to the new century.* Honolulu: Second Language Teaching & Curriculum Center, University of Hawai'i.

Ozar, D. T. 1993. Building awareness of ethical standards and conduct. In L. Curry et al., *Evaluating professionals* (pp. 148–177). San Francisco: Jossey-Bass.

Pak, J. 1986. *Find out how you teach*. Adelaide: National Curriculum Resource Center.

Paquette, M. 1987. Voluntary collegial support groups for teachers. *Educational Leadership, 45*, 36–39.

Paris, S. C., & Turner, J. C. 1994. Situated motivation. In P. R. Pintrich, D. R. Brown, & C. E. Weinstein (eds.), *Student motivation, cognition, and learning* (pp. 213–237). Hillsdale, NJ: Erlbaum.

Pascarelli, J. 1998. A four-stage mentoring model that works. In S. Goodlad (ed.), *Mentoring and tutoring by students* (pp. 231–243). London: Kogan Page.

Passmore, J. 1980. *The philosophy of teaching*. Cambridge, MA: Harvard University Press.

Peacock, M. 1997. The effect of authentic materials on the motivation of EFL learners. *ELT Journal, 51*(2), 144–156.

Pedersen, P. 1982. Cross-cultural triad model. In E. K. Marshall, P. D. Kurtz and associates, *Interpersonal helping skills* (pp. 238–284). San Francisco, CA: Jossey-Bass.

Pedraza, P., & Ayala, J. 1996. Motivation as an emergent issue in an after-school program in El Barrio. In L. Schauble & R. Glaser (eds.), *Innovations in learning* (pp. 75–91). Mahwah, NJ: Erlbaum.

Pelletier, C. M. 1995. *Handbook of techniques and strategies for coaching student teachers*. Prentice Hall.

Pennington, M. C. 1990. A professional development focus for the language teaching practicum. J. C. Richards & D. Nunan (eds.), *Second language teacher education* (pp. 132–153). Cambridge University Press.

Pennington, M. C. 1996a. *Modeling teacher change: relating input to output*. Hong Kong: City University of Hong Kong, Dept. of English.

Pennington, M. C. 1996b. When input becomes intake: tracing the sources of teachers' attitude change. In D. Freeman & J. C. Richards (eds.), *Teacher learning in language teaching* (pp. 320–347). Cambridge: Cambridge University Press.

Perloff, R. M. 1993. *The dynamics of persuasion*. Hillsdale, NJ: Erlbaum.

Peterman, F. 1997. The lived curriculum of constructivist teacher education. In V. Richardson (ed.), *Constructivist teacher education* (pp. 154–163). London: Falmer Press.

Peters, K. H., & March, J. K. 1999. *Collaborative observation*. Thousand Oaks, CA: Corwin Press/Sage.

Phelan, A., McEwan, H., & Pateman, N. 1996. Collaboration in student teaching: learning to teach in the context of changing curriculum practice. *Teaching and Teacher Education, 12*(4), 335–353.

Philadelphia Teachers' Learning Cooperative. 1984. On becoming teacher experts: Buying time. *Language Arts, 61*, 731–736.

Philips, S. 1983. *The invisible culture: communication in the classroom and on the Warm Springs Indian reservation.* New York: Longman.

Phillips, D.C. (ed.) 2000. *Constructivism in education: opinions and second opinions on controversial issues.* Chicago, IL: National Society for the Study of Education/University of Chicago Press.

Phillipson, R. 1992. ELT: the native speaker's burden? *ELT Journal, 46*(1), 12–18.

Phillipson, R. 1992. *Linguistic imperialism.* Oxford University Press.

Phillipson, R., & Skutnabb-Knagas, T. 1996. English only worldwide or language ecology. *TESOL Quarterly, 13*(3), 371–380.

Pierce, B. N. 1995. Social identity, investment, and language learning. *TESOL Quarterly, 29*(1), 9–33.

Pierce, B. N. 1996. Interpreting data: the role of theory. *TESOL Quarterly, 30*(2), 337–340.

Pintrich, P. R., & Schunk, D. H. 1996. *Motivation in education: theory, research and applications.* Englewood Cliffs: NJ: Prentice-Hall.

Plumb, K. 1988. Starting a teacher development group. *TESOL France News, 8*, 17.

Polio, C., & Wilson-Duffy, C. 1998. Teaching ESL in an unfamiliar context: international students in a North American MA TESOL practicum. *TESOL Journal, 7*(4), 24–29.

Polkinghorne, D. 1988. *Narrative knowing and the human sciences.* Albany, NY: SUNY Press.

Popkin, R. H., & Vanderjagt, A. (eds.) 1993. *Scepticism and irreligion in the seventeenth and eighteenth centuries.* New York: E. J. Brill.

Porter, P. A., Goldstein, L., M., Leatherman, J., & Conrad, S. (1990). An ongoing dialog: learning logs for teacher preparation. In J. C. Richards & D. Nunan (eds.), *Second language teacher education* (pp. 227–240). Cambridge University Press.

Posner, G. J. 1987. Pacing and sequencing. In M. J. Dunkin (ed.), *International encyclopedia of teaching and teacher education* (pp. 266–272). Oxford: Pergamon.

Posner, G. J. 1996. *Field experience* (4th. edn.). New York: Longman.

Potthoff, D., & Alley, R. 1996. Selecting placement sites for student teachers and pre-student teachers: six considerations. *The Teacher Educator, 32*(2), 85–98.

Power, E. J. (1982). *Philosophy of education: studies in philosophies, schooling, and educational policies.* Englewood Cliffs, NJ: Prentice-Hall.

Pratte, R. 1992. *Philosophy of education: two traditions.* Springfield, IL: C. C. Thomas.

Prodromou, L. 1992. What culture? Which culture? Cross-cultural factors in language learning. *ELT Journal, 46*, 39–50.

Pruitt, D. G., & Carnevale, P. J. 1993. *Negotiation in social conflict.* Buckingham, UK: Open University Press.

Pugh, A. K. 1996. A history of English teaching. In N. Mercer & J. Swan (eds.), *Learning English: development and diversity* (pp. 159–204). London: Routledge.

Raiser, L. 1987. A teacher support network. *Teaching Exceptional Children, 19*, 48–49.

Rajal, J. 1983. The andragogy/pedagogy debate. *Lifelong Learning, 6*(9), 14–15.

Ramage, K. 1991. Motivational factors and persistence in second language learning. *Language Learning, 40*(2), 189–219.

Rampton, B. 1990. Displacing the 'native speaker': expertise, affiliation, and inheritance. *ELT Journal, 44*(2), 97–101.

Rampton, B. 1999. Dichotomies, difference, and ritual in second language learning and teaching. *Applied Linguistics, 20*(3), 316–340.

Reagan, T. 1996. *Non-western educational traditions.* Mahwah, NJ: Erlbaum.

Reiman, A. and Thies-Sprinthall, L. 1998. *Mentoring and supervision for teacher development.* New York: Longman.

Rest, J. R., & Narváez, D. (eds.). 1994. *Moral development and the professions.* Hillsdale, NJ: Erlbaum.

Reynolds, A. 1992. What is competent beginning teaching? A review of the literature. *Review of Educational Research, 62*(1), 1–35.

Reynolds, M. C. (ed.). 1989. *Knowledge base for the beginning teacher.* Oxford: Pergamon.

Reznich, C. 1985. Facilitation. In Experiment in International Living, *Teaching Teachers* (pp. 85–88). Brattleboro, VT: Experiment in International Living.

Rich, J. M. 1984. *Professional ethics in education.* Springfield, IL: C. C. Thomas.

Richards, J. C. 1970. *The language factor in Maori schooling.* Quebec: Centre International de Recherche sur le Bilinguisme.

Richards, J. C. 1998. *Beyond training.* Cambridge: Cambridge University Press.

Richards, J. C., & Crookes, G. 1988. The role of the practicum in ESL teacher training programs. *TESOL Quarterly, 22*(1), 9–27.

Richards, J. C. & Lockhart, C. 1994. *Reflective teaching in second language classrooms.* Cambridge University Press.

Richards, J. C. & Rodgers, T. 1986. *Approaches and methods in language teaching.* Cambridge University Press.

Richterich, R. 1972. *Language needs and types of adults.* London: British Council.

Ricoeur, P. 1984. *Time and narrative* (trans. K. McLaughlin & D. Pellauer). Chicago: University of Chicago Press.

Rilling, S., & Pratt, S. 1998. Meeting student expectations and behavioral challenges within a newly defined curriculum. In J. C. Richards (ed.), *Teaching in action: case studies in second language classrooms* (pp. 219–224). Washington, DC: TESOL.

Ritchie, J. S., & Wilson, D. E. 2000. *Teacher narrative as critical inquiry.* New York: Teachers College Press.

Roberts, C. 1998. Language acquisition or language socialization in and through discourse. *Working Papers in Applied Linguistics* (Thames Valley University, London) *4*, 31–42.

Robinson, P. 1987. Needs analysis: from product to process. In A.-M. Cornu (ed.), *Beads or bracelet: how do we approach LSP?* (pp. 32–44). Copenhagen: Oxford University Press.

Rogers, B. 1998. *You know the fair rule* (2nd. edn.). London: Pitman.

Rogers, J. 1982. "The world for sick proper." *ELT Journal, 36*(3), 144–151.

Röhrs, H., & Lenhart, V. (eds.). 1995. *Progressive education across the continents.* Frankfurt: Lang.

Rojot, J. 1991. *Negotiation: From theory to practice.* London: Macmillan.

Rosaldo, R. 1989. *Culture and truth.* Boston, MA: Beacon Press.

Ross, E. W., Cornett, J. W., & McCutcheon, G. (eds.). 1992. *Teacher personal theorizing.* Albany, NY: SUNY Press.

Rousseau, J.-J. 1762/1938. *Emile* (B. Foxley, trans.). New York: E. P. Dutton.

Rueda, R., & Moll, L. 1994. A sociocultural perspective on motivation. In H. F. O'Neill & M. Drillings (eds.), *Motivation: theory and research* (pp. 117–137). Hillsdale, NJ: Erlbaum.

Rule, S. H. 1994. Rethinking the lesson plan. *TESOL Journal, 4*(1), 48–49.

Ryan, C. W., Jackson, B. L., and Levinson, E. M. 1986. Human relations skills training in teacher education: The link to effective practice. *Journal of Counseling and Development, 65*, 114–116.

Said, E. W. 1999. *Out of place: a memoir.* New York: Knopf.

Sánchez, E., Rosales, J., & Cañedo, I. 1999. Understanding and communication in expositive discourse: an analysis of the strategies used by expert and preservice teachers. *Teaching and Teacher Education, 15*, 37–58.

Sartre, J.-P. (K. Gore, ed.). 1947/1987. *Huis-clos.* London: Methuen.

Sawyer, R. K. 1997. *Pretend play as improvisation.* Mahwah, NJ: Erlbaum.

Schafer, R. 1983. *The analytic attitude.* New York: Basic Books.

Schecter, S. R., & Ramirez, R. (1992). A teacher-research group in action. In D. Nunan (ed.), *Collaborative language learning and teaching* (pp. 192–207). Cambridge: Cambridge University Press.

Schmuck, R. A., & Schmuck, P. A. 1983. *Group processes in the classroom* (4th. edn.). Dubuque, IA: Brown.

Schniedewind, N. 1993. Teaching feminist process in the 1990s. *Women's Studies Quarterly, 21* (3 & 4), 17–30.

Schoenhoff, D. M. 1993. *The barefoot expert: the interface of computerized knowledge systems and indigenous knowledge systems.* Westport, CN: Greenwood Press.

Schön, D. A. 1983. *The reflective practitioner: how professionals think in action.* New York: Basic Books.

Schön, D. A. 1987. *Educating the reflective practitioner.* San Francisco, CA: Jossey-Bass.

Schubert, W. 1991. Teacher lore: a basis for understanding praxis. In C. Witherell & N. Noddings (eds.), *Stories lives tell* (pp. 207–231). New York: Teachers College Press.

Schubert, W. H., & Ayers, W. (eds.). 1992. *Teacher lore: learning from our own experience.* White Plains, NY: Longman.

Schumann, J. 1978. The acculturation model for second language acquisition. In R. Gingras (ed.), *Second language acquisition and foreign language teaching* (pp. 27–50). Arlington, VA: Center for Applied Linguistics.

Schutz, P. A. 1994. Goals as the transaction point between motivation and cognition. In P. R. Pintrich, D. R. Brown, & C. E. Weinstein (eds.), *Student motivation, cognition, and learning* (pp. 135–156). Hillsdale, NJ Erlbaum.

Seeberg, V., Swadener, B., Vanden-Wyngaard, M., & Rickel, T. 1998. Multicultural education in the United States. In K. Cushner (ed.), *International perspectives on international education.* (pp. 259–300). Mahwah, NJ: Erlbaum.

Selin, H. 1992. *Science across cultures: an annotated bibliography of books on non-western science, technology, and medicine.* New York: Garland.

Senior, R. 1997. Transforming language classes into bonded groups. *ELT Journal, 51*(1), 3–11.

Shade, B. R. J. 1989. Afro-American cognitive patterns. In B. R. J. Shade (ed.), *Culture, style, and the educative process (pp. 87–115).* Springfield, IL: C. C. Thomas.

Shaeffer, S. 1990. Participatory approaches to in-service teacher training. In V. D. Rust & P. Dalin (eds.), *Teachers and teaching in the developing world* (pp. 95–114). New York: Garland.

Shamim, F. 1996. Learner resistance to innovation in classroom methodology. In H. Coleman (ed.), *Society and the language classroom.* (pp. 105–121). Cambridge: Cambridge University Press.

Shapiro, S. B. 1999. *Pedagogy and the politics of the body: a critical praxis.* New York: Garland.

Sharan, S. 1980. Cooperative learning in small groups: Recent methods and effects on achievement, attitudes, and ethnic relations. *Review of Educational Research, 50,* 241–271.

Sharan, S., Shachar, H., & Levine, T. 1999. *The innovative school: organization and instruction*. London: Bergin & Garvey.

Shavelson, R. J. & Stern, P. 1981. Research on teachers' pedagogical thoughts, judgments and decisions and behavior. *Review of Educational Research, 51*, 455–498.

Shawar, Z. 1991. Adapting individualization techniques for large classes. *English Teaching Forum, 29*(3), 16–21.

Shecter, S. R., & Ramirez, R. 1992. A teacher-research group in action. In D. Nunan (ed.), *Collaborative language learning and teaching* (pp. 192–207). New York: Cambridge University Press.

Shell, G. R. 1999. *Bargaining for advantage*. New York: Viking.

Sheridan, J. E. 1975. *China in disintegration*. New York: Free Press.

Shilling, C. 1993. *The body and social theory*. London: Sage Publications.

Shimahara, N. K. 1995. Teacher education reform in Japan: ideological and control issues. In N. K. Shimahara & I. Z. Holowinsky (eds.), *Teacher education in industrialized nations: issues in changing social contexts* (pp. 155–193). New York: Garland.

Shimahara, N. K. 1998a. The Japanese model of professional development: teaching as craft. *Teaching and Teacher Education, 14*(5), 451–462.

Shimahara, N. K. 1998b. *Politics of classroom life*. New York: Garland.

Shimahara, N., & Sakai, A. 1995. *Learning to teach in two cultures: Japan and the United States*. New York: Garland.

Shor, I. 1992. *Empowering education*. Chicago: University of Chicago Press.

Shotton, John. 1993. *No master high or low: libertarian education and schooling in Britain 1890–1990*. Bristol, UK: Libertarian Education.

Shriewer, J. (ed.). 2000. *Discourse formation in comparative education*. New York: Peter Lang.

Shulman, L. S. 1987. Knowledge and teaching: Foundations of the new reform. *Harvard Educational Review, 57*(1), 1–22.

Shulman, L. S. 1988. A union of insufficiencies: Strategies for teacher assessment in a period of educational reform. *Educational Leadership, 46*(3), 36–41.

Sinclair, J. McH. & Coulthard, R. M. 1975. *Towards an analysis of discourse: the English used by teachers and pupils*. London: Oxford University Press.

Skrtic, T. M., & Ware, L. P. 1992. Reflective teaching and the problem of school organization. In E. W. Ross, J. W. Cornett, & G. McCutcheon (eds.), *Teacher personal theorizing* (pp. 207–218). Albany, NY: SUNY Press.

Slavin, R. E. 1983. *Cooperative learning*. New York: Longman.

Sleeter, C. E. 1996. *Multicultural education as social activism*. Albany, NY: SUNY Press.

Slimani, A. 1992. Evaluation of classroom interaction. In J. C. Alderson & A. Beretta (eds.), *Evaluating second language education* (pp. 197–220). Cambridge: Cambridge University Press.

Sloggett, B. B., Gallimore, R., & Kubany, E. S. (1970). A comparative analysis of fantasy need achievement amount high and low achieving male Hawaiian-Americans. *Journal of Cross-Cultural Psychology, 1,* 53–61.

Smith, D. B. 1996. Teacher decision making in the adult ESL classroom. In D. Freeman, & J. C. Richards (eds.), *Teacher learning in language teaching* (pp. 197–216). New York: Cambridge University Press.

Smith, D. C. 1991. *The Confucian continuum: educational modernization in Taiwan.* New York: Praeger.

Smith, M. P. 1983. *The libertarians and education.* London: George Allen & Unwin.

Smylie, M. A. 1995. Teacher learning in the workplace. In T. R. Guskey & M. Huberman (eds.), *Professional development in education* (pp. 92–113). New York: Teachers College.

Smyth, J. (ed.). 1993. *A socially-critical view of the self-managing school.* London: Falmer Press.

So, W. W-M. 1997. A study of teacher cognition in planning elementary science lessons. *Research in Science Education, 27*(1), 71–86.

Sockett, H. 1990. Accountability, trust, and ethical codes of practice. In J. I. Goodlad, R. Soder, & K. A. Sirotnik (eds.), *The moral dimensions of teaching* (pp. 224–250). San Francisco, CA: Jossey-Bass.

Sorensen, G. 1989. The relationships among teachers' self-disclosure statements, student perceptions, and affective learning. *Communication Education, 38,* 260–276.

Sorensen, G. A., & Christophel, D. M. 1992. The communication perspective. In V. P. Richmond & J. C. McCroskey (Eds), *Power in the classroom* (pp. 35–46). Hillsdale, NJ: Erlbaum.

Sparks-Langer, G. M. 1992. In the eye of the beholder: cognitive, critical, and narrative approaches to teacher reflection. In L. Valli (ed.), *Reflective teacher education: causes and critiques* (pp. 147–160). Albany, NY: SUNY Press.

Spolsky, B. 1989. *Conditions for second language learning: introduction to a general theory.* New York: Oxford University Press.

Spring, J. 1998. *Education and the rise of the global economy.* Mahwah, NJ: Lawrence Erlbaum Assocs.

Springer, E., et al. 1997. *Community-based ethnography.* Mahwah, NJ: Erlbaum.

Srivastava, A. 1997. Anti-racism inside and outside the classroom. In L. G. Roman & L. Eyre (eds.), *Dangerous territories: struggles for difference and equality in education* (pp.113–126). London: Routledge.

Stern, H. H. 1983. *Fundamental concepts of language teaching.* Oxford: Oxford University Press.

Storey, R. 1997. *The art of persuasive discourse.* London: Gower.

Stoynoff, S. 1999. The TESOL practicum: an integrated model in the U.S. *TESOL Quarterly, 33*(1), 145–151.

Strevens, P. D. 1976. A theoretical model of the language learning/teaching process. *Working Papers on Bilingualism, 11*, 129–152.

Strike, K. A., & Soltis, J. F. 1992. *The ethics of teaching* (2nd. edn.). New York: Teachers College Press.

Sudnow, D. 1981. *Ways of the hand: the organization of improvised conduct.* New York: Harper & Row.

Swadener, B. B., & Lubeck, S. 1995. *Children and families "at promise": deconstructing the discourse of risk.* Albany, NY: SUNY Press.

Swaffar, J., Arens, K., & Byrnes, H. 1991. *Reading for meaning.* Englewood Cliffs, NJ: Prentice-Hall.

Syed, Z. 2001. Notions of self in foreign language learning: a qualitative analysis. In Z. Dörnyei & R. Schmidt, (eds.), *Motivation and second language acquisition* (pp. 127–148). Honolulu: National Foreign Language Resource Center/ University of Hawai'i Press.

Sykes, G. 1999. The 'new professionalism' in education: an appraisal. In J. Murphey & K. S. Louis (eds.), *Handbook of educational administration* (2nd. edn.; pp. 227–249). San Francisco: Jossey-Bass.

Tallon, A. 1997. *Head and heart.* New York: Fordham University Press.

Tam, H. 1998. *Communitarianism.* New York: New York University Press.

Tang, C. 1997. The identity of the nonnative ESL teacher – on the power and status of nonnative ESL teachers. *TESOL Quarterly, 31*(3), 577–580.

TESOL. 1980. Guidelines for ethical research in ESL. *TESOL Quarterly, 14*(3), 383–389.

Tesser, A., & Shaffer, D. R. 1990. Attitudes and attitude change. *Annual Review of Psychology 41*, 479–523.

Tharp, R., & Gallimore, R. 1988. *Rousing minds to life.* Cambridge University Press.

Thomas, M. 1998. Programmatic ahistoricity in second language acquisition theory. *Studies in Second Language Acquisition, 20*, 387–405.

Thorkildsen, T. A., & Johnson, C. 1995. Is there a right way to collaborate? When the experts speak, can the customers be right? In J. G. Nicholls & T. A. Thorkildsen (eds.), *"Reasons for learning": expanding the conversation on student-teacher collaboration* (pp. 137–161). New York: Teachers College Press.

Ting-Toomey, S. and Korzenny, F. (eds.) 1991. *Cross-cultural interpersonal communication.* Newbury Park, CA: Sage.

Titone, R. 1968. *Teaching foreign languages: an historical sketch.* Washington, DC: Georgetown University Press.

Tollefson, J. W. 1991. *Planning language, planning inequality* (Ch. 4: Modernization and English language teaching). London: Longman.

Tollefson, N., & Kleinsasser, A. 1992. Cooperating teachers' descriptions of "outstanding" interns. *Journal of Personnel Evaluation in Education, 5*(4), 359–367.

Tom, A. R. 1984. *Teaching as a moral craft.* New York: Longman.

Tomlinson, B. (ed.). 1998. *Materials development in language teaching.* Cambridge: Cambridge University Press.

Tu, W. 1993. *Way, learning, and politics: essays on the Confucian intellectual.* New York: SUNY Press.

Tudor, I. 1996. *Learner-centredness as language education.* Cambridge University Press.

Turski, W. G. 1994. *Towards a rationality of emotions: an essay in the philosophy of mind.* Athens, GA: Ohio University Press.

Tyler, R. W. 1950. *Basic principles of curriculum and instruction.* Chicago: University of Chicago Press.

Ulichny, P. 1996. What's in a methodology? In D. Freeman & J. C. Richards (eds.), *Teacher learning in language teaching* (pp. 178–196). Cambridge: Cambridge University Press.

Underhill, A. 1992. The role of groups in developing teacher self-awareness. *ELT Journal, 46*(1), 71–80.

Valdes, J. M. (ed.). 1986. *Culture bound.* Cambridge University Press.

Vandrick, S. 1997. The role of hidden identities in the postsecondary ESL classroom. *TESOL Quarterly, 31*(1), 153–157.

Wadden, P., & McGovern, S. 1991. The quandary of negative class participation: coming to terms with misbehavior in the language classroom. *ELT Journal, 45*(2), 119–127.

Wajnryb, R. 1992. *Classroom observation tasks.* Cambridge University Press.

Walker, C. J., & Quinn, J. W. 1996. Fostering instructional vitality and motivation. In R. J. Menges and associates, *Teaching on solid ground* (pp. 315–336). San Francisco, SF: Jossey-Bass.

Wallace, M. J. 1991. *Teaching foreign language teachers.* Cambridge: Cambridge University Press.

Wallace, M. J. 1998. *Action research for language teachers.* Cambridge University Press.

Watson, D., & Bixby, M. 1994. Teachers! A support group needs you! *Teaching K–8, 24*, 86–88.

Wauticher, H. (ed.). 1998. *Tribal epistemologies: essays in the philosophy of anthropology.* Brookfield, VT: Ashgate.

Webne-Behrman, H. 1998. *The practice of facilitation: managing group process and solving problems.* Westport, CN: Quorum Books.

Weiner, B. 1984. Principles for a theory of student motivation and their application within an attributional framework. In R. Ames & C. Ames (eds.),

Research on motivation in education (vol. 1, pp. 15–38). New York: Academic Press.

Wheeler, C. E., & Chinn, P. L. 1988. *Peace and power: a handbook of feminist process* (2nd. edn.). New York: National League for Nursing.

White, J. J. 1989. Student teaching as a rite of passage. *Anthropology and Education Quarterly, 20*(3), 177–195.

White, J. J. 1991. War stories: invitations to reflect on practice. In B. R. Tabachnick & K. M. Zeichner (eds.), *Issues and practices in inquiry-oriented teacher education* (pp. 226–252). Philadelphia: Falmer Press.

Whitty, G., Power, S., & Halpin, D. 1998. *Devolution and choice in education.* Melbourne: Australian Council for Educational Press/Open University Press.

Wiener, W. J., & Rosenwald, G. C. 1993. A moment's monument: the psychology of keeping a diary. In R. Josselson & A. Lieblich (eds.), *The narrative study of lives* (pp. 30–58). Newbury Park, CA: Sage.

Wilkins, D. 1976. *Notional syllabuses.* Oxford: Oxford University Press.

Willerman, M., McNeely, S. L., & Koffman, E. C. 1991. *Teachers helping teachers: peer observation and assistance.* New York: Praeger.

Williams, M., & Burden, R. L. 1997. *Psychology for language teachers.* Cambridge University Press.

Willing, K. 1992. *Talking it through: clarification and problem-solving in professional work.* Sydney NSW [Australia]: National Centre for English Language Teaching and Research.

Wiseman, D., Cooner, D. D., & Knight, S. L. 1999. *Becoming a teacher in a field-based program.* New York: Wadsworth.

Witherel, C., & Noddings, N. (eds.). 1991. *Stories lives tell: narrative and dialogue in education.* New York: Teachers College Press.

Wlodkowski, R. J. 1985. *Enhancing adult motivation to learn.* San Francisco, CA: Jossey-Bass.

Wolfe, P. 1987. What the "seven-step lesson plan" isn't! *Educational Leadership, 44*(5), 70–71.

Wolfe-Quintero, K., & Brown, J. D. 1998. Teacher portfolios. *TESOL Journal, 7*(6), 24–27.

Wolff, L. B., & Vera, J. L. 1989. Teachers' groups in Spain. *The Teacher Trainer, 3*, 14–16.

Wolfgang, C. H. 1995. *Solving discipline problems* (3rd. edn.). New York: Allyn & Bacon.

Womack, D. F. 1990. Communication and negotiation. In D. O'Hair and G. L. Kreps (eds.), *Applied communication theory and research* (pp. 77–101). Hillsdale, NJ: Erlbaum.

Wong-Filmore, L. 1985. When does teacher talk work as input? In S. Gass & C. Madden (eds.), *Input in second language acquisition* (pp. 17–50). Rowley, MA: Newbury House.

Wood, P. O. 1991. The cooperating teacher's role in nurturing reflective teaching. In B. R. Tabachnik & K. M. Zeichner (eds.), *Issues and practices in inquiry-oriented teacher education* (pp. 202–210). Philadelphia, PA: Falmer Press.

Woods, D. 1996. *Teacher cognition in language teaching: beliefs, decision-making, and classroom practice.* Cambridge: Cambridge University Press.

Woodward, G. C. 1990. *Persuasive encounters: case studies in constructive confrontation.* New York: Praeger.

Woodward, T. 1991. *Models and metaphors in language teacher training.* Cambridge: Cambridge University Press.

Wright, A. 1976. *Visual materials for the language teacher.* London: Longman.

Wyman, E. D. 1998. Trips to reality for immigrant secondary students. In J. C. Richards (ed.), *Teaching in action: case studies from second language classrooms* (pp. 180–183). Washington DC: TESOL.

Yee, A. 1969. Do cooperating teachers influence the attitude of student teachers? *Journal of Educational Psychology, 60,* 327–332.

Yee, S. M. 1990. *Careers in the classroom.* New York: Teachers College Press.

Yule, G. 1998. *Explaining English grammar.* Oxford University Press.

Zahorik, J. A. 1988. The observing-conferencing role of university supervisors. *Journal of Teacher Education, 39*(2), 9–16.

Zinn, L. M. 1990. Identifying your philosophical orientation. In M. W. Galbraith (ed.), *Adult learning methods* (pp. 39–76). Malabar, FA: Krieger.

Zuck, J. G. 1984. Comments on Peter Master's "The etiquette of observing." *TESOL Quarterly, 18*(2), 337–341.

Index

academic literature. *See also*
    educational research
    of applied linguistics, 181, 240n3
    of classroom management (ES/FL),
        143, 150–4
    consulting, 194–5
    on morality (TESOL), 48–9
    political/ethical dimensions of
        (ES/FL), 85, 236n1
    skepticism and, 8, 43–4, 195
action research, 40–2, 194
activities, classroom, 131–2, 144–5,
    239n2
adhocracy, 185, 186
administrative systems
    adhocracy, 186
    machine bureaucracy, 185
    professional bureaucracy, 185
    school-based management, 188–90
administrators, school
    American Association of School
        Administrators (AASA) for,
        237n6
    divisions with teachers, 205
    former teachers as, 186
    of S/FL programs, 184
    teacher study groups with, 204–5
adult education, 17, 18, 87, 142, 165,
    170, 240n7
affiliation, need for, 132
Agee, J.M., 226
alienation, teacher, 204–5
Alley, R., 222, 230
allocation, of classroom resources, 86

Allwright, Dick, 237n9
alternative education, 17–18, 58
American Association of School
    Administrators (AASA), 237n6
American Association of University
    Professors, 237n6
Ames, C., 137
"analytic philosophy," of education,
    52–3
Applegate, J.H., 225–6
applied ethics, 93
applied linguistics
    educational linguistics in, 117
    in field of education, 2
    language policy debates in, 85
    literature of, 181, 240n3
    "talk of learners" in, 78
"apprenticeship of observation," 196
Armour, M., 205, 207, 211–12
Ashton-Warner, Sylvia, 74, 114
Ashworth, Mary, 97, 98
assessment
    "authentic"/alternative, 135
    portfolio-based, 135
attendance, required v. voluntary, 142
Australian teachers
    ES/FL, study of, 163
    ESL, study of, 102
autonomy, student, 17–18

Bailey, F., 37, 38
BAK (beliefs/assumptions/knowledge)
    networks, 114
Barnes, D., 78

curiosity, 131, 239n4
demotivated, 137
elementary, teachers of, 86–7, 142
feedback, 70
fourth/fifth grade (U.S.), study of, 132
gay/lesbian/bisexual, 92, 237n5
goals, shared with teacher, 14, 17–18, 19
goal-setting v. teacher, 12–14, 17–18
immigrant, 85, 137
international, in-group discussion, 37
Japanese, study of, 132
journals, 43
motivation, 128–40
motives for S/FL learning, 128
portfolios, 199
pre-schoolers, study of (rewards), 133
self-perceptions/conceptions, 136–8
student teachers
benefiting cooperating teachers, 224–5, 243n5
benefiting from cooperating teachers, 226
finding placements for, 222
importance of voice in, 77
lesson planning by, 103, 238n2
working with cooperating teachers, 219–30
student teachers' comments, 3
on conceptual frameworks, 125–7, 127f
on cultural differences, 156–9
on dominant/nondominant speaking groups, 37–8
on goals, 15–16
on issues of control, 159–60
on lesson planning, 109–10
on personal practical theories, 125–7, 127f

on social skills, 167–9
on teachers as role model in Korea, 94
student-student relationships, 169–71
student/teacher "feedback loop," 42–3
subjective theories, 114
summary model-based review, 193–8
discussion questions for, 198
supervised teaching, duration of, 5, 21
supportive discipline, 148
syllabus/bi
goal-setting in course, 14
modified for motivation, 136
motivation and, 135–6
"multistrand" syllabus as, 27
philosophy of teaching in written, 48
Syed, Z., 139

T2/T3 theories, Stern, H. H. on, 122
talking, as reflection process, 33–40
"talking to learn," 78
"task," classroom, 144
teacher(s), 78–81. *See also* action research; cooperating teachers; student teachers
of adults, 87, 142
alienation, 204–5
Australian (ES/FL), study of, 163
Australian (ESL), study of, 102
British (ESL), questionnaire surveying, 163
burn-out, 204
Canadian (ESL), study of, 102
change, 175–6
as "change agents" (ESL), 172, 174
as cultural boundary crossers (S/FL), 7, 141, 145
dealing with government policy (ESL), 85
decision-making (ESL), 169
different groups of (ES/FL), 46–7
divisions with administrators, 205
effectiveness, research, 66
elementary, 86–7, 142